Thurid Vogt

Real-time automatic emotion recognition from speech

AF092727

Thurid Vogt

Real-time automatic emotion recognition from speech

The recognition of emotions from speech in view of real-time applications

Südwestdeutscher Verlag für Hochschulschriften

Imprint
Any brand names and product names mentioned in this book are subject to trademark, brand or patent protection and are trademarks or registered trademarks of their respective holders. The use of brand names, product names, common names, trade names, product descriptions etc. even without a particular marking in this work is in no way to be construed to mean that such names may be regarded as unrestricted in respect of trademark and brand protection legislation and could thus be used by anyone.

Publisher:
Südwestdeutscher Verlag für Hochschulschriften
is a trademark of
Dodo Books Indian Ocean Ltd., member of the OmniScriptum S.R.L Publishing group
str. A.Russo 15, of. 61, Chisinau-2068, Republic of Moldova Europe
Printed at: see last page
ISBN: 978-3-8381-2545-9

Zugl. / Approved by: Bielefeld, Universität, Diss., 2010

Copyright © Thurid Vogt
Copyright © 2011 Dodo Books Indian Ocean Ltd., member of the OmniScriptum S.R.L Publishing group

Contents

1 Introduction   **1**
    1.1   Research questions 3
    1.2   Outline of the book 4

2 Basics of emotions in speech   **7**
    2.1   A psychological view on emotions: Models of emotions 8
    2.2   The expression of emotion 13
         2.2.1   Language and speech 13
         2.2.2   Extra-linguistic modalities 15
    2.3   Automatic emotion recognition from speech 16
         2.3.1   Overview of a statistical speech emotion recognition system 16
         2.3.2   Feature calculation 18
    2.4   Databases with emotional speech 27
         2.4.1   Types of emotion databases 28
         2.4.2   Labelling emotional databases 31
    2.5   Summary 35

3 Approaches to speech emotion recognition   **37**
    3.1   Emotion units 37
    3.2   Features 39
         3.2.1   Global statistics features 40

		3.2.2	Short-term features	44

        3.2.2   Short-term features 44

        3.2.3   Non-acoustic features 45

        3.2.4   Feature selection 46

  3.3   Classification 46

        3.3.1   Static classification 46

        3.3.2   Dynamic classification 47

        3.3.3   Trends in speech emotion classification 48

  3.4   Speaker types, languages and target classes 50

  3.5   Real-time speech emotion recognition 52

  3.6   Applications for speech emotion recognition 53

  3.7   Multimodal emotion recognition 55

  3.8   Conclusion 56

4 Databases and methods for speech emotion recognition   59

  4.1   Databases 59

        4.1.1   Berlin Database of Emotional Speech 61

        4.1.2   FAU Aibo Emotion Corpus 62

        4.1.3   SmartKom Corpus 65

  4.2   Audio segmentation 67

  4.3   Features 71

        4.3.1   Feature extraction 72

        4.3.2   Feature selection 81

  4.4   Classification 84

        4.4.1   Support Vector Machines 85

        4.4.2   Naïve Bayes 87

  4.5   Summary 88

5 Experimental results — 89

- 5.1 Evaluation measures 89
- 5.2 Emotion units 91
- 5.3 Feature evaluation 94
  - 5.3.1 Individual feature ranking 95
  - 5.3.2 Intra-feature type comparisons 97
  - 5.3.3 Inter-feature type comparison 101
  - 5.3.4 Reducing the number of statistical measures 103
  - 5.3.5 Automatically selected features 105
  - 5.3.6 Feature subsets 111
- 5.4 Classifiers 116
- 5.5 Conclusion 118

6 EMOVOICE — Real-time speech emotion recognition — 121

- 6.1 Architecture 122
- 6.2 Data acquisition 126
- 6.3 Sample applications and prototypes 130
  - 6.3.1 Conversational applications 130
  - 6.3.2 Artistic applications 133
- 6.4 Emotion expressions under realistic conditions 136
- 6.5 Evaluation studies 138
  - 6.5.1 Barthoc jr. 139
  - 6.5.2 E-Tree 140
  - 6.5.3 EmoEmma 142
- 6.6 Conclusion 144

7 Multimodal emotion recognition — 145

7.1 Gender information — 146
- 7.1.1 Combined gender and emotion recognition — 147
- 7.1.2 Relevant features — 148
- 7.1.3 Results and discussion — 150
- 7.1.4 Conclusion — 152

7.2 Biosignals — 153
- 7.2.1 Experiment for data collection — 154
- 7.2.2 Recognition of emotions from speech and biosignals — 155
- 7.2.3 Results and discussion — 156
- 7.2.4 Conclusion — 157

7.3 Linguistic information — 157
- 7.3.1 The SAL database — 158
- 7.3.2 Feature sets — 159
- 7.3.3 Results and discussion — 160
- 7.3.4 Conclusion — 161

7.4 Facial expressions — 161
- 7.4.1 The DaFEx database — 162
- 7.4.2 Recognition of emotions from facial expressions and speech — 163
- 7.4.3 Results and discussion — 164
- 7.4.4 Conclusion — 165

7.5 Conclusion — 165

8 Final conclusion and outlook — 167

Bibliography — 169

List of Figures

2.1	Universal facial expressions of emotions	9
2.2	Plutchik's wheel of emotions	10
2.3	Dimensional models of emotions	11
2.4	Overview of a speech emotion recognition system	17
2.5	Representation of a signal as a waveform and as a spectrogram	19
2.6	Emotion relevant acoustic properties in neutral, happy and bored speech	21
2.7	An example for a decomposition into frequency scales by wavelet transformation	24
2.8	The frequency spectrum of an /a/ in neutral, happy and bored speech	24
2.9	The times of glottal pulses	25
2.10	PCA: a mapping of the original two dimensions onto the principal component axes	27
2.11	Types of databases used for emotion recognition and their complexity/difficulty	32
2.12	Tracking the emotional state over time with Feeltrace	33
4.1	Steps in training and testing of the speech emotion recognition system	60
4.2	Recording conditions during the creation of the Berlin Database of Emotional Speech	62
4.3	Sony's pet robot Aibo	63
4.4	Design study of the SmartKom-Mobile scenario	65
4.5	Transformation of time value series using pitch as example	75
4.6	Support vectors $\vec{s_1}$, $\vec{s_2}$ and $\vec{s_3}$ for a SVM classifier maximise the distance between two classes	86

5.1 Average duration of units in seconds for the Berlin, Aibo and SmartKom databases 93

5.2 Distribution on feature types of the 100 best ranked features according to their information gain for the Berlin, Aibo and SmartKom databases 97

5.3 Distribution on feature types of the three subset selection strategies for Berlin . . 106

5.4 Distribution on feature types of the three subset selection strategies for Aibo . . . 107

5.5 Distribution on feature types of the three subset selection strategies for SmartKom 107

5.6 Distribution on feature types of the full feature set 108

5.7 Proportion of discarded features in each feature type 108

5.8 Proportion of feature types in discarded features 109

5.9 Proportion and frequency of selected features for raw, logarithmised and median subtracted logarithmised pitch 109

5.10 Mean number of selected features for each single MFCC coefficient and for the average of all coefficients per database split 110

6.1 Overview of tools in EMOVOICE 123

6.2 Overview of `emo_online`, the online speech emotion recognition module of EMOVOICE 125

6.3 Graphical user interfaces supporting speech database creation and classifier building 126

6.4 Examples for emotional stimuli sentences inspired by the Velten mood induction technique 128

6.5 The humanoid robot head Barthoc jr. and the virtual agent Greta as empathic listeners mirroring the user's emotional state with their facial expressions 131

6.6 EmoEmma, karaoke singers and Affective Interactive Narrative installation . . . 132

6.7 EmoSkype, an add-on to the internet voice messaging software Skype™, gives feedback on how a user acts on his/her phone conversation partner 133

6.8 An animated kaleidoscope to visualise online recognised emotional states 134

6.9 Showcases of interactive art in the CALLAS project making use of EMOVOICE . 136

6.10 Questionnaire results of the first and second E-Tree user study 142

6.11 Averaged answers to the evaluation study of EmoEmma 143

7.1 Combination of a gender detection system and two gender-specific emotion classifiers into a single emotion recognition system 148

7.2 Examples for facial expressions of actors in the DaFEx database 162

7.3 Overview of the architecture of the emotional facial expression recognition system 164

List of Tables

2.1	Some definitions of basic emotions	9
2.2	Variables of appraisal theory	12
2.3	Variations of acoustic variables observed in emotional expressions compared to neutral speech	14
3.1	Overview of emotion units	39
3.2	Difficulties of real-time speech emotion recognition	57
4.1	The 10 utterances recorded in the Berlin database of emotional speech	61
4.2	The distribution and duration of emotions in the Berlin Database of Emotional Speech	62
4.3	The distribution of emotions in the AMEN words of the FAU Aibo Emotion corpus.	64
4.4	The distribution and duration of emotions in the turns containing at least one AMEN word of the FAU Aibo Emotion corpus	64
4.5	The number and duration of turns with AMEN words in the two schools	64
4.6	Duration and number of emotional episodes in the headset-recorded sessions within the mobile scenario of the SmartKom database	66
4.7	Emotion units explored for the Berlin, SmartKom, and Aibo database	69
4.8	The words in the turn "jetzt *gehd g'radeaus stopp stopp" in the Aibo corpus	70
4.9	Label mapping in the Aibo database from word based labels onto the different units	71
4.10	Transformations of pitch features	76
4.11	Transformations of energy features	76

4.12 Transformations of MFCC features 77
4.13 Explicit duration features 78
4.14 Transformations of spectral features 79
4.15 Transformations of voicing features 80
4.16 Transformations of voice quality features 80
4.17 Number of features in each feature type 81
4.18 Denotation of features 82

5.1 Numbers of instances per emotion unit in Berlin 91
5.2 Numbers of instances per emotion unit in Aibo 91
5.3 Numbers of instances per emotion unit in SmartKom 92
5.4 Comparison of segmentation levels 94
5.5 10 best features from information gain ranking for the Berlin database 95
5.6 10 best features from information gain ranking for the Aibo database 95
5.7 10 best features from information gain ranking for the SmartKom database 96
5.8 Different pitch transformations to compensate for speaker differences: recognition rates 98
5.9 Different pitch transformations to compensate for speaker differences: information gain 98
5.10 Mean, median, first quartile, 3rd quartile of different pitch normalisations to compensate for speaker differences: recognition rates 99
5.11 Mean, median, first quartile, 3rd quartile of different pitch normalisations to compensate for speaker differences: information gain 99
5.12 Comparison of different representations of MFCCs: recognition rates 100
5.13 Comparison of different representations of MFCCs: information gain 100
5.14 Feature type comparison for the Berlin database 101
5.15 Feature type comparison for the Aibo database 102
5.16 Feature type comparison for the SmartKom database 103
5.17 Individual evaluation of statistical measures 104

List of Tables

5.18	Group evaluation of statistical measures	105
5.19	Manually selected feature set based on experience	113
5.20	Comparison of "simple" feature sets	113
5.21	Comparison of feature subsets selected from the full feature set	114
5.22	Comparison of feature subsets selected from the restricted feature set	114
5.23	Ranking of selection strategies	115
5.24	Selection and classification time of different feature selection strategies	115
5.25	Comparison of classifiers	117
5.26	Comparison of training and test times of the classifiers	117
7.1	Relevant features for gender detection in the Berlin and SmartKom databases	149
7.2	Relevant features for gender-independent, male and female emotion classification on the Berlin database	149
7.3	Relevant features for gender-independent, male and female emotion classification on the SmartKom database	150
7.4	Accuracy for gender detection from mean pitch only and from the optimised feature set on the Berlin and SmartKom databases	151
7.5	Gender-independent, gender-dependent and combined gender and emotion recognition: recognition accuracies	152
7.6	Uni- and bimodal recognition results for speech and physiological signals	156
7.7	Distribution of turns in the SAL database on 5 emotion classes	158
7.8	Results for acoustic, lexical, stylometric and deictic feature sets and their fusion on feature and decision level	160
7.9	Unimodal and bimodal recognition results of speech and facial expressions on the DaFEx database	164

Chapter 1

Introduction

> *"Affect makes us smart; that's the lesson of my current research into the role of affect. This is because affect is always passing judgements, presenting us with immediate information about the world: here is potential danger, there is potential comfort. This is nice; that is bad."* Don Norman, 2002 [166]

Emotion is omnipresent in our lives, we evaluate the emotionality of everything we encounter. Emotion also influences seemingly rational processes. The above statement was written by Don Norman as motivation for the successor of his book "The Design of Everyday Things" [165] which is about the usability and function of things or software. However, he had to acknowledge that users rate nice things, with same functionality, as more usable. This applies in general, and in particular to computers and software.

Up to the turn of the millennium, the predominant paradigm in human-computer interaction was that of rational information processing. The goal was to input and output information in an efficient way. Rational thinking was considered as the central human activity [100]. Since then, a shift of paradigms can be observed, manifested for example by Rosalind Picard's seminal work "Affective Computing" [178] which lent its name to a new kind of computing that abandons the image of a purely rational human user.

Considering affective processes in computing is necessary both for a better and more adequate user experience as well as for problem solving in computer-internal processes. With respect to the user experience this means interaction should rely less on the traditional input devices keyboard and mouse in favour of more natural forms of interaction such as language or gestures, compatible with a ubiquitous and unobtrusive computing environment. In order to make such interfaces natural, it is necessary that they also respond to the expression of the emotional state of the user. Users would perceive a mismatch if a system talks naturally with them, but would not recognise when they, for example, are becoming impatient or speak angrily or happily. This concerns just as much the output side, where, for instance, the facial expressions of an embodied character or the speech output of an application should match the emotionality of the message it is trying to convey and should respond to the user's state as well as the situation. As an example, it is perceived as irritating by some users if the voice output of a navigation system in a car repeats "please turn around" several times with a friendly, unchanged voice when instructions have not been followed. Though, of course, the system is indifferent about that, to some extent the user attributes human traits to the system because of its natural speech output.

Affective information even supports internal computer reasoning or problem solving processes. "Affective reasoning is effective reasoning" as Elliott and Brzezinski [71] state. Affect helps humans to make faster decisions, for example to detect dangers, which usually require fast reactions. Likewise it is possible to base computer heuristics on it.

This book is concerned with the recognition of emotions by a computer, more precisely with the recognition of emotions from the acoustic characteristics of speech which may be pitch, loudness, but also the spectral distribution of frequencies, for instance. Examples for applications where this is useful include call centres, or learning and game software. Knowledge about the emotional state can help to connect angry callers of an automatic dialogue system to a human operator, to motivate a student at the right time, or to develop a fun game that is influenced by emotional expressions. However, emotion recognition from speech is a very challenging tasks. First and foremost, this is due to the infinite variability of emotional expressions within and among speakers, even for the same emotion. Other factors are the complexity of emotions as they may occur blended, or social influences may cause persons to shade or suppress their real emotional state. In order to recognise vocally expressed emotions automatically, affective information has to be separated from other influences on the voice, such as anomalies of the voice organs or physical effort which may be for instance a reason for breathlessness. Furthermore, in real-life, it is not trivial to find an objective ground truth on what the current emotional state of a particular person is though this is a prerequisite for automatic recognition. For these reasons, recognition accuracies of current systems are still relatively low, so that affect recognition is hardly used in commercial products. Furthermore, it has not been possible to recognise arbitrary affect categories in real-time, which is necessary for most applications.

What has been achieved so far is the recognition of clearly pronounced acted emotions where very high accuracies can be obtained. More realistic emotions, usually induced within a user study, have also been examined, though with lesser accuracies, and research has often concentrated on the prototypical cases within the data. Accuracies depend not only on the emotion types but also on the number of emotion classes: up to eight emotion classes have been successfully recognised from acted emotion, while with natural emotions, no more than five classes can seriously be classified and even these with accuracies below 50 %. Developed methodology has been tested to work equally well on men, women and children. However, so far usage of technology is largely limited to laboratory settings with quiet background conditions and a clearly audible single speaker.

As a result of these considerations, the emotion recognition framework EMOVOICE was developed, which provides an acoustic feature extraction that can be used to calculate many features in real-time. This feature set can then be restricted to the most relevant ones for any particular application or scenario. Furthermore, the recogniser is able to find meaningful classification units from speech without prior word recognition. The units are segmented incrementally in real-time from the digitised speech signal.

Of course there are many more possibilities to detect emotions than just from acoustic features, including word information, facial gestures, etc. As humans use available information in its entirety, a holistic approach is also promising for automatic emotion recognition. For this reason, a few research studies on multimodal approaches as combinations of EMOVOICE with other modalities will be discussed here as well. In order to develop the framework and conduct subsequent evaluations and multimodal studies, a number of research questions had to be answered first, that will be detailed in the next section. Finally, this introductory chapter is ended by an outline of the rest of the book.

1.1 Research questions

The goal of this book is to develop a framework for real-time emotion recognition from speech, that allows for easy integration into applications and thus boosts the design of affective applications. Therefore the following questions are researched:

1. **What is suitable methodology for emotion recognition when considering real-time constraints?**

    Methodology for speech emotion recognition includes audio segmentation to find units for analysis, extraction of emotion-relevant features, and classification. Several units for speech emotion classification have been proposed, among them linguistically motivated units such as utterances or words, and acoustically motivated segments such as fixed length segments or segments based on pause detection. While linguistically motivated units require preprocessing by an automatic speech recognition system to obtain unit boundaries, acoustically motivated units can be obtained from the speech signal alone. However, in the case of acoustic units it may be necessary to abandon psychological validity.

In the main part of this book, only acoustic features for emotion recognition will be exploited. While psychology has studied the acoustic correlates that humans employ when perceiving emotions, it is not clear whether the same variables are relevant for recognition by machines. Therefore, a multitude of possible feature types is explored here and whether these contribute complementary information to the task. Since in the past, many studies have been conducted with acted emotions, it should be investigated if acted emotions are good substitutes for real emotions and if the same features are relevant for both.

With regard to the classifier, speech emotion recognition does not pose any particular requirements. Still, some algorithms have proved to be more successful than others. The consideration of real-time constraints as well as uncontrolled input data that occurs during run-time in applications could, however, give preference to other algorithms.

Findings on good methodology will be used to construct a framework for real-time speech emotion recognition which raises further questions.

2. **To what extent is it possible to build application dependent recognisers? How can these recognisers be trained?**

   While it is technically possible to build an online speech emotion recognition system, it is not clear to what extent useful results can be expected from such a system. It cannot yet be the aim here to build a general Swiss-knife emotion recognition system, but rather to be able to easily build task and application dependent recognisers. However, there will not be training databases with emotional speech available for arbitrary tasks, applications and conditions (e.g. microphones). Therefore, a procedure to quickly record a database with not overly acted emotional speech is developed.

3. **How much can further information such as words, gender, bio sensor data and facial gestures contribute to improve speech emotion recognition?**

   Obviously, unimodal emotion recognition from acoustic information alone cannot yield results that are comparable to humans if these in turn use much more information. Therefore, several bimodal recognition experiments are conducted and it is investigated if and how much each modality adds new information to the acoustic channel.

The first question is covered in Chapter 5, while Chapter 6 presents a solution to question 2. Finally, question 3 will be discussed in Chapter 7.

1.2 Outline of the book

This book is organised as follows:

1.2. Outline of the book

- **Chapter 2** introduces to theoretical and practical considerations necessary for the automatic recognition of emotions in speech. Thus, first psychological models of emotions are presented to define the concept of "emotion" and evaluated with respect to their usefulness for automatic recognition. Then, modalities where human emotions can be observed are summarised, among them for example language or facial expressions. Based on these notions, a general speech emotion recognition system and relevant acoustic features for emotions are described. Further emphasis is given to the topic of database types and labelling, as good databases with emotional speech are crucial to the task of emotion recognition from speech.

- **Chapter 3** gives an overview of the literature related to speech emotion recognition. The literature will be reviewed under different aspects, among them emotion units, features, classifiers, speaker types, languages and target classes. Furthermore, challenges in real-time processing and affective applications making use of speech emotion recognition are addressed. Finally, a few approaches to multimodal emotion recognition including speech will be presented. Starting from this discussion, it is motivated why and how the work presented here goes beyond the existing literature.

- **Chapter 4** presents the databases and the methodology for speech emotion recognition that are evaluated in this book. In order to be able to make as general assertions as possible, evaluation experiments are conducted on three databases of different types with acted and spontaneous emotions. Methodology includes several strategies for emotion units that are suitable for real-time applications. Furthermore, possible acoustic correlates of emotions in speech that can be extraced fast and automatically such as pitch or energy are identified and the exact features that are derived from these correlates and form the feature vector are described in detail. As this leads to a very high-dimensional vector, procedures to select the most relevant features for a given purpose are motivated. Lastly, the algorithms of some real-time classifiers are explained.

- In **Chapter 5**, experimental results are described and discussed to find the best settings for the methodology introduced in the previous chapter. Thus, first emotion units are compared with special respect to their fast and robust segmentation. Then, several feature evaluation experiments are conducted, that aim at finding feature types that are relevant for particular database types or in general. A comparison of classifiers ends the chapter.

- **Chapter 6** shows how methodology and experimental results were used to construct a framework for online speech emotion recognition. The chapter further addresses the issue of building small emotional speech databases for training speaker or application dependent recognisers. It is also demonstrated by means of examples how the framework can be used to build affective applications and first insights are given on how users interact with and accept such applications.

- **Chapter 7** presents four studies that combine acoustic information with other information relevant for holistic emotion recognition as multimodal emotion recognition promises higher accuracy. The examined modalities are context (gender information), word, facial and biosignal information.

- **Chapter 8** finally concludes this book with respect to the research questions of the previous section and gives an outlook on future work.

Chapter 2

Basics of emotions in speech

This chapter introduces to theoretical and practical considerations necessary for the automatic recognition of emotions in speech. In order to recognise emotions, one first needs a precise idea of what they are, that is a theory of emotions. Emotion theories have a long tradition in psychology, having produced elaborate models that can be used as basis for automatic emotion recognition. The most relevant ones in view of speech are presented in the first section of this chapter. They are also discussed regarding to what extent they are feasible to realise in practical applications, which is not fully the case for the more recent and complex theories.

The next question to deal with is where emotions can be observed. They are expressed in language, through acoustic, syntactic or semantic information, but also on other levels of human behaviour as facial or body gestures. These are the channels which are at the disposal of a human communication partners. Machines, however, can also exploit information obtained by measuring body signals like heart rate or perspiration to deduce the emotional state of a person.

Having introduced these notions, a closer look on automatic emotion recognition from speech is appropriate. After presenting a general system design, ranging from audio segmentation over feature extraction to the actual classification, possible features as acoustic correlates of emotions in speech are described in detail, since the extraction of relevant features is a major part of the work presented here.

A related topic is the design of databases with examples of emotional vocal expression as they are an important input to automatic classifiers. Therefore it is important to discuss the major design questions, which are 1) the type of the included emotions, that is whether they are acted or natural, induced or spontaneous, and 2) the labelling of the emotions found within the database. The latter is dependent on the underlying emotion model and on the scenario of the corpus. Of course, it is harder to find adequate descriptions for natural emotions.

2.1 A psychological view on emotions: Models of emotions

Humans are experts in emotions, as we experience them every moment of a day. We can also most of the time name the emotional state that we or the people we interact with are in. It is, however, not easy to describe this in a systematic way. Still, in order to classify emotions automatically a precise idea of what emotions are is needed. So what is an emotion? A psychologist would definitely give a different answer than a linguist, a computer scientist or the average man on the street. Let's start with a general definition. Merriam-Webster's Online Dictionary [155] states, among others: "a conscious mental reaction (as anger or fear) subjectively experienced as strong feeling usually directed toward a specific object and typically accompanied by physiological and behavioural changes in the body". A more elaborate, psychological definition is for example to define emotions as "episodes of massive, synchronised recruitment of mental and somatic resources allowing to adapt to or cope with a stimulus event subjectively appraised as being highly pertinent to the needs, goals, and values of the individuals" from Roesch et al. [189].

From both definitions it is certainly agreed that the word *emotion* describes a short-term, consciously perceived, valenced state, either positive or negative, like for example joy or anger, in contrast to moods which can last one or several days (cheerfulness/depression), preferences that describe our attitudes in relation to objects (liking/hating) over a longer period or dispositions like nervousness or anxiousness which describe personality traits [189]. The fact that emotions lead to changes in the body, and that these changes can actually be observed, is indeed what makes the work described here possible.

Note that the notions *emotion*, *affect* and *feeling* are often used interchangeably. However, slight distinctions can still be made. *Affect* is usually used as a general term. Damasio [57] defines *emotion* as a bodily affective reaction in contrast to *feeling* as a mental affective reaction. Therefore, *emotion* refers rather to what can be observed from outside — and thus is more applicable in the context here —, while *feeling* refers to an internal state.

Psychologists have a long tradition in research on emotions and they have proposed various models or theories for the description of emotions. Until the last few decades the concept of basic emotions was the most accepted of these. It is inspired by evolution theory, and already Darwin [58] supposed that there exist basic innate emotions which have a specific physiological response pattern, like for example contractions of the arm muscles while experiencing anger as preparation for fighting. Ekman, the most prominent representative of the basic emotion theory, classified emotions as having a distinct facial expression associated that can be recognised uniformly across cultures [70], as illustrated by Figure 2.1. Besides physiological and facial evidence, a third source of information for psychologists to identify basic emotions is to find emotion terms that are most widely agreed among subjects [54]. Other emotions would then be either mixtures of

2.1. A psychological view on emotions: Models of emotions

Figure 2.1: Facial expressions of emotions that are universal according to Ekman et al. [70]. Upper row: anger, fear, surprise; lower row: disgust, joy, sadness, boredom.

Authors	Basic emotions
Plutchik [181]	acceptance, anger, anticipation, disgust, joy, fear, sadness, surprise
Ekman et al. [70]	anger, disgust, fear, joy, sadness, surprise
Oatley and Johnson-Laird [168]	anger, disgust, anxiety, happiness, sadness
Weiner and Graham [253]	happiness, sadness

Table 2.1: Some definitions of basic emotions (from Ortony and Turner [169]).

these basic emotions or cultural dependent emotions.

Table 2.1 shows an overview of Ortony and Turner [169]'s synopsis of which basic emotions were identified in different studies. Obviously, anger, disgust, fear/anxiety, joy/happiness and sadness are most often included into a basic set of emotions.

An example system for describing emotions through basic emotion terms is Plutchik's wheel of emotions (see Figure 2.2) with 8 emotions in opposite pairs (acceptance vs. disgust, anger vs. fear, anticipation vs. surprise, joy vs. sadness) arranged in a wheel with the strength of the emotions modeled by the distance from the centre of the wheel [181].

The concept of basic emotions is easy to conceive, however, from the multitude of terms in Table 2.1 one can already suspect that the so-called basic emotions are not that basic at all. Indeed, the concept's validity is questioned. Ortony and Turner [169] argue that basic emotion terms (which are anger, fear, joy and so on) are not to be confused with basic emotions, and that the expression of emotions (for example the facial expression) is not the same as the emotions themselves. They claim that for example occurrences of specific facial expressions that are recognised around the

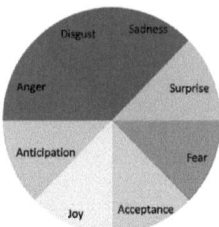

Figure 2.2: Plutchik's wheel of emotions [181].

world and seem universal are not linked to emotions but rather to certain conditions that also elicit emotions. A further argument against basic emotion theories is that most of the so-called basic emotions as found in Table 2.1 are contained in some other emotional state. As an example, distress would be a more basic concept of anger and fear.

Furthermore, it is often inadequate to describe emotions of every-day life by mixtures of basic emotions as these are assumed to be full-blown, and in everyday life, full-blown emotions occur very rarely. A real emotion might be between anger and fear, shadowed by disgust, and the intensity of all the components is important as well.

An approach that can remedy some of these short-comings are dimensional models where an emotion is a point in an emotion space described by two or three variables. Variables in a two-dimensional space are usually valence/evaluation/pleasure and arousal/activation; for a third dimension, dominance, stance, power or control are usually added. On the one hand, these enable a more fine-grained description, because they allow for the simultaneous modelling of more than one aspect of emotions in a continuous range of values. On the other hand, however, they are simplifying as they capture only those aspects encoded in the dimensions. For instance, in a two-dimensional model, differences between anger and fear can hardly be modelled: both are highly negative and come with high arousal. A three-dimensional model can cope better with this discrimination, as can be seen in Figure 2.3 which shows a two- and a three-dimensional emotion space. Basic emotions can still be represented in a dimensional model, as a point or rather area in the emotion space. An example for a dimensional model is Mehrabian's widely used PAD (**P**leasure-**A**rousal-**D**ominance) model [153].

Both basic emotions as well as dimensional models are simplified representations of emotions that of course do not cover all their aspects. In particular, both do not consider the goals and effects of emotions. Hence, appraisal theory describes emotions basically to be "elicited by evaluations (*appraisals*) of events and situations" [190]. It tries to overcome simplifications made by alternative models by providing a very differentiated elaboration – not directly of emotions

2.1. A psychological view on emotions: Models of emotions

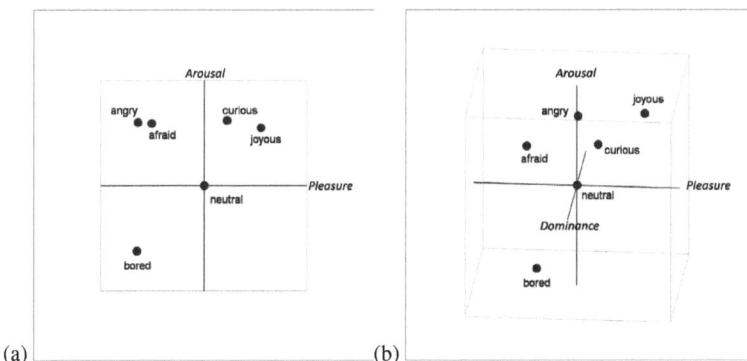

Figure 2.3: Dimensional model of emotions; (a) 2 dimensions, (b) 3 dimensions.

but of the causes of emotions through a set of variables that consider the cognitive evaluation of events by dimensions, criteria, or checks. Each emotion is thus associated with a distinct pattern of appraisals.

Several varieties of appraisal theory exist, e. g. from Frijda [81], Scherer [196], Roseman et al. [191], and Smith and Ellsworth [223] that differ mainly in the set of appraisal variables they define. As an example, Scherer's set is reproduced in Table 2.2 which allows a very fine-grained "18-dimensional" description of emotions. A further important appraisal model is the so-called OCC model [170] that defines emotions as "valenced reactions to consequences of events, actions of agents, and aspects of objects" and looks at the cognitive structure and implications of emotions. Through the multitude of criteria, appraisal theory can obviously easily model blended emotions and also many other aspects of emotions.

The above mentioned models all describe emotions more or less adequately for psychological purposes. However, they are not to the same extent suitable for automatic emotion processing. Thus, though the idea of basic emotions or discrete emotional classes is simplifying, it is the one that yields, at the current state of the art, most satisfactory results for automatic emotion recognition because the higher number of variables or dimensions provided by other models cannot reliably be estimated. Furthermore, if humans are supposed to use the results or to annotate the training data of a statistical classifier, it is also much more intuitive and faster for naïve persons to interpret terms of basic, or common, emotions than to look at points in an emotion space or a set of appraisal variables. For these reasons, discrete emotional classes are the most widely spread model, and commonly used categories in recognition tasks are for example anger, joy, sadness [173, 215].

Still, an approximation of the dimensional model is very useful in practice by defining areas in

Criteria	Variables	Values
novelty	suddenness	high, medium, low
	familiarity	high, medium, low
	predictability	high, medium, low
intrinsic pleasantness	global	high, medium, low
goal significance	concern relevance	person concerns, relationship concerns, social order concerns
	outcome probability	high, medium, low
	relation to expectation	consonant, dissonant
	conduciveness to goals	conducive, obstructive
	urgency	high, medium, low
coping potential	cause: agent	self, other, nature
	cause: motive	intent, negligence
	controllability of event	high, medium, low
	power of agent	high, medium, low
	adjustment possible to agent's own goals?	high, medium, low
compatibility with standards	external (norms or demands of a reference group)	high, medium, low
	internal (self ideal or internalised moral code)	high, medium, low

Table 2.2: Variables of appraisal theory (from Scherer [196]).

the emotion space as classes, for example the four quadrants in Figure 2.3 (a) (positive pleasure/high arousal, negative pleasure/high arousal, positive pleasure/low arousal, negative pleasure/low arousal). Of course, there are also some studies on using dimensional models for automatic recognition [91, 256]. Usually only the two dimensions valence and arousal are included. However, with continuous values as input, no discrete output can be produced so that a regression over the continuous range of values has to be performed. This is more difficult to interpret for humans and thus better suited for direct exploitation by computers.

The OCC model is mainly applied to emotion synthesis, for instance for embodied conversational agents, as it specifies valenced reactions to the situations in which an agent can be [13], but has also been applied to affective user modeling by Conati and Zhou [52]. The possibilities of full appraisal theory exceed those of current automatic emotion recognition, however, estimation of only few variables would be feasible. Besides, effects of appraisal on the voice are still largely unexplored, even from a psycholinguistically point of view, though it might be the theory for future emotion recognisers. Scherer [195] already examined some predictions for appraisal effects on acoustic parameters. Again, however, appraisal theory is already used for modeling embodied agent behaviour [90]. In the end, the choice of the most appropriate model or subset of occurring emotion classes should be application-driven.

2.2 The expression of emotion

After having reviewed how emotions can be described, the next question is where emotions can be observed. As "bodily reactions" they manifest themselves in all physiological modalities, including language and speech, which is the main emphasis here and will be discussed first, but also extra-linguistic modalities such as facial and body gestures, or biosignals.

2.2.1 Language and speech

Information on emotion is encoded in all aspects of language, in what we say and in how we say or pronounce it, and the "how" is even more important than the "what". Looking at all levels of language, from pragmatics down to the phonetic/acoustic level, the following things can be considered: Starting with *pragmatics*, a speakers' intention is highly correlated with his emotional state [199]. In this context, Gibbs et al. [85] found that figurative language such as metaphors or irony conveys emotions much more subtle than literal expressions; for example the metaphoric expression "I had reached the boiling point" is more tailored at the specific situation than the literal expression "I was really angry". *Semantics*, or the literal meaning of an utterance or of words, feature the most obvious display of emotions, so statements or keywords such as "I am happy" can be analysed as emotion indicators [171]. However, literal emotion expression can also be meant ironically or express not the real emotions a speaker feels but rather those he wants others to believe he feels, as this level of language is the one which is most easily manipulated deliberately. Fries [80] lists exclamatory and optative phrases as special *syntactic* constructs that most often have an emotional meaning associated. For example, "That fits so well!" tells of much higher arousal of its speaker than the utterance "That fits well.". Furthermore, certain part-of-speech categories such as interjections are very likely to imply emotions, and *morphologically*, prefixes like "super-" (e. g. in "superman") have an intensifying positive meaning (which of course can also be employed ironically).

Emotion	Pitch	Intensity	Speaking rate	Voice quality
Anger	higher mean wider range abrupt changes	higher	slightly faster	breathy chest tone
Joy	higher mean wider range	higher	faster or slower	breathy blaring
Sadness	lower mean narrower range	lower	slower	resonant
Fear	higher mean wider range	normal	faster	irregular voicing
Disgust	lower mean wider range	lower	slower	grumbled chest tone

Table 2.3: Variations of acoustic variables observed in emotional expressions compared to neutral speech. Synopsis of Murray and Arnott [159]'s summary table.

The tone of a voice, that is the *phonetic and acoustic* properties of spoken language, is another indicator of emotions beyond the literal meaning. Thus, for instance a cracking voice is evidence of high arousal. Acoustic emotion recognition is the main focus of this book and the relevant features will now be discussed in greater detail. The vocal parameters that have been best researched in psychological studies and which are also intuitively the most important ones are prosody (pitch, intensity, speaking rate) and voice quality. Murray and Arnott [159] wrote an often cited review of literature on emotions in speech and refer to a number of studies which seemingly have identified almost unambiguous acoustic correlates of emotions. They summarise their review as displayed in Table 2.3 which shows prosody and voice quality to be most important to distinguish between emotions according to human perception. In particular, pitch and intensity seem to be correlated to activation, so that high pitch and intensity values imply high, low pitch and intensity values low activation.

The automatic recognition of emotion seems straight-forward when looking at Table 2.3. However, when examining closer different studies on acoustic correlates of emotions of multiple authors, also those described by Murray and Arnott [159], often contradicting results can be found, as for example Cowie et al. [56] noticed. This is partly due to different variants of certain emotions such as hot and cold anger, but as well to the intrinsically great variability of emotional expressions. Thus, as will also be shown later in this book, there is just no direct mapping between acoustics and emotions.

2.2.2 Extra-linguistic modalities

Of course, the expression of emotions is not restricted to language. Facial and body gestures may at first seem to be not as important as speech, but psychological experiments showed that they reveal the real emotional state even more reliably, because the physiological processes that take place for speech production can better be controlled consciously than for example facial expressions. Words are hence often employed to distract from the real emotion. Among visual approaches, emotion recognition from faces is most frequently found [117, 214, 265] but also from body gestures [94].

The physiological state of a person also reflects strongly his/her emotional state. It is measurable through signals like pulse, electro-myogram (EMG; for muscle activity), skin conductance (to measure perspiration) or respiratory frequency as described by Wagner et al. [249] and Hönig et al. [104]. Though, these are channels that humans cannot exploit to get hints on the affective state of another person. Event-related brain potentials from the electro-encephalogram (EEG) also encode affect [4]. At first, these sensors may seem to be very invasive, but as computers become more and more ubiquitous, it is imaginable that in the future, they might even be integrated in clothes, so that this information could easily be exploited in many situations for automatic emotion recognition, and serve of course also other purposes.

Emotional behaviour can also be observed in human-computer interaction with traditional devices, for instance from patterns of mouse-clickings which Schuller [203] relates the user state to. Furthermore, the user's expression of emotion can be enabled or supported by gestures made with novel interaction devices. Examples are Nintendo's Wiimote which Rehm et al. [188] have used to measure the user's expressivity and Sentoy, a tangible doll equipped with sensors that allow users to express themselves emotionally introduced by Paiva et al. [174]. Lv et al. [150] use novel pressure sensor keyboards and relate the emotional state of the user to the pressure and timing sequence of key strokes.

Information on emotions can be deduced from all available modalities alone. But, as Hudlicka [107] states, reliable emotion detection requires the concurrent use of multiple modalities. Which modalities should be used in a specific scenario depends on the types of emotions that should be recognised as some are easier recognised by a certain modality, on the feasibility of application of the technical instruments necessary to track the modalities, possibly on real-time requirements and on the availability of the multimodal data, as for example on the telephone, of course no facial data is available. Furthermore, machines cannot be expected to yield human-comparable results, when humans employ all information they have at hand, but machines are limited to only one modality. Nevertheless, one needs knowledge and expertise about every single channel and the goal of this dissertation is to contribute to the speech channel.

2.3 Automatic emotion recognition from speech

As already mentioned in the previous sections the study of emotions has a long tradition in psychology. However, in information technology, emotions have rather been regarded as useless or even contradicting to "serious" technical applications. Picard introduced the notion of *Affective Computing* in her ground-breaking book [178] of the same title in the nineties. Since then, it is accepted for an intelligent user interface to consider emotions, which means recognising and reacting to the emotional state of the user and exhibiting itself emotional behaviour. This is necessary both for efficiency and for convenience reasons. In the last decade a number of approaches to affective computing have emerged, identifying physiological and cognitive human variables to exploit, applications in existing technology, possible usage scenarios and investigating resources for research and applications such as databases with emotional speech. In this section, first a general overview of a system for emotion recognition from speech is given. Subsequently, an overview of feature extraction, selection and reduction methods is given in more detail, to lay foundations for later discussions of this topic. An extensive overview of existing literature will be given in the next chapter.

2.3.1 Overview of a statistical speech emotion recognition system

One of the first practical works on automatic emotion recognition was conducted by Dellaert et al. [62] in 1996. Their data collection comprised 1250 sentences of five speakers in five different acted emotions, namely happiness, sadness, anger, fear, and neutral. They computed features related to the smoothed pitch contour and to timing (or rhythm) aspects such as speaking rate for every sentence. With this feature set they came close to 80 % recognition accuracy. Note that all features, also the rhythm related features, were based exclusively on pitch. Of course, the underlying data was very idealistic, however, the features and the methodology including feature selection is similar to many current approaches.

Thus, a speech emotion recognition system in the tradition of pattern recognition systems consists of three principal parts, as shown in Figure 2.4: signal processing, feature calculation and classification.

Signal processing involves digitisation of the recorded signal, potentially acoustic preprocessing such as filtering, and the segmentation of the input signal into meaningful units. While the first three steps are standard procedures, the last step is the most crucial with respect to speech emotion recognition.

The aim of the feature calculation is to find those properties of the digitised and preprocessed acoustic signal that are characteristic of emotions and to represent them in an n-dimensional fea-

2.3. Automatic emotion recognition from speech

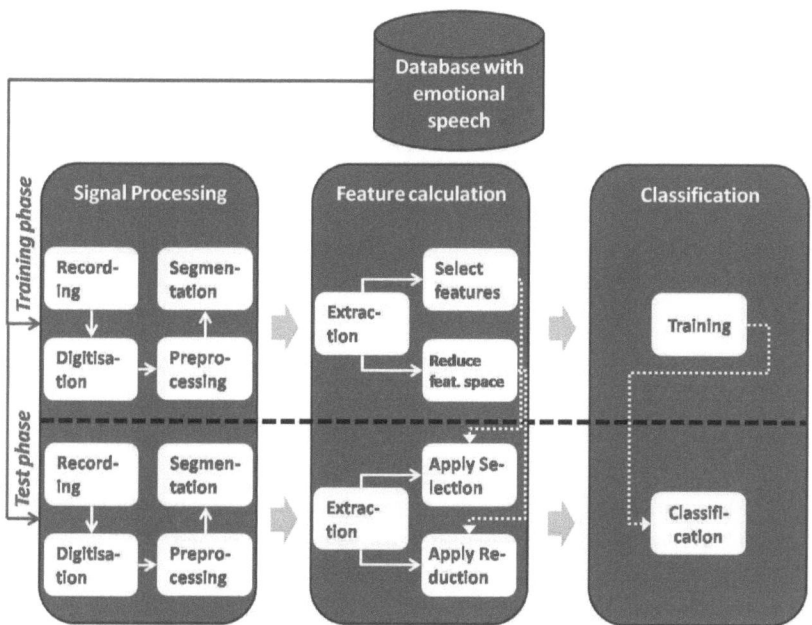

Figure 2.4: Overview of a speech emotion recognition system.

ture vector. So far, there is not yet a general agreement on which features are the most important ones and good features seem to be highly data dependent, for which the current book provides evidence and which is also a topic of Devillers et al. [63]. As a consequence, most approaches compute a high number of features and apply then a feature selection algorithm, in order to reduce the dimensionality of the input data. The feature selection algorithm chooses the most significant features with respect to the data for the given task. Alternatively, a feature reduction algorithm like principal components analysis (PCA) can be used to encode the main information of the feature space more compactly.

After the feature calculation, each emotion unit is represented by one or more feature vectors, and the problem of emotion recognition can now be considered a general pattern classification problem. Static as well as dynamic classification approaches are considered. In static modeling, one feature vector represents one emotion unit, while in dynamic modeling, one emotion unit is represented by a sequence of feature vectors. The latter therefore consider also the temporal behaviour of the features. As timing is very important for emotions, temporal information has to be encoded in the feature vector for static modeling, which usually leads to high-dimensional vectors, while the feature vectors used in dynamic modeling are generally smaller. So, in principle, any classifier can be used, though Support Vector Machines, Neural Networks and Bayesian classifiers for static modeling and HMMs for dynamic modeling are most commonly found in the literature on emotional speech recognition. Currently, static modeling approaches prevail. The parameters of the classifier are learnt from training data which is the topic of Section 2.4 in this chapter.

For real-time emotion recognition, online capabilities of used algorithms have to be considered in all steps. Additionally, methods need to be more robust against changing noise and other interferences because in applications, influences on the situation cannot be controlled afterwards.

Before going into the details of feature calculation for acoustic emotion recognition, a final note should be given to offline validation methods of classifiers for pattern recognition and, in particular, emotion recognition. In order to get a prediction on how a trained classifier will perform on new unseen data, it has to be tested with data that was not used during training. As data recording usually involves a huge effort and it is consequently not possible to acquire unlimited new test data, normally an existing database is partitioned into disjunct training and test sets. On the other hand, the quality of the classifier usually increases with the size of the training data and with such a percentage split a considerable amount of the data is not available for training. Furthermore, the evaluation results depends strongly on the chosen split. Another possibility is the so-called cross-validation where the database is split into n parts and by iterating over all parts, always $n-1$ parts are used for training and the remaining part is used for testing. The overall recognition accuracy then results from the combination of the accuracies on all test splits. A most frequently found value for n is 10; in this book mostly $n=3$ or $n=5$ is assumed. Usually, all splits are made of equal size and it is also considered that the class distribution remains equal. This proceeding is called stratified cross-validation. However, in particular in emotion recognition it is often important for the quality of the predictions to consider other criteria as well, for instance to observer speaker independence, or age and gender distribution. In this case, it can occur that the splits are only approximately of equal size and also the class distribution is not maintained completely.

2.3.2 Feature calculation

Features for emotion recognition are calculated from speech signals as produced by a speaker. The speech signal can be assumed to be a waveform that is momentarily periodic. As every waveform it has certain properties such as amplitude, time, and (usually superposed) frequencies that serve to characterise it and also help to distinguish between different emotions. The graphical representation of a waveform in Figure 2.5, upper part, shows time on the x-axis and amplitude on the y-axis. Frequency is implicitly given by the oscillation of the signal.

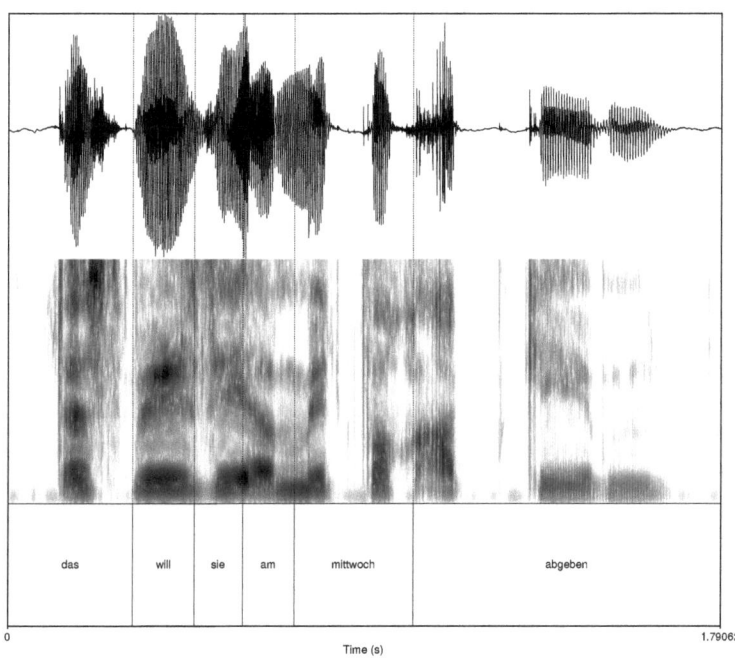

Figure 2.5: Representation of a signal as a waveform and as a spectrogram.

For computational purposes, the waveform is digitised. Consequently, the rate at which samples are taken is an important characteristic of the signal. According to the Nyquist theorem, a continuous singal can be sampled without loss of information only if it does not contain frequency components above one half of the sampling rate. Although the human ear perceives frequencies up to about 20 kHz (though this ability degrades with age), only frequencies below 8 kHz are used for the perception of speech. Thus, a sampling rate of 16 kHz is sufficient for most speech processing purposes. Telephone lines usually transmit only 8 kHz sampled sound signals, which makes some phonemes sound equal (e. g. /s/ and /f/), though humans are able to differentiate them by means of the context.

Another form of representation of a signal that is especially suitable for speech analysis is the spectrogram which is shown in the central part of Figure 2.5. It shows the energy of small frequency bands of for example 20 Hz over short time intervals (e. g. 5 msec), so it is a representation of frequency over time. Amplitude is encoded by the colouring: the darker a frequency is coloured in the spectrogram, the higher the energy of the frequency is. Different phonemes or speaking styles have very distinct frequency patterns that are visible in the spectrogram.

Various other acoustic measures can be derived from amplitude, time and frequencies.[1] Among them are pitch, energy, voice quality, duration and other spectral properties. According to Table 2.3, the recognition of emotions from acoustic measures seems to be straight-forward, as one needs only search for certain prosodic patterns. But, unfortunately, the problem is much more complex. As with many tasks, what is relatively easy for humans is really hard for computers, since either the variables humans employ to recognise emotions have not yet been identified correctly or they are inadequate for machine processing. Looking closer at the studies examined by Murray and Arnott [159], one can notice that they are to some extent contradicting. This is most obvious for anger where it is in part due to the different appearances of anger (e. g. cold/hot anger), but can also be found for the speech rate in a joyous or fearful state. In addition to this, the acoustic effects of anger, joy and fear are very similar, though these emotions are usually not hard to distinguish for humans. Furthermore, it is not mentioned whether the studies looked at data from actors or on naturalistic data. While even professional actors cannot put themselves in an emotional state that is completely natural, the competence of lay actors to produce realistic emotions is highly argued. They rather produce prototypical, full-blown emotions and not those mixed or shadowed, just noticeable emotions that occur in real life.

Therefore, there is no easy mapping from acoustics to emotions. In the following those acoustic measures that are the basis of most features used for automatic emotion recognition will be described. For human perception their importance is quite well explored, the extent of their respective significance for automatic emotion recognition however is not yet ultimately resolved. Regarding their temporal structure the measures belong to two broad groups: pitch, formants, loudness, Mel-frequency cepstral coefficients, wavelets and other spectral features are measured for short fixed-length time intervals, while duration, speaking rate and voice quality are usually supra-segmental measures.

Pitch

The term pitch refers to the ear's perception of tone height [49]. For most purposes, this is just the fundamental frequency f_0, though the two terms are not identical since f_0 can be measured as a property of an acoustic wave, while pitch is grounded by human perception. Pitch is a very obvious property of speech, also for non-experts, and it is often erroneously considered to be most important for emotion perception. Examples of pitch contours are given in Figure 2.6 (a). The contours of acted neutral, happy and bored speech are quite distinctive, with higher pitch

---

[1]The most commonly used features for speech emotion recognition are derived from prosody, that is energy, pitch and rhythm, so features in general are often denoted as prosodic features, in contrast to linguistic features derived from word information. However, as also many non-prosodic acoustic features are relevant, it will always be refer to acoustic features here.

2.3. Automatic emotion recognition from speech

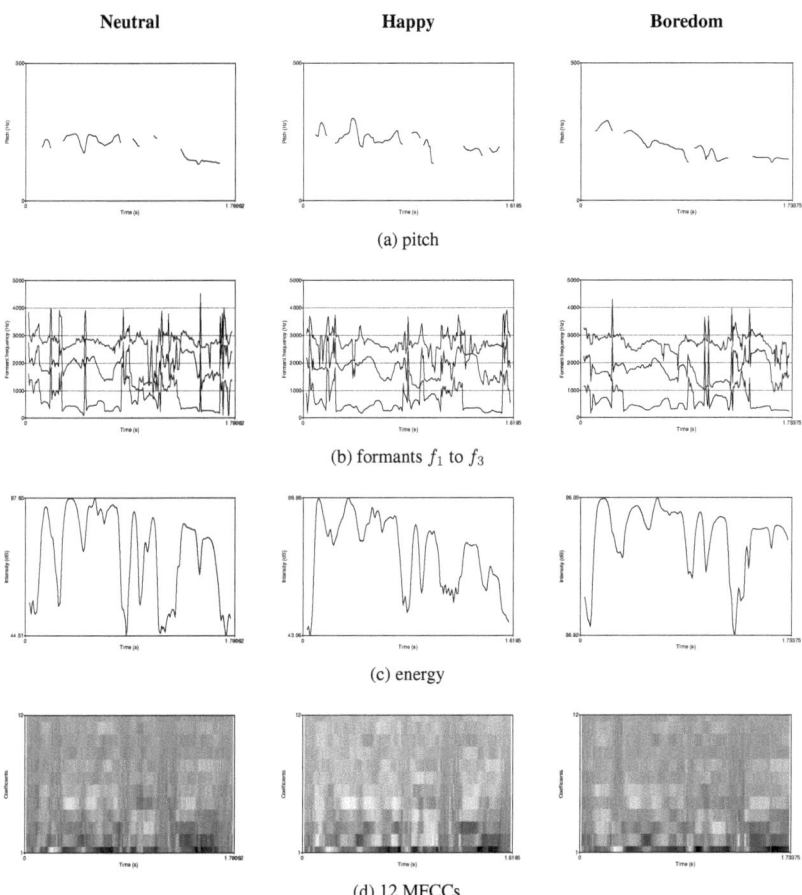

Figure 2.6: Emotion relevant acoustic properties shown for a neutral, a happy and a bored utterance of an actress taken from the Berlin Database of Emotional Speech [31]. The text spoken in each of the utterances was "Das will sie am Mittwoch abgeben." ("She will hand it in on Wednesday.").

and greater variance for happiness, but little variance and a falling-off curve for boredom, both compared to neutral. Pitch does definitely have some importance for emotions, but it is probably not as huge as typically assumed. Generally, a rise in pitch is an indicator for higher arousal, but also the course of the pitch contour reveals information on affect.

Pitch can be calculated from the time or the frequency domain. In the time domain pitch can for example be calculated from the zero-crossings rate. This method is however more suited for musical pitch detection. For speech, pitch is usually determined by looking at the maxima of the auto-correlated frequency spectrum. Either the global maximum is taken, or, for better results, a path through the strongest local maxima is searched which considers that big pitch changes such as octave jumps or voiced-unvoiced transitions and pitch during silence occur seldom. Obviously pitch does not exist for the unvoiced parts of the speech signal.

Formants

Formants are local maxima in the frequency spectrum caused by resonance during speech production [49]. The fundamental frequency f_0 (related to pitch) is usually the global maximum, and the further formants f_1, f_2, f_3, ... are the following local maxima, sorted by frequency. Figure 2.6 (b) gives examples for the first three formants. Especially for vowels the distribution of the formants is very characteristic. For instance, the first formant of /i/ is low, while it is high in /o/ and f_2 and f_3 are close. The degree of significance of formants for emotions is often estimated low although for example Biersack and Kempe [25] associate higher first formants, and Waaramaa et al. [248] higher third formants with positive emotions. Goudbeek et al. [89] find a direct relationship between high arousal and a high first formant in vowels, as well as positive valence and a high second formant. Articulatory reduction, which is also related to formant positions, has been observed in sadness and fear in the Berlin Database of Emotional Speech by Kienast et al. [125]. However, all this studies have been conducted on acted speech, so it is questionable if this finding can be transferred to spontaneous emotions. However, articulation, and thus formant position, is influenced by the physiological state of a speaker, which in turn is influenced by emotions [88]. Consequently, there does exist a connection between formants and emotions, though it may not be obvious or unambiguous.

Loudness

Loudness is the strength of a sound as perceived by the human ear. It is hard to measure directly, therefore the signal energy is often used as a related feature. Energy can be calculated from the spectrum after a Fourier transformation of the original signal. However, it differs from loudness in that all existing noises add to the signal energy, while the ear perceives the loudness of speech as just that.

The energy curve depends on many factors, such as phonemes, speaking style, utterance type (e. g. declarative, interrogative, exclamatory), but also on the affective state of the speaker. Again, like pitch, high energy roughly correlates with high arousal, but also variations of the energy curve give hints on the speaker's emotion. For example, as can be seen in Figure 2.6 (c), variations of energy may be lower for bored speech.

Mel-frequency cepstral coefficients

Mel-frequency cepstral coefficients (MFCCs, [154]) are a parametric representation of the speech signal, that is commonly used in automatic speech recognition, but they have proved to be successful for other purposes as well, among them speaker identification and emotion recognition.

MFCCs are calculated by applying a Mel-scale filter bank to the Fourier transform of a windowed signal. Subsequently, a DCT (discrete cosine transform) transforms the logarithmised spectrum into a cepstrum. The MFCCs are then the amplitudes of the cepstrum. Usually, only the first 12 coefficients are used. Through the mapping onto the Mel-scale, which is an adaptation of the Hertz-scale for frequency to the human sense of hearing, MFCCs enable a signal representation that is closer to human perception.

MFCCs filter out pitch and other influences in speech that are not linguistically relevant, hence they are very suitable for speech recognition. Though this should make them useless for emotion recognition, they turned out to yield also very good results in several approaches [138, 162, 203]. This can be seen as further evidence that the relationship between speech and emotions is not as clear as could be expected from human evaluation of acted emotional speech and that traditional features are not sufficient for automatic recognition.

Differences of MFCCs depending on the speaker's affect are visualised in Figure 2.6 (d).

Wavelets

Wavelet transformation [60], like Fourier transformation, yields representation of a signal in terms of other functions, which are sine and cosine functions for Fourier transformation, and a set of orthonormal square-integrable basis functions for wavelet transformation. Common so-called "mother-wavelets" are for example Haar-, Daubechies-, or "Mexican Hat"-wavelets. Wavelets have the advantage over Fourier transforms of being localised in both frequency and time, not just in frequency. This is achieved by breaking a signal into shifted and scaled versions of the mother wavelet ending up in a time-scale view of the signal. In this way short duration and high frequency as well as longer duration and lower frequency information can be captured at the same time. Thus, a wavelet transform holds more information than a Fourier transform. An example of such a decomposition is illustrated in Figure 2.7.

Since wavelet transforms contain many aspects of the speech signal, in particular information on timing which is very important for emotions, they could be very promising features for speech emotion recognition. So far, however, they are still novel features that have not been used often [76].

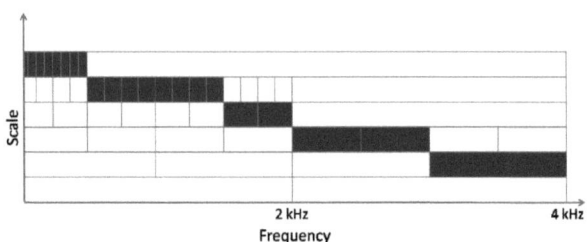

Figure 2.7: An example for a decomposition into frequency scales by wavelet transformation.

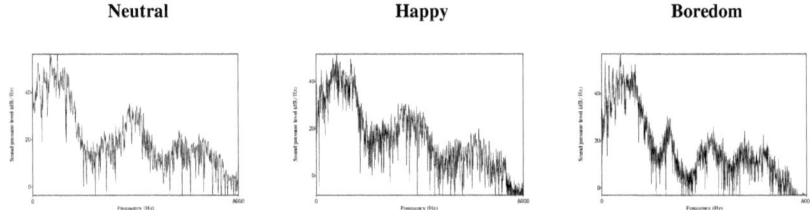

Figure 2.8: The frequency spectrum of an /a/ in neutral, happy and bored speech.

Other spectral features

Besides the already mentioned features related to the frequency spectrum (in a broader sense these include also MFCCs and wavelets), a number of other measures can be derived from the spectrum. These include the spectral slope, mean, centre of gravity or further measurements of the distribution of frequencies in the spectrum which would for example reflect a rise in the proportion of high frequencies that should occur with high arousal as in Figure 2.8.

Duration and speaking rate

Timing certainly plays a huge role in the expression of emotion. This concerns the duration of speech units like utterance length, average word length in an utterance or average syllable length in a word, but also the speaking rate. Speaking rate can be measured e. g. by the word or syllable rate, if word information is available. To automatically compute it exclusively from the signal, energy-peak counting approximates speaking rate. A gross measure is for example the distance between (low-passed) local energy maxima which roughly coincide with the syllable rate. This can be further refined by combining multiple estimators [157]. Furthermore, the distribution of voiced and unvoiced segments from pitch calculation approximates speaking rate.

Speaking rate and duration itself but also various temporal patterns of words or utterances can

2.3. Automatic emotion recognition from speech

Figure 2.9: The times of glottal pulses (blue lines) marked in the same speech signals as in Figure 2.6.

help to distinguish between emotional user states. Luengo et al. [146] derive rhythm features from vowel duration. In Figure 2.6, for example, the duration of the happy utterance is slightly shorter than that of the other utterances. Similarly, the duration and distribution of pauses is significant: it makes a difference whether few long pauses or many short pauses occur. The first might be an indication of pondering, while the latter may result from a chopped speaking style.

Voice quality

The quality of a voice can sound breathy, creaky, harsh, whispery. Relations of voice quality to emotions are diverse, for example, breathiness may result from excitement, harshness from anger, or a frightened speaker might whisper. Voice quality can be measured in several ways, jitter, shimmer and harmonics-to-noise ratio (HNR) being the most frequent ones in automatic classification approaches. Usually, voice quality measurements like voice breaks, jitter and shimmer are performed on long vowels only and are originally used for the analysis of pathological voices, but they can also give information about emotions. Voice breaks are measured by the proportion of unvoiced regions in typically voiced vowels. Jitter and shimmer measure the variability in distance and amplitude of the glottal pulses which are shown in Figure 2.9.

HNR can be computed on the whole signal or on small parts of it. It relates the energy of the harmonic parts of a signal to the energy of the noise parts and thus measures the pureness of the voice.

Though voice quality is intuitively a good indicator for emotions, such features are not part of standard feature sets for emotion recognition.

Feature selection and reduction

Most of the described acoustic parameters including pitch, energy, formants, MFCCs, HNR, are short-term measures over frames of around 20 msec. In emotion recognition, however, usually not short-term values are of interest, but rather statistical functions of them like mean, maximum, minimum, variance and so on over a longer segment as emotions are considered to be suprasegmental phenomena expressed over longer time periods. Thereby a huge number of features can potentially be generated. This is on the one hand costly for the classifier in terms of time, but may also degrade its accuracy by over-fitting to the training data, the so-called "curse of dimensionality" [24]. However, there is not yet an agreement which is the best set of features for vocal emotion recognition. For this reason, there exist mainly two approaches to finding a good feature set. One is to carefully design a manually chosen feature set, the other is to provide a multitude of features and let an automatic selection procedure decide which are the most relevant ones for the given task. But even if many manually chosen features are provided, a selection process can be helpful.

The selection procedure can either operate by ranking all features individually according to an evaluation function or by evaluating feature subsets rather than individual features. For the latter, a search algorithm through the space of possible feature subsets is needed. An exhaustive search, though it would find the optimal subset by evaluating all possible subsets, is out of question for computational reasons. Thus, heuristic search functions like best-first search, random search or genetic search are preferably applied. A possible evaluation function for feature subsets is the recognition rate of a classifier but it can also be the correlation of the features within the subset. In order not to evaluate all subsets, a stop criterion is defined, for example to stop after N iterations of no improvement. For single features, the evaluation function can also be classifier performance, but more often information theoretic measures like the information gain of the feature or other entropy based measures are used. The obtained ranking is then used to select a predefined number of features or all features with an evaluation score above a certain threshold.

The most popular selection algorithm for emotion features is sequential forward selection (SFS). This procedure starts with an empty set, and at every iteration, one feature is added. During an iteration sequentially the effect of joining each remaining feature individually to the current set is evaluated and at the end the best feature is chosen. The search stops if there has been no improvement in one (or N – to reduce the possibility of getting stuck in a local minimum) subsequent runs. A variation of this method starts with the full set and sequentially removes features, thus it is called sequential backward selection (SBS). In order to further avoid local minima, sequential forward floating search (SFFS) allows also removal of features in every iteration, sequential backward floating search (SBFS) works analogously. This is usually more successful, but also more time-consuming.

If there is a huge number of features, evaluating feature subsets by the performance of sophisticated classifiers like Support Vector Machines or Neural Networks can be too costly. Therefore, a simplistic classifier like K-Nearest-Neighbour or Naïve Bayes can be used for the selection,

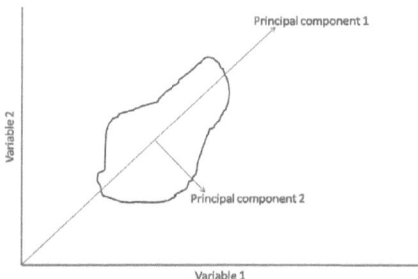

Figure 2.10: PCA: a mapping of the original two dimensions onto the principal component axes.

while later classification on the reduced feature set is performed with the better classifier. The drawback, however, is that the resulting feature subset from the selection is optimised for another classifier than is used for the final classification. This can lead to lower performance and in just not having an optimal subset. Another possibility is to first reduce the number of features by correlation analysis and subsequently perform the feature selection with the target classifier.

As an alternative to selecting some features and discarding the rest, a dimension reduction of the feature space can also be achieved by a transformation of the features such as principal component analysis (PCA). PCA [255, p. 307] transforms the original feature space into a new coordinate system with principal axes placed along the greatest variance of the features. The principal axes are calculated as the eigenvectors of the diagonalised covariance matrix. This is illustrated by Figure 2.10.

2.4 Databases with emotional speech

Databases with recorded material of emotional speech are essential to statistical emotion recognition. General emotion-specific relations between acoustic parameters can only be learnt from a large set of examples. Thereby, the quality of the recordings is crucial to the trained classifier, since it can not learn more than the training data provides. The more specific the data fits to the particular scenario or the more representative it is to the general expression of emotions, the better does it allow a classifier to generalise to unseen instances. Furthermore, research is restricted to those emotions that can be found in available databases. All this contributes to the importance of the training corpora.

This section gives an overview of different types of emotional speech databases and presents some important design decisions to be made when creating a database. This includes mainly the type of speech and the type of emotions to be produced, that is whether they are supposed to be acted or spontaneous. Furthermore, the issue of finding an appropriate set of labels for the emotions in the databases is a key aspect for the validity of classification and is described in the second part of this section. The procedure of assigning labels from this set to emotion occurrences requires special care and should usually be done by more than one person.

2.4.1 Types of emotion databases

Databases with emotional speech are not only essential for psychological studies, but also to automatically predict emotions, as standard methods are statistical and need to learn by examples. Trained classifiers can only reliably classify data which is similar to the training data. It is not possible to predict the accuracy of a classifier on test data that is very different to the training data. So the design or choice of the training data for a given application is a very important step. Similarity means here recorded under similar conditions (same microphone, environment and background noises) with the same kind of speakers (concerning age, gender, etc.) and the same kind of speech (spontaneous, read, acted).

Designing a database with emotional speech is a very complex task [64]. The first decision to be made concerns how the emotions should be produced: usually they have to be elicited in some more or less obvious manner. The easiest way is to ask subjects to pretend emotions. Generally, research deals with databases of acted, induced or completely spontaneous emotions. Of course, the complexity of the task increases with the naturalness. At the beginning of the research on automatic vocal emotion recognition, which started seriously in the mid-90s, work began with acted speech [62] and shifts now towards more realistic data [63, 143] though acted emotions are still widely used. In order to rule out influences of the content, the spoken utterances are usually of emotionally neutral content because the linguistic content often guides people more than paralinguistic features when asked to classify the emotions of their conversation partner. Thus, the performance of an automatic classifier on utterances of emotional content could not be compared to that of humans. Besides, if one emotion was recognised worse than others, it would not be possible to differentiate whether the reason was that this particular emotion is harder to recognise or whether the emotional content was not chosen well.

Professional actors are said to really immerse in an emotion they pretend to such an extent that they have even similar physiological responses as when in real emotional states. Therefore, some people argue that these emotions are better suited for examination and training than real-life emotions because they are pure, that is free from other uncontrollable influences [10]. However, it is disputed how far this is true, as acted emotions usually comprise only basic and very pronounced emotions whereas in real life emotions are often weak, shadowed and a mixture of several emotions. Evidence of the differences of acted and spontaneous emotions has been sup-

2.4. Databases with emotional speech

plied by Wilting et al. [254] who showed in human listening tests that the perception of acted emotions is different than that from natural emotions. In an experiment based on the Velten mood induction method [237] they had one group of test persons utter a set of positive or negative emotional sentences, and another group that was told to utter the same sentences, but act positively for the negative sentences, and negatively for the positive sentences. After the experiment, the first group stated that they actually felt positive or negative, while the other group felt neutral. Furthermore, in a perception experiment, listeners judged acted emotions to be stronger than natural emotions which suggests that actors tend to exaggerate. So, assumptions that hold for acted emotions do not necessarily transfer to natural emotions which are obviously of greater interest to human-computer interaction. Further evidence on the differences between acted and spontaneous emotions will also be given later on.

In variation to producing simulated emotions, another possibility is to have subjects read a text with more or less emotional content. If they are asked to read the text expressively, also non-professional speakers can produce noticeable emotions. They succeed easier if the text is emotionally coloured. Of course, neither speech nor emotions are spontaneous in such a setting.

A relatively large number of databases with acted speech exist. Among them is the popular Danish Emotional Speech database (DES) [72] which contains speech from four actors uttering two single words ("yes"/"no"), nine sentences and two passages of fluent speech in five emotions and has been processed in various papers on automatic emotion recognition [e. g. 59, 239]. The language is, of course, Danish. For stress classification, the SUSAS (Speech Under Simulated and Actual Stress Database) database [99] has been used extensively [e. g. 134, 269]. It contains speech of simulated stress in eight different speaking styles such as slow, fast, low, and angry. Utterances all consist of isolated aircraft communication words. Another example for a database with acted speech is the Berlin Database of Emotional Speech [31] which is described in detail in Section 4.1.1.

The conventional approach to collecting acted emotional speech databases is to let actors read a set of sentences portraying particular emotional states. This usually results in very prototypical and artificial data. In order to enhance the realism of this approach, it has been suggested to use special acting techniques. For example, Busso and Narayanan [34] let their subjects (professional actors and drama students) play improvised or scripted drama, and compared the two approaches. They found improvised drama to be more natural, but less controlled, for example overlapped speech occurred frequently. Scripted drama is easier to analyse as the lexical content is known and overlapped speech occurred rarely. Both approaches, however, need experienced actors, either for realistic improvisation or for memorising the script. Emotions occurring in the spontaneous sessions showed to be more intense than in the scripted sessions.

Acted data is relatively easy to record. Trying to get more spontaneous emotions is much more difficult, because emotions somehow have to be induced. Methods include showing subjects pictures or movies with very emotional content and let them discuss the content. Another emotion induction technique is the Sensitive Artificial Listener (SAL) developed at Queens University, Belfast, within the ERMIS (Emotionally Rich Man-machine Intelligent System) project [66]. Subjects talk to an artificial listener that can have four different simulated personalities to encourage the user to engage in corresponding emotional styles. The personalities are optimistic, confrontational, pragmatic, and depressed, and subjects can exchange them during the conversation as they like. The conversation is scripted from the listener side, that is, answers can be chosen from a predefined set. At present, however, these answers have always been chosen by a human operator. A fully automated listener is currently being developed by the EU project SEMAINE[2]. Though emotions elicited by SAL come from a wide range, they are not very intense, presumably because the situation is not realistic enough for subjects. So far, there exist English, Hebrew and Greek versions of SAL [67].

Amir et al. [6] used a recall technique to construct a database of emotional speech. Subjects were asked to recall and talk about an emotional situation they had experienced in their life. The recorded emotions comprised anger, fear, sadness, disgust, joy, as well as neutral. They are expressed quite distinctively and still to some extent natural.

The SUSAS database mentioned earlier contains not only simulated, but also actual stress which was induced by having subjects produce the aircraft communication words while performing different tasks as for example roller-coaster riding or helicopter flying.

Another widely used method to gather spontaneous emotions is a Wizard-of-Oz setting which was first introduced by Kelley (see e. g. [124]). For emotion elicitation, subjects are given a task, for instance interact with a novel software, and are told that certain features of that software are going to be tested. In truth, the software is operated remotely by a person that triggers the behaviour of the application in such a way that emotions are likely to occur, for example annoyance because a speech recognition system constantly fails, or joy because a game is played extraordinarily successful, beyond the usual abilities of the player. After the experiment its true nature is of course revealed to the subjects. Except for being in a laboratory situation, the behaviour of the participants is quite spontaneous and natural, while the situation is still very controlled. The drawback is that subjects usually do not engage a lot since a successful outcome of the fictitious task is not important to them. Examples for databases created with this method are the SmartKom database and the FAU Aibo Emotion database which are both described in detail in Section 4.1.

Real-life emotions would in principle not be too difficult to record. However, ethical reasons and personality rights prohibit to use them without asking the producers and most people would

---

[2]http://www.semaine-project.eu/

2.4. Databases with emotional speech

not agree as they do not like the idea of being recorded without their knowledge, especially as emotions are considered to be very personal. Besides, it is then hard to record good audio quality (constant close distance to the microphone, no distortion or other environmental noises). Call centre data contains very realistic emotions while having relatively controlled recording conditions [63]. In some countries like France, researchers are allowed to use this data without asking the callers for permission.

Another type of training corpora with copious data material comes from TV. As an example, people in talkshows behave seemingly natural and express lots of emotions. However, the presence of a camera always influences behaviour to be not totally natural. Besides, copyright reasons make it often difficult to use movie or TV data. The Belfast naturalistic database (English) and the EmoTV database (French) are examples for databases containing TV clips [65]. Conversations were chosen, among others, from chat shows and religious programs (Belfast naturalistic database) or from TV interviews (EmoTV) and exhibit a wide range of emotions. Recently, the publicly available "Vera am Mittag" audio-visual database [93] has been released. It contains recordings of the German talkshow "Vera am Mittag" and features spontaneous emotional expressions from discussions between the talkshow guests. The database is labelled by a large number of annotators along the three dimensions valence, activation and dominance.

Though TV data is also more or less suited for training a spontaneous emotions recogniser, finding emotions in movies can be an application in itself: the classification of the emotional content of a movie in a huge multimedia database may help to rate movies [252] or to sort them by genres.

Concluding, it can be said, the more spontaneous and natural the speech and the emotions are, the more classification results degrade, as illustrated by Figure 2.11. For a specific task, the best type of training database of course depends on the application the emotion recognition system is used in. If used as a toy or for a game acted emotions can even be suitable as users might actually play emotions. As for all pattern recognition tasks the best is to collect data from exactly that scenario the application will be developed for and to have a very limited scenario, though these are sometimes unfeasible requirements.

2.4.2 Labelling emotional databases

Once data has been collected, it needs to be labelled in order for a supervised classifier to learn dependencies between acoustic data and emotions. This is a crucial task, as of course, an automatic emotion recogniser can only be as good as its underlying data and the quality of the data's labels. For acted data, the labels are usually known beforehand.

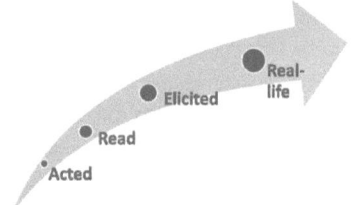

Figure 2.11: Types of databases used for emotion recognition and their complexity/difficulty.

The labelling of emotions can in principle follow any of the models described in Section 2.1, however normally, a small set of discrete emotion classes is used. Note that this holds only for the purpose of automatic classification. The most common emotion labels in acted speech comprise anger, joy, fear, sadness, disgust, boredom and neutral. In spontaneous speech, often distinctions on the evaluation dimension are made as this is most important in many applications. So neutral against negative, and less often against positive speech is labelled. Other common labels for spontaneous speech include anger, joy, or stress. Typically, two, three, or no more than four emotion labels are used for realistic emotions. The simplest, but still useful distinction is that between neutral and emotional speech.

Though current recognition systems of spontaneous emotions usually do not deal with more than four classes, current databases are tagged following more sophisticated strategies in view of future, more capable classifiers. An extended scheme for the annotation of real-life emotions is for example proposed by Devillers et al. [63]. MECAS (Multi-level Emotion and Context Annotation Scheme) allows the attribution of two labels to a segment, a major and a minor one, in order to cope with blended emotions that occur frequently in real-life. Additionally, task and speaker-dependent context information can also be included in this scheme.

Schröder et al. [200] propose EARL (Emotion Annotation and Representation Language), an XML-based scheme for representing and annotating emotions. This scheme is independent from the input modality, thus, it can not only be used for speech, but also for text, videos, pictures, or multimodal data. It allows for the representation of simple emotions, in terms of categories, emotion dimensions, or appraisals, but also of complex emotions that are composed by several simple emotions. Recently, EARL has been further developed into an Emotion Markup Language by the W3C Emotion Incubator group[3] which features the annotation of emotion categories, dimensions, appraisals or action tendencies and allows for coding additional information such as intensity, confidence, modality, timing and other meta-data [202].

The annotation tool Feeltrace [55] takes a different approach compared to common annotation

---

[3]http://www.w3.org/2005/Incubator/emotion/

2.4. Databases with emotional speech

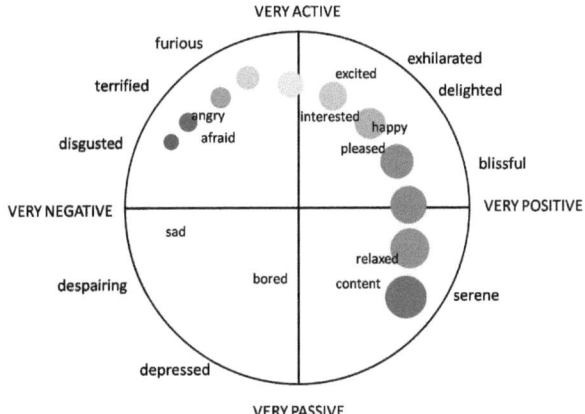

Figure 2.12: Tracking the emotional state over time with Feeltrace [55].

tools in two ways. First, it can be used to label data in a two-dimensional emotion space. Furthermore it allows continuous tracking of the emotional state over time as is shown in Figure 2.12. However, labellers need some experience in order to annotate fast and exactly.

Independent of the chosen approach, the labelling procedure can be supported by video recordings if available. In ambiguous situations, where a decision from speech alone is hard to take, video information can help to disambiguate [65, 228].

Just as the expression of emotion differs hugely between different persons, its perception is also very subjective. Busso and Narayanan [33] and Truong et al. [234] found that assessing the emotional state can differ considerably if done by the speaker himself or by other persons. The question is who may be a better judge of the "real" emotion because sometimes one may not be aware of one's own emotional state. However, since there is usually no information on self-assessment, the ground truth has to be established from labelling based on other persons' perception. Furthermore, Truong et al. [235] showed in further work that with current methods observed emotions can be better classified than felt emotions. Except for special cases, for example the evaluation of the emotions conveyed by infant cries when usually only the caregivers can judge the real emotion with high accuracy [194], labelling a database by only one labeller is dangerous as it might be strongly biased and, as Mower et al. [158] showed, can be less consistent. For this reason, collected data is usually annotated by at least two, better three or up to five different persons and for example majority voting is used to establish a ground truth which of course holds only for the specific scenario. The agreement between the labellers, i.e. the percentage of cases where labellers agree on the annotation, tells about the reliability of the labelling. Typical values for labeller agreement reported in the literature range from 57/67 %

[63] to 71 % [7] or 85 % [79].

The inter-labeller consistency is often also expressed in terms of the Kappa statistic which is defined as

$$\kappa = \frac{P(A) - P(E)}{1 - P(E)} \qquad (2.1)$$

where $P(A)$ is the relative and $P(E)$ the chance agreement between two labellers [39], thus measuring agreement above chance. The higher the Kappa value, the higher the agreement between raters is. This is both a quality measure of the rating as well as a measure of how hard the task of rating was, and will be for a machine. The Kappa value truly expresses if agreement exceeds chance level. However, the Kappa value must be interpreted with caution concerning how much chance level is exceeded, as it makes no distinction between different ways of disagreement. Kappa values reported in the literature for realistic data are around 0.4 [7, 137, 217] or around 0.7 [63, 79], depending on emotionality of the data, number of raters and classes.

As most classification algorithms only work on one target class for each instance, at the end of the labelling process the decisions of all labellers need to be mapped on a single label, which is usually done by majority voting. This is a good, but not ideal solution. On the one hand, majority voting does not hold all information, the "true" emotion might even be recognised by only one labeller. On the other hand a misclassification into a class that was actually assigned by some labeller(s) but not by the majority is actually not that bad as one none of the labeller came up with. Devillers et al. [63] therefore propose a weighted emotion vector holding all labels a segment was given, with weights according to their number of occurrence and whether they were major or minor emotions. Steidl et al. [226] aim at rescoring classification results. Using an entropy-based measure they relate the reference labels of the human raters and the recognised class in such a way that the entropy increases if none or only few reference labels are equal to the recognised class and vice versa. Doing the same with a human labeller that has not been used for the reference labels, they found their automatic classifier to perform comparably to humans though the traditional recognition rate was lower. The measure is therefore appropriate to evaluate performance for applications as it takes into account that misclassifications humans would also make are not that grave.

As can be easily understood from the above considerations, labelling of large, especially spontaneous emotional speech databases involves a lot of human effort. Co-training attempts to mitigate this problem by automatically labelling unlabelled data based on a small data set of labelled instances [145, 152]. This usually leads to an improvement compared to a classifier that was only trained on the small labelled data set. Of course, it is even better to have large set of labelled data.

2.5 Summary

This chapter introduced to basic concepts related to emotions and speech. First, different possibilities to describe emotions were presented. Though very fine-grained descriptions are possible by dimensional or appraisal models, in automatic recognition usually the simpler and more intuitive discrete emotion categories are used. Furthermore, potential sources for information on emotions were identified, which include language and speech, on all levels from acoustics to pragmatics, facial and body gestures, physiological sensors as well interaction patterns. Afterwards, a general speech emotion recognition system with the three major steps of signal processing, acoustic feature calculation and classification was described. In particular, possible acoustic features that are or could be important for emotions were discussed. While at first view, mainly acoustic measures such as pitch or energy that can be consciously controlled seem to be suitable, not directly manipulable features such as spectral features or voice quality turn out to be similarly or even more important, as will be shown later. The former features are especially important with acted speech, which actually consists of consciously produced emotions, while the latter are often more useful for natural emotions, as they can be assumed to give information about unconscious and uncontrollable components of emotions.

Finally, important issues for the design of emotional speech databases were presented. This concerns mainly the type of speech (spontaneous or read) and how emotions are produced (acted, elicited, natural). Further difficulties arise when labelling emotional speech databases. Since emotions are subjective experiences, perception is different among listeners, in particular between the producer and other persons. The next chapter will examine closer to what extent problems in automatic speech emotion recognition have been addressed in the literature.

Chapter 3
Approaches to speech emotion recognition

Automatic emotion recognition from speech is a rather new discipline, but interest has increased tremendously in the last decade. Thus, a substantial body of literature related to this work has emerged. This chapter intends to give an overview of existing related work on automatic emotion recognition from speech. For this purpose the available literature will be surveyed under different points of view, namely emotion units, feature extraction, classification, and other aspects such as speaker types, languages and target classes. Subsequently, special emphasis is given to a review of affective applications and approaches particularly targeted at real-time processing. Finally, various approaches to multimodal emotion recognition including speech will be presented. Starting from this discussion, the major topics of this book are motivated at the end of the chapter and it is explained how they differ from and go beyond existing approaches.

3.1 Emotion units

The segments, or the "units of emotion", are most commonly longer units such as turns, utterances or phrases [63, 77, 127, 134, 137, 143, 161, 173, 176, 177, 182, 207, 222, 229, 230, 267], but also words [15, 243]. Some approaches classify long units, but compute features only from parts of them, for example from the words of an utterance [15, 144, 163] or special phonemes such as vowels or voiced consonants [27, 138]. In order to find suitable phonemes, Busso et al. [37] compared phoneme classes on their relevance with respect to emotions and found vowels to hold more emotional information than for example nasals. Schuller et al. [211] even used phoneme and word specific emotion models. This, however, requires a database with a minimum occurrences of each word. As words may be very short, Batliner et al. [15] based their features on words with a varying number of surrounding words. They also compared turns as classification units with a chunking of the turns by two levels of boundaries. From this qualitative analysis they found smaller units to perform better or worse than turns depending on the chunking level, but as they have not further quantitatively explored this, they cannot provide general guidelines. Nicholas et al. [163] classified words, but their annotation was turn-wise, so every word in a turn got the same emotion label. They also followed a strategy to use only the features of the middle word of a turn to classify the whole turn. In both cases they achieved an improvement over turn-based features. The importance of word position was also shown by the work of Kim et al. [128] who found that sentence medial words are more important than sentence initial and final words.

There are not too many studies comparing various units [204, 243, 244]. Among these, Schuller and Rigoll [204] examined fixed time intervals and also combined features based on multiple time scales into a super-vector. These time scales consisted of the full utterance as well as first, second and third third, or first, central and last 500 milliseconds. Fixed time intervals turned out to perform worse than utterances, but are very useful in an online application context. The combination of multiple time scales which is also an approach to incorporate timing information exceeded the performance of utterances, showing that timing is evidently relevant for emotion recognition. The combination of utterance level features with those obtained from first, second and third third of the utterance thereby outperformed those of utterance level features combined with features obtained from fixed length frames at relative positions in the utterance. Furthermore, the second third of an utterance showed to have the highest relevance with respect to the emotional content and performed almost as good as the whole utterance. This finding is conform with the above mentioned studies of Nicholas et al. [163] and Kim et al. [128] where also the central part of the utterance proved to be most important. Vogt and André [244] compared utterances, words, words in context and fixed time intervals. This study is also part of this book and described in detail in Section 5.2.

Thus, it can be concluded that there are several alternatives of units for speech emotion recognition as listed in Table 3.1. In general, longer units such as utterances are preferable over shorter units and linguistically motivated come off slightly better than others, though this may vary in particular databases or scenarios. However, it also depends on the particular application purpose which units are feasible at all. Units are scarcely evaluated in view of online processing. Furthermore, it can be said that in longer units there are areas that reflect emotions stronger than others, for example vowels are more distinct than consonants and central parts more than initial or final parts.

Unit	Features based on
phonemes	phonemes
words	words
	words in context
	all phonemes
	vowels
	voiced consonants
utterances and turns	utterances
	all words
	central words
fixed length intervals	fixed length intervals
relative length intervals	relative length intervals

Table 3.1: Overview of emotion units.

3.2 Features

An optimal set of features for automatic classification of emotions in speech is not yet established. Therefore, on-going research explores the use of a multitude of different features. Originally, mainly pitch and energy related features were applied, and these continue to be the prominent features. Formants and MFCCs are also frequently found. Durational and pause related features are noted in several papers, as well as different types of voice quality features. Parametric representations other than MFCCs are less common and spectral measures have only recently gained more interest.

Feature extraction approaches fall in mainly two classes: features computed over short term speech segments and those computed on global level speech segments. To explain this in more detail, common acoustic feature types such as pitch are usually observations made on short time intervals of about 10–80 ms. These raw values can be used directly for emotion recognition by dynamic classifiers such as HMMs. Instead, however, usually one feature vector for a longer time segment such as a word or an utterance is classified with a static classifier (Support Vector Machines, Neural Networks, etc.). Thus, series of values have to be mapped onto single values to be represented in the feature vector. Timing information is lost by this approach, though it is essential for emotion classification, because emotions are phenomena that do not occur at single points in time only, but affect speech continuously and evolve over time. Thus, in static classification, time has to be encoded in the feature vector by computing statistical functions such as mean, maximum or minimum from the value series of the basic feature types.

The following sections describe approaches using global statistics and short term features. Subsequently, some literature on meta-features and specific feature selection algorithms is presented.

3.2.1 Global statistics features

To obtain global level features based on statistics, for each of the underlying segments, a feature vector is calculated by applying statistical functions to the base feature types. These statistics are typically mean, maximum, or minimum, quartiles, etc. of the segment, but can also be regression, derivations or other more complex functions. Now, first studies comparing feature types will be described.

Comparisons of feature types

Oudeyer [173] conducted one of the first data-mining experiments on feature types, different views on the feature types, and statistical functions. That study was the starting point of the work described here. The feature basis was formed by pitch, energy, at 250 Hz low-passed and high-passed energy as well as the norm of the absolute vector derivative of the first ten MFCCs. The raw time series of values of each of these measures was further transformed in a series of the local maxima, a series of the local minima and a series of the distances between local extrema of the 10 Hz smoothed curve. Then, ten functions were applied to each of the raw and transformed time series of an utterance: mean, maximum, minimum, range, variance, median, first quartile, third quartile, interquartile range and mean of the absolute value of the local derivative. Thus, altogether 200 features were analysed. When evaluating the relevance of the features, Oudeyer [173] came to the conclusion that features that are traditionally put forward, especially by psychoacoustics literature, such as pitch or overall energy were outperformed by features related to the low-passed energy. The cut-off frequency of 250 Hz for the low- and high-passed energy correlates to a division of pitch and formant energies. High results for low-passed energy features suggests that pitch energy is actually more important than the pitch values themselves. The low importance of high-passed energy implies the lesser relevance of formants. The lesser importance of raw pitch features was also supported by Fernandez and Picard [77], Schuller et al. [207] and Vogt and André [244] who found MFCC, voice quality or loudness features to be superior.

Unfortunately, it is rarely possible to compare published studies on features among each other, because conditions vary a lot and even slight changes in the general set-up can make results incomparable. Most researchers use their own recordings, and different databases or particularly types of emotions (acted, natural, ...) have a huge impact on the comparability of two approaches. For one database, 50 % accuracy may be excellent for a 4-class problem, while for

3.2. Features

another database, recognition rates of 80 % to 90 % can be reached for a 7-class problem. This does not mean that the database in the former case was not well designed, but rather that it is a harder task which can be due to many factors. For this reason one topic of this book is to examine the effects of different databases on the relevance of features.

Though, as said before, many researchers use their own recordings, there are a few available databases that are used relatively often, for example the Berlin Database of Emotional Speech [31], the Danish Emotional Speech database (DES) [72] and the Speech Under Simulated and Actual Stress Database (SUSAS) [99]. However, often evaluation strategies differ (for example some evaluations are speaker dependent, others speaker independent), so that no direct comparison is possible. The FAU Aibo Emotion Corpus [225] attempts to be the first benchmark corpus by defining the evaluation strategy to be used in all research studies. It has been released for the public recently within the INTERSPEECH Emotion Challenge 2009 [213], a competition to compare speech emotion methodology. However, mainly full systems or classifiers competed, so that no further insights on the relevance of features could be gained. Still, in the future, interesting results on features can be expected from evaluations of this database.

Not only databases, but also classifiers, target classes and speaker types differ in the various publications on automatic emotion recognition, so that a comparison of the literature does not allow a general statement on which features are most successful. Of course, comparisons of features within publications are made, for example through relevance ranking by the information gain of single features [173, 207] or by rank in a sequential selection method [77, 134]. Relevance ranking usually has the goal to see the salience of single features, usually per feature type. However, a single feature's relevance does not necessarily imply usefulness in a set of features. Another strategy is to have groups of features (e. g. prosodic, lexical, etc.) and to look at the different performance of the groups or combinations of groups [16, 137, 143]. So far, no general conclusions can be drawn from the work on feature evaluation, but as mentioned before, pitch features have on various occasions shown not to be that important as previously assumed. In the particular case of stress classification, though, a first general conclusion may be possible, as several papers have reported wavelets or TEO-based features to be superior to MFCCs [76, 192, 269]. Up to now, this results has however not been confirmed for other emotion classification tasks. The CEICES (Combining Efforts for Improving automatic Classification of Emotional user States) initiative [21] aimed at finding a more general evaluation of features by providing a database under fixed conditions and having different research sites use their own features and classifiers. In [208] they compared voice quality, pitch, spectral, formant, cepstral, wavelet, energy and duration features and found duration and energy to be most and voice quality to be least important. However, results were also partly classifier dependent. In contrast, Lugger and Yang [147] found pitch and voice quality features to be most relevant, though on acted data, whereas CEICES analysed elicited emotion data. So, as said before, no general conclusions on best feature types are possible. Rather, a review of the literature suggests to use a multitude of feature types each contribution some new information.

The suitability of features for real-time emotion classification and the possibility to extract them automatically was especially emphasised by Litman and Forbes-Riley [143]. There, as well as in this book, it is an important principle because feature sets are designed for use in online applications. Several other approaches partly access information from manual processing, for example disfluencies [208]. Of course, even in view of real-time processing feature selection and training of the classifier is done off-line.

Analysis of individual feature types

There are also studies that look at single feature types or explore novel features. In order to show the diversity of feature approaches, some of them will be presented now.

In a comparison of pitch features only, Busso and Narayanan [35] found that pitch features modeling dynamic statistics such as mean, maximum, minimum, range are superior to features modeling the pitch shape, thus validating the traditional approach to emotion recognition, and that pitch features obtained from whole utterances perform better than those obtained from voiced regions only. They also achieved high classification results with pitch features only across databases and three languages, which shows the general relevance of pitch features, though this analysis was conducted on acted data.

Pfitzinger and Kaernbach [177] argued that loudness features may often not unfold their full potential because the recording gain of the amplitude is readjusted for each speaker and emotion in order to mitigate clipping of loud passages or high background noise in low passages. They showed that amplitude and amplitude variation features hold indeed very relevant information for emotion processing and introduce a database without amplitude readjusting. However, this could only be achieved by absolutely quiet studio conditions during recordings. Thus, though they make a relevant contribution, their finding is not easily transferable to realistic conditions in applications.

Fernandez and Picard [77] also explored novel features related to loudness. In particular, they applied a loudness model that is more perceptually oriented than the commonly used signal energy as it takes into account masking effects and considers that the human ear gives unequal emphasis to perceived frequencies. Their feature vector includes then the overall loudness value according to this model, as well as loudness values for 13 frequency bands. These bands are critical in the frequency spectrum of the human ear and their width is defined by the Bark scale for tone height perception, each comprising 1 Bark. In addition, Fernandez and Picard compute a dissonance diagram of harmonic patterns in the frequency spectrum, which was also inspired by

3.2. Features

perception. These novel features combined with some standard features proved to be competitive and in a relevance ranking, some of the novel features indeed outperformed standard ones.

Cepstral features are increasingly becoming part of standard emotional feature sets that traditionally included only prosodic features. The most prominent cepstral feature type are MFCCs, but also Linear Prediction Cepstral Coefficients (LPCCs) can be found [167]. MFCCs are evaluated in feature sets with other feature types, but they are also relatively often used as only feature type. Compared to most other types, they have a greater potential to be sufficient because they are a parametric representation incorporating many different aspects of the speech signal. Neiberg and Elenius [161] obtained MFCCs from two filterbanks, one in the region of prosodic information between 20 and 600 Hz and one in the region of spectral and formant information between 300 and 3400 Hz. They could outperform a standard prosodic feature set, though not with identical classifiers. They also compared the two filterbank regions and found that the lower region gives slightly better results. Thus, they took this as further evidence that prosodic information is more important than spectral and formant information, which is in line with other work (e. g. [35]).

Spectral features are also becoming increasingly popular. Usually, a frequency spectrum of short time intervals (< 50 ms) is computed. Examples for features derived from the spectrum are the spectral slope [106], spectral entropy [139], spectral centre of gravity [216], the ratio of the spectral flatness to the spectral centre of gravity [127], or log frequency power coefficients [146, 167]. Most of these features encode the distribution and weighting of frequencies in the spectrum. They appear to be quite successful, though they are rarely directly compared to other features. One example for a comparison is the work of Nwe et al. [167] who propagate log frequency power coefficients (LFPC) that model the energy in logarithmised frequency bands for stress classification. In their experiments, the LFPCs outperformed classical MFCCs and LPCCs. Wu et al. [259] argued based on psychoacoustic and neurophysiological evidence of human speech processing that it is more adequate to calculate the spectrum from longer segments of 250 ms. Though they achieved an improvement with their long-term spectro-temporal features over their baseline system, they compare only to prosodic, not to short-term spectral features.

Except for jitter and shimmer, voice quality features are not very common yet. Even if used, their individual impact is seldom measured. Lugger and Yang [149] developed features based on voice quality parameters describing gradients of the glottal excitation spectrum and harmony features lent from music retrieval that exploit that humans perceive music as positive or negative based on its harmonic structure. The harmony features are dissonance, the valence of the sound perception of a tone pair, tension which parametrises that diminished and augmented triads are perceived as unresolved and thus negative, and modality which can be major or minor in resolved triads. They showed that these features raise recognition accuracy when added to a prosodic feature set. Sun et al. [229] also considered glottal parameters and compared them in several two-class emotion tasks with pitch and energy features, yielding a benefit in some, but not all tasks.

Zhou et al. [269] primarily examined better features for word recognition in speech under stress, but also employ them for stress classification, which is a task related to emotion recognition though not necessarily the same, as stress can also be experienced independent of an emotional state. They propose features based on the Teager energy operator (TEO) which assumes a nonlinear airflow caused by vortices during speech production. This is opposed to the common model of the air flowing through the vocal tract as a plain wave. A further type of TEO based features has been developed by Fernandez and Picard [76] who first calculate Daubechies-4 wavelets on which they then apply the TEO, again for stress-classification. These features performed quite well in the given task, but where not compared to other kinds of features. Wavelets have also successfully been employed for stress classification by Sarikaya and Gowdy [192].

As is obvious from the above review of single feature types, many have been explored so far, but the ultimate solution is still missing which suggests further work on this topic. Furthermore, many studies are still conducted with acted speech only. As will be shown, relevant features can be very different for acted and realistic emotions. Therefore, not all results of studies that achieved an improvement by special features can be regarded as generally valid. They rather apply to only the very particular conditions they were tested in.

3.2.2 Short-term features

Short-term features differ from global statistics features in that no statistical function is applied over a series of values, but the raw values themselves form the feature vector, and the segments are very short time intervals (10–30 ms) of a constant length. Thus, classification units are assigned sequences of feature vectors, not only one single vector. These sequences still hold the time contour of the basic feature types. Other classification strategies have to be used than for global statistics features, for example HMMs, and are explained in detail in Section 3.3. HMM features are most often MFCCs [138, 250, 264], but also wavelets [76], Teager energy operator (TEO) based features [76, 269], log frequency power coefficients (LFPC) [167] and linear prediction cepstral coefficients (LPCC) [167] have been explored. Neiberg et al. [162] included low frequency MFCCs to model F0 variations. Busso et al. [37] described a study where raw Mel filter bank features outperformed MFCCs in an HMM based classification approach. Prosodic features are also found among short-term features, though less frequently. For instance, Nogueiras et al. [164] and Schuller et al. [206] used low-level pitch and energy values, Huang and Ma [106] pitch, energy and zero-crossing rate of short-term frames in combination with HMMs.

3.2.3 Non-acoustic features

Acoustic features can be directly combined with other, non-acoustic features, in order to boost recognition accuracy. These may be manually labelled phonetic features, linguistic features or meta information known or automatically recognised from the context. Phonetic features include prosodic peculiarities, disfluency cues and extra-linguistic acoustic features, which were annotated by hand. Prosodic peculiarities of Batliner et al. [16] comprise hyper-clear speech, pauses inside words and syllable lengthening that were annotated by human labellers. Off-talk was also marked. The extra-linguistic acoustic features of Devillers et al. [63] were inspiration, expiration, mouth noise, laughter, crying and unintelligibility of voices which occurred in their data from call-centre recordings with human-human communication and were labelled manually. So, though these feature types may be relevant, they are not applicable in a real-time approach.

Valuable linguistic information that can be directly integrated with acoustic information is word or part-of-speech information [15]. However, it relies either on the (possibly faulty) output of an automatic speech recogniser or on manual transcription of the data. Word information can be processed simply as occurrence vectors [172], bag-of-words [207], n-grams or string kernels [212]. Grammatical or style features have been exploited by [172], a study that is also described later in Section 7.3. Lee and Narayanan [137] adopted the concept of "emotional salience" that chooses words appearing more frequently in one emotion class than in others. Though data sparsity is a problem here, combining acoustic features and emotional salience led to a considerable improvement. The authors argue further that extending emotional salience to word sequences would match human perception even more.

Furthermore, meta information that is available from the context can be used to improve acoustic emotion recognition. This includes for example gender [8, 105, 128, 133, 137, 222, 239, 245, 261, 262] or culture [123]. Shahid et al. [218] found out that both age and culture have an influence on how well humans can recognise certain emotions audio-visually. This finding is probably also true for machines. Other features from meta-data were applied by Litman and Forbes-Riley [143]. They collected a corpus from a spoken dialogue tutoring system in the physics domain and hence incorporated into their feature set further application dependent knowledge like the respective speaker, the gender and which of five available physics problems was treated. In later work [3], they also employed system and user performance in the tutoring system dialogues for emotion recognition. Lee and Narayanan [137] integrated five speech act categories occurring in the user responses to their dialogue system with acoustic and linguistic information but cannot boost accuracy with this discourse information. A further interesting contribution comes from Lee et al. [135] who model that dialogue partners mutually influence their emotional state. Context information can thus be considered very valuable, however, it depends on the particular scenario if and which information is available.

3.2.4 Feature selection

As already mentioned, in most work with global statistics features a selection process is applied to reduce the dimensionality of the feature space. Sequential forward selection or floating forward selection with a k-Nearest-Neighbour or Support Vector Machine classifier is a popular search method [137, 207, 240]. Oudeyer [173] and Álvarez et al. [5] alternatively use a genetic search, Tato et al. [230] select those features that significantly modify a linear regression model. Vogt and André [244] and Haindl et al. [97] used correlation based selection criteria. Haindl et al. showed mutual correlation of features to be inferior in accuracy, but much faster than sequential selection methods. For very large feature sets with more than 1000 features it is therefore a good strategy to first apply correlation based feature selection in order to reduce the set to a size that is tractable for sequential feature selection. A very different approach was taken by [270] who based their feature selection on rough set theory.

The feature space dimension can also be reduced by through Principal Components Analysis (PCA) [77, 137]. Another method for feature space reduction is explored by You et al. [263] who used Enhanced Lipschitz Embedding (ELE) based on geodesic distance estimation and showed it to be superior to for example PCA. Furthermore, the method proved to be robust again background noise. In any case, due to the "curse of dimensionality" and other reasons explained later, downsizing the dimensionality of large feature vectors, by selection or reduction, is usually mandatory.

3.3 Classification

As mentioned in Section 2.3.1 vocal emotion recognition does not need any specialised classifier. Therefore, usually algorithms developed for other domains are adapted to the task. In the following, first studies with static classifiers that use global statistics features and assign one class label to each feature vector are presented. Then, dynamic classification approaches are described that rely on sequences of short-term feature vectors and where time is modelled by the classifier, not by the features. Finally, current trends in emotion classification are discussed.

3.3.1 Static classification

So far, a number of generally available classification algorithms have been tested and compared, including variants of SVM [40, 173, 203, 243, 259, 270], Bayesian classifiers [12, 47, 148, 158, 180], Neural Networks [176, 261], Decision Trees [48, 221], Nearest-Neighbour classifiers [101], Linear Discriminant Analysis (LDA) [16, 137, 161] or Gaussian Mixture Models (GMM)

[50, 148, 161, 216, 243]. Still, some classifiers are more suitable than others. Requests to such a classifier include that it can deal with high-dimensional input data. To be also suitable for real-time recognition, it should be fast, at least during the classification stage. As training is usually done off-line this stage may be more time consuming.

The quality of a classifier can be determined in comparison to human raters in listening tests or to other classification algorithms. The former is more meaningful for practical purposes and shows also the complexity of the particular tasks but it usually involves much effort to conduct listening tests. Human rating performance has been reported in various studies to be around 65 % [167, 176] which is also supported by the findings of Scherer et al. [197] in a psychological study, about 70 % [182, 183], or 80 % [138, 164]. Of course, human performance also depends on the task. Interestingly, the automatic classification results presented in these papers reach about the same level or even exceed it. These figures, however, concern acted speech; for spontaneous emotions the gap is supposed to be larger.

A comparison of classifiers is usually only reasonable within one study, not between different studies, because settings vary too much so that different classification rates can have a number of other reasons besides the classifier. Large-scale classifier comparison experiments were often done with the data-mining software Weka [255] which has become a standard in the speech emotion recognition community. This approach is followed, for example, by Oudeyer [173] as well as Schuller et al. [207] and Casale et al. [40] who compared a number of popular classification strategies. They all showed SVM to outperform Decision Trees or simple classifiers like Naïve Bayes or k-NN as well as classifier boosting to improve recognition rates. Oudeyer, however, achieved with boosted Decision Trees even better results than with SVMs, while this was not the case for Schuller et al.. Devillers et al. [63] also found boosted Decision Trees to perform a bit better than SVMs, though not significantly. Lee and Narayanan [137] compared two simple classification algorithms, k-NN and LDA, where LDA came off slightly better. Petrushin [176] tested k-NN against Neural Networks and found the latter to reach higher accuracies. Neural networks indeed are promising in principle, but as they do no longer work time-efficiently in high-dimensional input spaces, now most approaches refrain from using them.

As a general tendency it can be observed that sophisticated classifiers do achieve higher recognition rates than simple classifiers but not much. SVM is the most popular and the most often successfully applied algorithm, so it can be considered a kind of standard.

3.3.2 Dynamic classification

The most popular dynamic classification algorithm for speech emotion recognition are Hidden Markov Models (HMM) [76, 134, 138, 167, 206, 250, 264, 269]. A number of studies compare these with static classification algorithms. In [134] HMMs were shown to classify short utterances more accurately than SVM, and SVM to be more accurately than LDA. But in variable length utterances, SVM outperformed HMMs. Fernandez and Picard [76] and Lee et al. [138] compared HMMs with SVM. In both cases the HMMs performed better, but it is hard to assess whether the classifiers or the features account for that, as for HMMs short-term features were used, and for SVM, global statistics features were computed. Schuller et al. [206] contrarily found HMMs with short-term features to perform worse than GMMs with global statistics features. A comprehensive study of different HMM designs was conducted by Wagner et al. [250]. There, the best design proved to be highly database and task dependent, but in accordance with the earlier mentioned study of Kwon et al. [134], HMMs also performed better on short units than on longer ones, compared to static classification. This may be a generally valid finding.

Varieties from standard HMMs have also been explored. In [183] suprasegmental HMMs are introduced that model suprasegmental information on top of acoustic models. A suprasegmental state thus contains several states of the acoustic HMMs. The observations for the acoustic model are short-term features while the observations for the suprasegmental models are statistical values of pitch and intensity over that segment. To obtain a single output probability, the probabilities of both models are added on the leave of a suprasegmental state. Fernandez and Picard [76] test different architectures of HMMs. In particular they use conventional HMMs, autoregressive HMMs, where not only the internal states but also the observations depend on their predecessors, models with multiple state variables (factorial HMM and hidden Markov Decision Tree) and mixtures of conventional HMMs, with the last being the most successful.

Whether static or dynamic classification approaches are preferably can not yet ultimately be answered. So far, static approaches are applied more frequently. Maybe combinations of both approaches model contours and timing information best.

3.3.3 Trends in speech emotion classification

In the following, some topics from recent literature on speech emotion classification are presented to illustrate current research trends.

Hierarchical classification Recently, hierarchical classification approaches have come into vogue and seem very promising. Hierarchical classification means splitting the original classification problem into several smaller problems. This can be done along the emotion dimensions activation, evaluation and potency [8, 127, 148]. For example, when classifying into the classes anxiety, anger, happiness, boredom, sadness and neutral, Lugger and Yang [148] first distinguished between high and low activation (anxiety/happiness/anger vs. neutral/boredom/sadness),

3.3. Classification

then between high and low potency (happiness/anger vs. anxiety and neutral/boredom vs. sadness) and finally between positive and negative evaluation (happiness vs. anger and neutral vs. boredom). By that, they achieved a considerable improvement over non-hierarchical classification of 14 %. Xiao et al. [261] chose the individual classification problems automatically based on recognition accuracy. Interestingly, this still results in distinctions along emotion dimension axes. Instead of looking at the activation and valence dimensions, Lee et al. [136] proposed to use task-dependent hierarchies that start with easier classification problems and leave the harder problems for the final steps. Among all described studies, it is common that feature sets in hierarchical classification are optimised by selection for each individual step.

Regression In order to receive continuous output in terms of a dimensional emotion model, it is also possible to use regression to model the relationship between features and each dimension, both with continuous ranges of values. Results can no longer be expressed in terms of accuracy but in terms of correlation between true and estimated value. Continuous valued output allows to adjust software reaction to the affective user state in a more fine-grained way. It is also possible to map intervals of the regression output onto discrete classes and thus compare to classification techniques. As databases begin to be labelled by trace data from continuous emotion models (e. g. Feeltrace, see Section 2.4.2), regression models become more applicable, but are still scarcely found. Two examples are the studies of Grimm et al. [92] and Giannakopoulos et al. [84].

Classification levels Instead of computing statistical functions from basic feature type values over global level acoustic segments such as utterances or using dynamic classification approaches, some authors explore alternatives for mapping feature sequences onto utterance level classification results. For example, Schuller and Rigoll [205] investigated a multi-instance learning technique (MI-SVM) on "bag-of-frames" short-term features for interest recognition. However, they could not outperform a regular SVM classifier on global statistic features with this technique. Another approach has been taken by Sato and Obuchi [193] who classified each frame individually based on short-term features and then apply voting schemes to obtain utterance level classification results. Compared to a conventional classification scheme, they achieved a slight improvement.

In order to obtain a mapping from short-term features to a single feature vector for an utterance, Hu et al. [105] first train a GMM with the short-term MFCC features of an utterance and then feed the GMM output as feature vector into a SVM classifier. The GMM is adapted from a universal background model trained with a large amount of neutral speech. This method achieved an improvement over a conventional GMM approach, and could be extended in the future by using more feature types than MFCCs. Dumouchel et al. [69] combine this approach with global statistics feature classification at the decision level. Vlasenko et al. [242] take a different approach but also combine short-term with long-term features successfully. Thus, it seems that at all levels, short-term as well as global, there is relevant information for emotions available and that this information is not redundant.

Time Though emotions are short-term events opposed to long-term moods, they are not likely to change strongly within short time intervals. This assumption is modelled by Long Short-Term Memory Recurrent Neural Networks [256] which include memory cells into a Neural Network to consider emotional history. Thus, huge changes along the evaluation or activation axis in a dialogue context are made difficult.

Multi-corpora approaches A further interesting topic regarding classification has been examined by Shami and Verhelst [219]. They assessed how good classifiers can generalise from specific corpora. Dealing with two different corpora for this purpose, they compared results obtained by training and classification within one corpus with those obtained by training on one corpus and classifying on the other (off corpus) and by merging the two corpora. In the off corpus task, the classifiers actually managed to capture information general to the particular emotion class from a single corpus, as performance was higher than just classifying always in the most frequent class. Results of the integration of the two corpora lay between the results obtained from each corpus alone which suggests that it is possible to construct a robust classifier from different data sets recorded under different conditions but with the same set of emotional classes.

Finally, Busso et al. [37] also investigated a multi-corpora approach: they train a neutral model from a large database with neutral speech (TIMIT database [83]) and apply discriminant analysis on two other emotional speech databases to separate emotional from neutral speech. This can be used as a first step in a hierarchical classification system, where the following step(s) would involve classification of only the emotional speech into further emotion classes.

3.4 Speaker types, languages and target classes

Besides features and classification, other essential aspects for the evaluation of work on emotion recognition are for example speaker types, languages, and target classes. In most work, speakers are adults, but also children's speech is analysed [19, 262, 267] or even infants' cries [194]. The greater variability in children's speech may be accounted for by applying vocal tract length normalisation [267]. However, data collection with children is more laborious.

3.4. Speaker types, languages and target classes

Naturally, the best explored language for emotion recognition is English, but also studies on German [16, 18, 19, 21, 93, 203, 230], French [63], Japanese [173], Danish [239], Swedish [162], Finnish [215], Italian [8], Spanish and Basque [5], Polish [48] as well as Burmese and Mandarin [167] can be found. Though the feature values are of course different for different languages, methods are alike. Databases in uncommon languages are often recordings from actors, as the production involves less effort. Busso and Narayanan [35] did a cross-language study, that is they trained with a database in one language and tested on another database in another language. When discriminating between neutral and emotional speech, they found a two-step approach based on the similarity to reference models for neutral speech not to degrade if training and test language differed, while conventional methods did degrade considerably.

Target classes are usually dependent on the particular tasks. So for acted speech, usually so-called primary emotions based on the definition of Ekman et al. [70] are discerned. These include happiness, anger, sadness and neutral [173, 215], but eventually, also fear, disgust, boredom, or surprise are added [167, 176, 230, 239, 244], or happiness is omitted [182]. Tato et al. [230] took up a dimensional approach and partitioned their initial set of emotion classes (happiness, anger, sadness, boredom and neutral) along an arousal as well as an evaluation axis.

In dimensional approaches, the most frequent dimensions are activation and valence [256], but also dominance [91], involvement [11] or interaction [22]. The latter two dimensions are task-dependent and may not be useful or applicable in all conditions: involvement was measured during prank phone calls in a radio show, while interaction models addressing oneself or the communication partner. Generally, elicited and spontaneous emotion databases usually exhibit very specific, task or situation dependent emotional behaviour patterns, that fall not only into pure emotional categories, but also into emotion-related states. Furthermore, typically not all but only those emotions or states that are of interest for the particular application are labelled. For example, the interest in telephone applications lies mainly in the distinction of negative to non-negative emotions, since the main purpose here is to identify problems so that the call can be handed over to a human operator [32]. Meeting recordings, otherwise, are searched for parts of high involvement of the participants [257], or agreement vs. disagreement [103]. In spoken dialogue systems, important emotions are especially task-dependent and comprise such notions as confidence, confusion, frustration [267], uncertainty [184], motherese [19], or politeness [262]. Stress [76, 192, 269] and interest [205] recognition are further emotion-related tasks. Generally, it is easier to distinguish between emotions or states that differ in arousal than in evaluation though the latter often has more importance in applications.

3.5 Real-time speech emotion recognition

So far, most research on speech emotion recognition has been concerned with the offline analysis of available or specifically created speech corpora. However, most applications that could make use of affective information would require an online analysis of the user's emotional state. Therefore, the consideration of real-time constraints is also important for emotion recognition. Of course, recognition rates must be expected to be lower than for offline analysis, and tasks should be limited to very few emotional states. Schuller et al. [210] listed spontaneous speech, realistic emotions, noise and microphone conditions as well as speaker independence as major challenges of online recognition in applications and propose methods to cope with them. Robustness against background noise was also addressed by You et al. [263].

A further challenge of online recognition is that it is not known beforehand which emotions will occur. That means that classifiers are usually designed to recognise a closed set of emotions, however, during run-time arbitrary emotions may occur and also those that human labellers would not be able to establish a majority decision on [227]. One possibility is to consider a rest class besides the target emotions that consists of all emotional occurrences found in the training database that do not belong to the target classes, provided there are such occurrences. Truong and van Leeuwen [233] proposed to abandon classification in favour of detection, where for each emotion a classifier is trained that distinguishes between the particular emotion and all other emotions, the "open set". They show that so far unseen emotions are classified with high accuracy into the open set and that this approach is also transferable to new databases that were not used for training. A further aspect that is related to unknown emotions is that in natural settings, emotions are not limited to the big-five Ekmanian emotions, but also unusual, task-specific, thus non-prototypical emotions occur that are of course not as well explored [227].

The above mentioned studies have investigated topics that are important for real-time processing, still most of their underlying technology is not yet ready for online recognition. Recently, Eyben et al. [73] introduced OpenEAR[1], an open-source package for building complete automatic speech emotion recognition engines with real-time capabilities. While, or because, the package contains a comprehensive and powerful set of tools for signal processing and feature extraction it is primarily intended to support experts in speech emotion recognition with their experiments and with building online applications. Besides the EMOVOICE framework described later, it is the most comprehensive toolbox for real-time speech emotion recognition. While OpenEAR concentrates on providing a huge range of analysis methods and has more algorithms integrated, the emphasis of EMOVOICE is, as will be described later in more detail, the easy integration into applications by software developers, as well as the possibility for non-experts to build personalised

---
[1] http://sourceforge.net/projects/openart/

or speaker-independent recognisers with the help of a workflow and graphical user interface for audio corpus acquisition. In OpenEAR, this requires more familiarisation with the toolbox and is so far only possible with console applications.

A final aspect of real-time systems is their evaluation which is more complex than that of an offline system, because no ground truth is readily available for the emotions occurring during run-time. Instead, they would have to be labelled afterwards and compared with the recognised emotions. To assess the quality of their online system, Kim et al. [132] therefore feed it with utterances of a test database to simulate real-time conditions. It is also possible to evaluate the system based on questionnaires of the users' impression of its performance [86].

3.6 Applications for speech emotion recognition

As said before, so far only few online applications have been realised. Among these is the work of Huang and Ma [106] who presented a real-time conversation monitor that distinguishes between eight basic emotions. It is based on HMMs as classifier and outputs a result every 1.5 seconds. The program was not formally evaluated but authors state that accuracy is higher than guessing randomly. Another example for a real-time application is the Jerk-O-Meter that monitors attention (activity and stress) in a phone conversation, based on speech feature analysis, and gives the user feedback allowing her to change her manners if deemed appropriate [151]. One of the few commercial products already exploiting affective speech analysis is the KishKish Lie Detector, which is a free add-on for the internet based voice and instant messaging software Skype^{TM}. It should detect the stress level of the conversation partner who is informed of this monitoring and may dissent. Though no information is given on its analysis methods, it seems to mainly monitor the energy level. Finally, Jones and colleagues have explored online emotion detection in games [120] and for giving feedback in human-robot interaction[119]. In an offline validation of their systems, they claim 70/80/90 % accuracy for 5/4/3 emotion groups for the classifier integrated into the game and 75 % accuracy for 5 emotions in human-robot interaction. However, in a user study comparing one robot with and one without emotion recognition, users rated the robot with emotion recognition as only slightly more emotionally responsive than the other. All described studies are very specifically targeted to a particular application or classification scenario. A systematic analysis of the online suitability of the methods has not been conducted. In contrast, EMOVOICE, the framework presented later in this book, is deployable independent of the task or classes, because it calculates many features and not for example only those suitable for stress or activity detection.

Most offline studies also envisage application scenarios, for online as well as offline emotion recognition. Among these are call centre conversations, by e. g. providing call centre employees with information regarding the emotions their voice might portray, or by automatically switching from computer to human operators, if a caller exhibits high arousal in his voice, an indication for a problem [16, 18, 32, 63, 137, 162, 176]. As examples, call centre conversations in medical emergencies, stock exchange or flight booking have been analysed.

Another important domain are spoken dialogue systems [3, 45, 143, 262, 267], mostly for games or computer-enhanced learning software, but also for robots [9, 19, 47] or emotionally aware in-car systems [121, 122, 209, 231], for example to measure driving fun, or stress [77]. Emotion recognition may also be useful in a surveillance context, for instance for monitoring infants [194] or for detecting fear to ensure public safety [50].

A holistic approach is followed by the EU project SEMAINE[2] that aims to build a multimodal sensitive artificial listener (SAL) as a virtual character that interacts with human users in a natural way and also reacts appropriately to their emotional state [201]. Once fully implemented, the sensitive artificial listener could be used in many application context.

Furthermore, emotion recognition can also boost accuracy in speech recognition or speaker identification, as these tasks are harder for emotional speech than for neutral speech [109, 260].

Finally, some examples for offline applications making use of emotion recognition are the automatic annotation of court transcripts [8] or search in multimedia databases: the classification of the emotional content of a movie may help to rate movies [252] or to sort them by genres. A forthcoming popular field of application is the automatic processing of meeting recordings as in [162, 257].

As this outline shows, emotion recognition can be very useful and already a lot of applications making use of it have been conceived, though few have been realised so far, and virtually none are ready for the market. This is to a large part due to the low accuracy of current recognition systems, but also the full potential of emotion recognition for applications has not been tapped yet. In order to help application designers to think of new ways to deal with emotional awareness, Batliner et al. [20] proposed criteria for a taxonomy of applications that make use of emotions. The criteria are whether the system is *online* or *offline*, that is if it responds to the user's emotional state while or after interaction, whether the system is *mirroring* or not, which means if explicit feedback to emotions is given or not, whether the system reacts itself *emotional* in some way or not, and finally whether emotion processing is *critical* or not, that is if wrong processing impairs the applications aims or not.

---

[2]http://www.semaine-project.eu/

3.7 Multimodal emotion recognition

Though there is wide agreement that different sources of information need to be exploited to reach automatic classification performance comparable to human rating, work on multimodal emotion recognition is still relatively scarce and concentrates mostly on rather unnaturalistic data. On the one hand, this is due to the fact that approaches to single modality recognition do not yet reach satisfying recognition rates. However, synchronisation and fusion of the modalities pose even more serious problems.

Synchronisation is an issue because not all modalities are available at an arbitrary point in time. One might for example want to know about the emotional state of a person who is not speaking, or during speaking, but when the face is turned away from the video camera. Though this is indeed rather beneficial, as in the absence of one modality, there is a good chance that another modality can take over, the organisation of the different channels becomes a challenge. Furthermore the units of analysis may be distinct. Speech units may be at the utterance level while facial features are usually extracted from still images or video frames. Biosignals on the other hand require longer time periods than even utterances for reliable prediction.

If more than one modality is available at the same time, information should be fused in some way. This fusion can take place at the feature level, when a combined feature vector is formed by merging the features of the individual channels, or on the decision level. In the latter case, the feature vectors for each channel are classified separately and the outcomes are integrated into an overall result either by averaging over the confidence scores of the classes or by using for every class that modality that best predicts it in unimodal recognition, or by some other criterion.

One solution to these problems was proposed by Gilroy et al. [86] who designed a fusion scheme based on the PAD model (see Section 2.1) that maps the (possibly discrete) output of the various modalities onto vectors in the PAD model weighted by the confidence of the classification result. To address the problem of synchronisation, a decay is introduced at the time of fusion that gives lower weighting to modalities whose last classification event occurred longer ago. Modalities integrated into this model are speech (acoustic and lexical) and video analysis.

Wagner et al. [251] aim at facilitating the development of multimodal online emotion recognition systems by providing the open source framework Smart Sensor Integration (SSI). SSI offers tools for data segmentation, feature extraction and classification for online as well as offline applications. Furthermore, it is able to fuse input from various modalities.

One of the most common combination of modalities is acoustic and lexical information of language that are often regarded as two separate modalities though they both belong to language. Here, synchronisation is of course no problem though segmentation can be, if acoustic units smaller or incongruent to words are used. The fusion is usually performed at the feature level and can be found in a number of papers (as presented in Section 3.2.3). Though it often leads to a slight improvement, the effect is not huge, for example Schuller et al. [207] reached an improvement of 3.5 % over acoustic features only recognition with 90 % when combined with linguistic features (65 %). Osherenko et al. [172] achieved only a slight improvement by combining acoustic and linguistic information (67 %) compared to the single modalities (acoustic: 66 %; linguistic: 64 %). This study is described in detail later in Section 7.3.

The integration of audio and visual emotion information has been attempted several times in recent years [36, 38, 82, 186]. Caridakis et al. [38] segmented into "tunes" that are each assigned one emotion label. Then they computed a visual vector for every video frame and merged it with an acoustic vector that was computed over the whole tune. So the acoustic vector was repeated for every frame in the tune. With bimodal recognition, they achieved with a 79 % a significant improvement over the singel modalities (visual: 67 %; audio: 73 %). Busso et al. [36] recorded an actress and computed for every utterance a visual and an acoustic feature vector which are integrated on the feature and the decision level. Again, the bimodal recognition rate (89 %) exceeded the single modalities (visual: 84 %; audio: 71 %), while there was no difference for feature and decision level fusion. Rabie et al. [186] combined a facial emotion recogniser with the speech emotion recogniser of this book and they could also show bimodal recognition to yield slightly higher results than unimodal recognition (78 % vs 74 % visual and 62 % audio). The study is the topic of Section 7.4.

Probably the first combination of speech with biosignals has been undertaken by Kim et al. [131] with modality fusion on the feature and the decision level. On feature level fusion, they achieve 66 % compared to 53 % for biosignals only and 52 % for speech only. A detailed description of this study will follow in Section 7.2.

3.8 Conclusion

As the discussion in this chapter revealed, by now there exists a considerable amount of literature related to speech emotion recognition. So far, however, most research is still concerned with the study of offline recognition. So, currently, the design of affective applications by non-experts in emotion recognition is difficult. Since researchers in speech emotion recognition will not be able to conceive of all possible application scenarios, a framework that allows for easy building of a task and application dependent real-time recogniser, including data collection, would enable non-experts to integrate emotion recognition into their applications according to their needs. The development of such a framework is the goal of this book. The resulting applications could give insights about the real challenges of real-time speech emotion recognition and also about how

3.8. Conclusion

System aspects	Challenge
Units	should be fast to segment
	should be fully automatically to segment
Features	should be fast to extract
	should cover most relevant aspects of emotion in speech
Classification	should be fast and robust
Conditions	should work speaker-, language- and age-independent
	should work on non-acted speech
	should be adaptable to many applications

Table 3.2: Difficulties of real-time speech emotion recognition.

affective applications should be designed, how users interact with them, and in particular if and how they accept them. Based on these insights, the system can be improved more specifically.

In order to achieve this, first a real-time emotion recognition system is needed. Such a system was not available at the beginning of this work, and only very recently, a few systems have emerged, among them only one that is freely available [73]. Thus, a system that is suitable to serve as testbed for online methodology and that addresses the major challenges of real-time speech emotion recognition as listed in Table 3.2 is developed here. Until recent years, many approaches still relied at some point on manually obtained information. Here, of course, a fully automatic approach will be followed without any such information at any step. Units that are suitable for real-time processing have so far been scarcely explored. Therefore, a novel unit based on voice activity detection is tested here and a systematic comparison of different units is conducted. Feature extraction approaches in related work showed that a multitude of feature types is relevant for emotions and that each contributes complementary information. For this reason, the choice of strategy for feature extraction here falls on a generative approach with many feature types, including some novel features based on voicing and spectral regression. Generative means that starting from basic feature types, features are systematically produced by applying statistical functions, yielding a high number of generated features. All features are examined in view of their usefulness for real-time recognition. Furthermore, features should be applicable not only for acted, but also for spontaneous emotions. That there exist differences between relevant features for acted and spontaneous emotions and how to find features for the specific task, is a further topic of this book.

Requirements for the classifier are that it should be fast and robust. Analysis of the literature revealed that simple algorithms can be very successful in the task, so standard classifiers are employed here, as classification is not the main focus. More complex approaches such as hierarchical classification are very promising, but are beyond the scope of this book. The emotion model is determined by the annotation of the analysed databases which were all labelled according to discrete emotion classes.

With the chosen methodology, an open-source framework for real-time emotion recognition should be provided and tested in some prototypical applications. In order to make it easy to use for non-experts, furthermore a standardised procedure to construct training databases with emotional speech is developed and supported by a graphical user interface, thus boosting the development of affective applications.

Finally, the literature overview revealed multimodal approaches to show promise for more robust and accurate systems as at least slight improvements could be gained. For this reason, the usefulness of combining acoustic information with gender, linguistic, video and biosignal information is studied here.

Chapter 4

Databases and methods for speech emotion recognition

This chapter presents methodology for online as well as offline speech emotion recognition and databases used for its evaluation in this book. The goal is firstly, to find acoustic emotion units that are suitable for real-time applications, secondly, to identify possible acoustic features for emotion recognition that can be extraced fast and automatically, as well as to assess a good procedure to select the most relevant features for a given purpose, and lastly, to choose a fast, but accurate classification algorithm. Thus, the methodology used for all three steps as in the overview in Figure 4.1 is described for both the training and the test phase. In order to be able to make as general assertions as possible, evaluation experiments are conducted on three databases of different types with acted and spontaneous emotions. Experimental results will be reported in the next chapter.

In the following, after the presentation of the databases in Section 4.1, first possibilities to segment audio signals into units of emotions that are suitable for automatic purposes will be presented (Section 4.2). Afterwards, the calculation of the basic feature types such as pitch, energy, MFCCs etc. will be explained in Section 4.3, as well as the exact features that are derived from the basic types and form the feature vector. Except for a classifier comparison study, classifiers have been restricted to two common algorithms, Naïve Bayes and SVM. These will be described in Section 4.4.

4.1 Databases

Three databases were used to evaluate methodology in this book. The first one, the Berlin database of emotional speech, is a database of acted read emotions, the other two were recorded

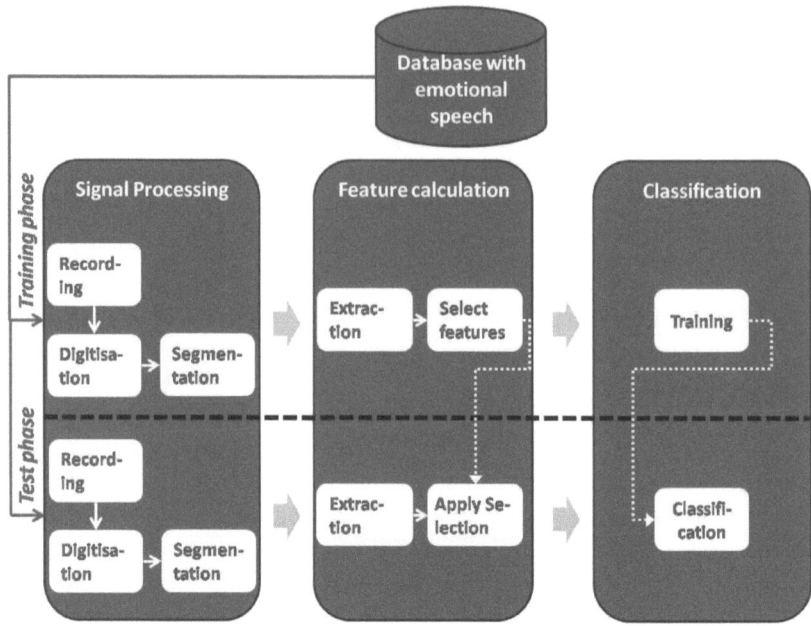

Figure 4.1: Steps in training and testing of the speech emotion recognition system.

in Wizard-of-Oz settings. The SmartKom database has only few emotions and contains speech of adults, while the FAU Aibo Emotion Corpus is more emotional and contains speech of children. Figures 4.2, 4.3 and 4.4 illustrate each scenario. All three databases are German, however, the methods described later in this chapter work language-independently.

At the beginning of the work reported here, databases with spontaneous emotional speech were sparsely available. Nowadays, the situation has improved, though it is still far from abundant. Besides the databases already mentioned in Section 2.4.1, an overview of the most important corpora has been compiled by Ververidis and Kotropoulos [238].

While classification on the Berlin database is a relatively easy task, it is not very realistic as it contains acted speech obtained under ideal conditions, a scenario one would scarcely find in an application. Furthermore, it is limited in size. The Aibo and the SmartKom database are much harder tasks, because emotions are not as prototypical and clear, but they are larger and close to realistic conditions. Thus, by evaluating these three databases, that are described in detail in the following, a wide variety of emotions is covered and results can be expected to be general.

4.1. Databases

#	German	Translation into English
1	Der Lappen liegt auf dem Eisschrank.	The tablecloth is lying on the fridge.
2	Das will sie am Mittwoch abgeben.	She will hand it in on Wednesday.
3	Heute abend könnte ich es ihm sagen.	Tonight I could tell him.
4	Das schwarze Stück Papier befindet sich da oben neben dem Holzstück.	The black sheet of paper is located up there besides the piece of timber.
5	In sieben Stunden wird es soweit sein.	In seven hours it will be.
6	Was sind denn das für Tüten, die da unter dem Tisch stehen?	What about the bags standing there under the table?
7	Sie haben es gerade hochgetragen und jetzt gehen sie wieder runter.	They just carried it upstairs and now they are going down again.
8	An den Wochenenden bin ich jetzt immer nach Hause gefahren und habe Agnes besucht.	Currently at the weekends I always went home and saw Agnes.
9	Ich will das eben wegbringen und dann mit Karl was trinken gehen.	I will just discard this and then go for a drink with Karl.
10	Die wird auf dem Platz sein, wo wir sie immer hinlegen.	It will be in the place where we always store it.

Table 4.1: The 10 utterances recorded in the Berlin database of emotional speech.

4.1.1 Berlin Database of Emotional Speech

The Berlin Database of Emotional Speech[1] was recorded at the Technical University of Berlin [31]. It contains acted emotional German speech of ten carefully chosen speakers (5 male, 5 female) that were asked to pretend six different emotions (anger, joy, sadness, fear, disgust and boredom) as well as a neutral state in ten utterances each. Five of the ten utterances consisted of one phrase, the other five of two phrases. The content of the utterances was emotionally neutral. The utterances in German and their translation to English can be found in Table 4.1. As the recordings were intended for phonetic analysis of emotions and emotional speech synthesis they were conducted under very controlled conditions and so are marked by a very high audio quality (Figure 4.2).

After the recordings a listening test was performed with 20 human subjects who should recognise the emotion of every utterance and rate it for its naturalness. Those utterances from the collected material that were misclassified by more than 20 % of the test persons or perceived as unnatural by more than 40 % were discarded, ending up with 493 utterances (female: 286/male: 207). On average, 94.25 % of the 493 utterances were recognised correctly and 78.83 % were perceived as

---
[1] http://database.syntheticspeech.de

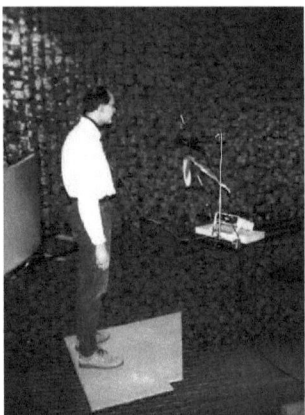

Figure 4.2: Recording conditions during the creation of the Berlin Database of Emotional Speech.[2]

	Joy	Anger	Fear	Disgust	Boredom	Sadness	Neutral	Σ
#	64	127	55	38	79	52	78	493
[min]	3'1"	5'36"	2'34"	2'34"	3'45"	4'11"	3'7"	24'48"

Table 4.2: The distribution and duration of emotions in the Berlin Database of Emotional Speech.

natural. The distribution of emotions is, except for anger, relatively equal, as can be seen in Table 4.2. Furthermore, manually labelled word boundary information is available for this database.

This database is a comparably easy task for emotional speech recognition, but quite far from realistic settings. It is evaluated by 5-fold cross-validation leaving always two speakers out (one male, one female). Though not intended by the creators who, as said before, designed this highly artificial database for speech synthesis it is used commonly in speech emotion recognition [e. g. 207] because it is freely available. Usually, it is evaluated with 10-fold speaker-dependent cross-validation.

4.1.2 FAU Aibo Emotion Corpus

The FAU Aibo Emotion Corpus was recorded at FAU Erlangen, Germany, in a Wizard-of-Oz (WoZ) setting within the EU project PF-Star [17, 22, 225]. It contains speech from children interacting with Sony's robot dog Aibo (Figure 4.3). The children had to direct the dog with

[2]©http://database.syntheticspeech.de/, 2010

4.1. Databases

Figure 4.3: Sony's pet robot Aibo.[3]

verbal commands in order to fulfil a task. In fact, however, the robot was operated remotely by another person and the sequence of its moves was predetermined. For the children, it thus looked like the dog was "disobedient" or incapable to do what they wanted it to do. This caused them to try to teach the robot, usually using baby talk (so-called "motherese"), to be angry with the dog when it disobeyed them, or to compliment it when it by chance made the right moves.

Recordings were obtained from 51 children in the age of 10 to 13 years from two schools (25 children from school "Mont" and 26 children from school "Ohm"), 31 of them girls, 20 of them boys. In total, it contains about 9.2 hours of speech in 13642 turns. Subsequently, each word was annotated by five independent raters with the labels joyful, surprised, emphatic, helpless, touchy/irritated, angry, motherese, bored, reprimanding, rest, and neutral. Word segmentation was obtained from an automatic speech recogniser and then manually corrected.

This corpus was initially only available for processing within the CEICES (Combining Efforts for Improving automatic Classification of Emotional user States) initiative [21] from the EU network of excellence HUMAINE which aimed at the joint evaluation of the database under fixed conditions in order to better compare results. Since the distribution of emotions is unequal, — neutral words prevail, — for the purpose of CEICES a subcorpus was chosen on which also the reference corpus throughout this work is based on. The so-called AMEN subcorpus contains only those words labelled with the four most frequent classes **A**ngry (formed by merging touchy, reprimanding and angry), **M**otherese, **E**mphatic and **N**eutral by at least three of the five labellers. The use of emphatic and motherese as emotion classes may at first seem strange, but emphatic was chosen because situations with emphatic speech often precede angry situations, and have

---
[3]©http://www.sonynet.com, 1999

	Angry	Motherese	Emphatic	Neutral	Σ
#	1557	1223	1645	1645	6070

Table 4.3: The distribution of emotions in the AMEN words of the FAU Aibo Emotion corpus.

	Angry	Motherese	Emphatic	Neutral	Σ
#	867	487	1334	1307	3995
[min]	38'	25'	63'	62'	188'

Table 4.4: The distribution and duration of emotions in the turns containing at least one AMEN word of the FAU Aibo Emotion corpus.

	Mont	Ohm
#	1739	2256
[min]	71'	117'

Table 4.5: The number and duration of turns with AMEN words in the two schools.

thus some kind of signalling function, and motherese marks situations when the child wants to compliment Aibo or make it obey in a positive way. These descriptions fit into the definition of emotion as a "short-term, consciously perceived, valenced state, either positive or negative" (see Section 2.1). In a stricter sense, they are "emotion-related user states" [225]. The classes emphatic and neutral were down-sampled in order to obtain a more balanced distribution of emotions, as is shown in Table 4.3. Thus, the AMEN corpus contains 6070 words which is about 15 % of the whole corpus. Evaluations of the Aibo database in this book refer to those turns that contain at least one of the AMEN words, not only to the AMEN words. Further segmentations (also words) are all based on these turns. Tables 4.4 and 4.5 show the distribution and duration of emotions, and the fraction of the two schools in the AMEN turns, respectively.

There also exists a semi-automatically segmentation into chunks for the whole Aibo corpus considering pauses and syntactic boundaries. The chunks therefore approximate a segmentation into utterances. Labels for the various units explored later were assigned on the basis of the word labels. The exact label mapping strategy will be described along with further segmentations in Section 4.2. As evaluation strategy for this corpus three-fold cross-validation was chosen, in order to have always one split as test set and the other two as a training set that can further be divided into a training and an evaluation set for feature selection. The splits were created with the gender, school and emotion distribution (given in order of priority) conserved as much as possible in the same way as by Schuller et al. [208].

As said before, the use of the database has been restricted until recently to the CEICES initiative.

4.1. Databases

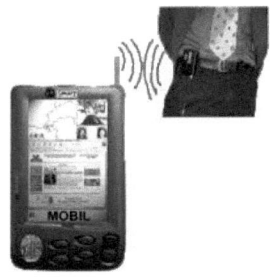

Figure 4.4: Design study of the SmartKom-Mobile scenario.[4]

In the course of the INTERSPEECH 2009 emotion challenge [213] on the full corpus it has been made publically available.

4.1.3 SmartKom Corpus

The goal of the SmartKom project was to develop a multimodal dialogue system for three different scenarios: a *public* information interface, a *home*-based and a *mobile* communication assistant (see Figure 4.4). The system was meant to understand speech and gestures, as well as to be responsive to emotions. Within the project, a large multimodal corpus was collected in a Wizard-of-Oz setting at the University of Munich [198]. 222 subjects were recorded in 447 sessions. Each session was about 4.5 minutes in length, however, the speech part is much less. Audio was captured with a directional microphone, a 4-channel microphone array and either a headset or a clip microphone. Because of better quality, only the headset microphone recordings are used here for analysis which restricts the data to 126 sessions of the mobile scenario by 66 speakers (37 female and 34 male). Three of the speakers were non-native German speakers. The age ranged from about 10 to 65 years, while the majority of speakers was between 12 and 27 years old. Thus, subjects were very heterogeneous. Videos were also recorded and supported the later annotation of emotions.

Subjects did not know during the recordings that their emotional state was observed. Besides from naturally occurring emotions it was tried occasionally to elicit emotions by slight disfunctions of the system like leading the subject all through a movie reservation process and telling them at the last step that this function was not available now. While the occurring emotions can be considered quite realistic, unfortunately, the biggest part of the speech is emotionally neutral.

The following emotions, referred to in SmartKom as "user states", were labelled [228]: joy/grati-

---
[4]©http://www.smartkom.org/mobil_de.html, 2010

	positive	neutral	negative	Σ
#	256	2086	776	3118
[min]	8'	139'	29'	176'

Table 4.6: Duration and number of emotional episodes in the headset-recorded sessions within the mobile scenario of the SmartKom database based on the holistic user state annotation.

fication, surprise, pondering/reflecting, helplessness, anger/irritation, and neutral, and unidentifiable episodes. The first five categories were further distinguished between strong and weak. Each session was labelled by three persons. Since some of the categories occurred only very rarely and a 12-class problem is not realistically tractable with current speech emotion recognition methods, especially in a database with very natural and weak emotions, a scheme base on Batliner et al. [16] was applied to merge the original categories into a 3-class problem. Thus, joy/gratification and surprise were mapped onto positive (or indicating "no problem"), pondering/reflecting, helplessness and anger/irritation onto negative (or indicating "problem"). The third class was neutral, unidentifiable episodes were dropped.

The annotation process had two stages. First, user states were annotated holistically, considering both audio and visual information. Then, the non-neutral segments were further labelled using only visual information. Due to this annotation procedure, the labels are often hardly identifiable from the speech signal alone, a fact also noted by the database creators [228]. As a consequence, this corpus represents a great challenge for automatic emotion recognition based on speech information only. Emotions are distributed very unequal, with more than two thirds of the speech being neutral, as can be seen in Table 4.6 which shows the distribution of the holistic user state annotation on the sessions of the mobile scenario.

Though this high proportion of neutral should occur in most real applications, in order to alleviate the difficulty of the task, only segments where both labels matched were selected for evaluation here, as these were regarded as less ambiguous. Obviously, in contrast to the other two databases labels in SmartKom are not based on linguistic units such as words or utterances. In addition to the annotation of user states, prosodic peculiarities were also labelled and supposed to enhance automatic emotion recognition. These were not used in this work as the emphasis is on fully automatically extractable features. Information on word boundaries was available from an automatic speech recogniser.

The SmartKom database was chosen for evaluation here because this natural corpus reflects the difficulties to be encountered in real world applications and therefore allows for a careful consideration of these problematic issues. Comparable results are available by the work of Batliner et al. [16] though their results were obtained from a different subset of the database, the public scenario. As Aibo, this corpus was evaluated with three-fold speaker-independent and gender-

4.2 Audio segmentation

As could already be seen in the Aibo and SmartKom databases in the previous section, speech segmentation is a non-trivial issue. The overview of the steps of the emotion recognition system in Figure 4.1 shows as the first step to segment the audio input signal into meaningful units to later derive the actual features from acoustic measurements of those units. The units are usually linguistically motivated medium-length time intervals such as words or utterances. Though the decision on which kind of unit to take is evidently important, it has not received much attention in past research on emotion recognition. Most approaches so far have dealt with utterances of acted emotions where the choice of unit is obviously just this utterance, a well-defined linguistic unit with no change of emotion within in this case. However, in spontaneous speech this kind of obvious unit does not exist. Neither is the segmentation into utterances straight-forward nor can a constant emotion be expected over an utterance. Generally speaking, a good emotion unit has to fulfil certain requirements. In particular, it should be

1. well-defined to be consistently extracted,
2. long enough so that features can reliably be calculated by means of statistical functions,
3. short enough to guarantee stable acoustic properties with respect to emotions within the segment,
4. consistent with the labelling of the training database.

The first point is important because the segmentation in training, test and application should be subject to the same rules, that is, it must have the same characteristics. Thereto the rules for segmentation need to be unequivocally defined. For example, the notion "sentence" does exist for spontaneous speech, however, a segmentation into sentences is often not feasible and if, it is often ambiguous. So a sentence would not be a good unit for spontaneous speech, though it is useful for acted speech.

Since here, as in many other work, the feature extraction approach of calculating global statistics for given time segments is taken, the classification units need to have a minimum length. The more values statistical measures are based on, the more expressive they are. On the other hand all alterations of the emotional state should possibly be captured, so the unit should be short enough that no change of emotion is likely to happen within. In addition, it should be so short that the acoustic properties of the segment with respect to emotions are stable, so that expressive features can be derived. This is particularly important for features based on statistical measures, since for instance the mean value of a very inhomogeneous segment yields an inadequate description. Thus, a compromise has to be found for these two conflicting requirements

Furthermore, for a given training database, arbitrary units cannot be used, since emotion labels are biased to some extent if they do not exist for exactly this segmentation. Hence a comparison of units on different databases must be drawn with care. For example, if the database is labelled on turn level, this does not mean that every word in the turn has this emotion. Some might be neutral if accounted for individually, especially short words without emphasis. In reverse, careful consideration is needed to derive a turn label from word labels, for example by simple majority voting over word labels. It is often better to reduce the influence of neutral words.

As the aim here is a real-time self-contained emotion recognition application which does not require further knowledge, for example about words and word boundaries, a further requirement is put onto the unit of choice as it should be automatically computed from the audio signal alone.

In general, potential units can be linguistically motivated and thus be phonemes, syllables, words, or utterances, or be set to frames with a fixed length, for example 0.5 or 1 seconds. The latter have the advantage that their automatic extraction is straight-forward which is favourable for realistic applications. Furthermore, a unit can be considered with its context, that means for example for a word, to consider the preceding and succeeding word(s) as well. In the context of dialogue systems, for which emotion recognition is especially applicable, whole dialogue turns can also serve as emotion classification units. The length and nature of turns, however, strongly depend on the dialogue system. In order to have a unit in spontaneous speech that approximates utterances in acted speech a — manual or automatic — boundary detection can be carried out. A strategy for automatic boundary detection is to segment by pauses, that is sections of low signal energy, that are at least 0.2 to 1 seconds long. For this purpose, voice activity detection (VAD) algorithms can be used, as breaks in voice activity can mark the boundaries.

Generally, it strongly depends on the data which unit fits best. Hence, various types of units will be explored here in view of their usefulness for different kinds of data, in particular fixed length units, words, utterances, segments marked by pauses, and turns. An overview of the examined units for each of the three databases can be found in Table 4.7.

Now, first the non-linguistic units are described. Three durations of fixed length units are tested: 0.5, 1 and 2 seconds. These were chosen because units of less than 0.5 seconds were considered as too short for the calculation of statistical measures, while changes of the emotional state may well occur in units longer than 2 seconds. Lastly, as an approximation of a linguistic unit, speech parts segmented by breaks in the voice activity detected automatically and on the acoustic

4.2. Audio segmentation

Unit	Berlin	Aibo	SmartKom
fixed length 0.5s	√	√	√
fixed length 1s	√	√	√
fixed length 2s	√	√	√
automatic pause segmentation by VAD	√	√	√
word	√	√	√
word in context (± 1 word)	√	√	√
manual syntactic/prosodic boundary detection (chunks)	—	√	—
pause segmentation by ASR (chunks)	—	—	√
utterance	√	—	—
turns	—	√	√

Table 4.7: Emotion units explored for the Berlin, SmartKom, and Aibo database.

signal only by the algorithm integrated into ESMERALDA, a framework for building automatic speech recognisers based on HMMs [78], are investigated. All these units are very suitable for an integrated online system.

Analysed linguistically motivated units comprise words, words in context, manual and automatic speech recognition (ASR) assisted pause segmentation as well as utterances and dialogue turns. These are analysed here offline and mainly as reference for the performance of the non-linguistic units and as reference to other related work. Words are often very short, that is why they are also investigated within the context of one preceding and succeeding word and the potential silent or non-verbal part in between. Among the units compared here, considering context is most reasonable for words, because the difference of adjacent words within an utterance in respect of their emotional tone will scarcely be huge. For dialogue turns, contrarily, this should be the case more often, as between succeeding turns, events that lead to a change in the emotional state may happen. Still, words are not desirable for the further goals of the work described here, because a speech recognition system is needed to determine word boundaries automatically. Since speech recognisers — especially for arbitrary application areas — are very prone to errors, their use will be avoided here so that a self-contained emotion recognition system can be built.

As higher-level linguistic units, chunks, utterances and turns are examined. On the Aibo database, chunks were obtained by a manually revised detection of syntactic and prosodic boundaries triggered by main clauses, free phrases and between successive occurrences of the word "Aibo", as these repetitions are likely to mark a change in the emotional state [208]. Prosodic boundaries were set when pauses between words exceeded 0.5 seconds. In SmartKom, chunks were defined by pauses longer than 0.5 seconds as detected by an ASR system, which is a fully automatical procedure. However, there were only a few emotionally neutral turns that were affected by this segmentation. Chunking is not available for the Berlin database, instead, utterances were used.

#	Word	Start	End	Labels
1	jetzt	0.49	0.75	NNNNN
2	*gehd	0.86	1.0	NNNNN
3	g'radeaus	1.12	1.92	EEENN
4	stopp	2.04	2.44	EEENE
5	stopp	2.56	2.93	EEENE

Table 4.8: The words in the turn "jetzt *gehd g'radeaus stopp stopp" in the Aibo corpus with start and end times in seconds, as well as labels from each of the five labellers.

Within dialogue turns changes of the emotional state have to be expected, but the classifier has to decide on only one emotion per turn. Turns containing more than one emotion are probably not acoustically homogeneous with respect to emotions so they assumedly produce lower recognition rates. If this indeed makes them a suboptimal unit for emotion recognition will be discussed by means of the results in the next chapter.

A very important point is how labels, which were always available for only one unit per database, are mapped onto other units. Labels in the Berlin database arise from that emotion that the actors were asked to pretend in the superordinate utterance. Finding a good label mapping strategy for the Aibo database is more complicated since labels are available on word level from each of the five annotators. The mapping is based on Steidl's strategy [225]. Thus, for word and 0.5 seconds, a majority voting of all available labels was used. The label of the word in context arises from the label of its central word. For VAD based units, chunks and 1.0 seconds, a unit was labelled as neutral, if at least 60 % of the votes were neutral; as motherese, if there were at least as many votes for motherese than for emphatic or angry; as angry, if there were equal or more votes for angry than for emphatic; and as emphatic in the remaining cases. For turns and 2.0 seconds, the same strategy was used, but the threshold for neutral was set to 70 %. Neutral is treated in a special way because for a whole chunk to be perceived emotional, not all words, especially function words, need to be pronounced emotionally. In the case of fixed length and VAD units, labels are weighted by the number of samples they occur in the unit. If more than one third of a unit was not labelled because it did not occur in a word, the unit was not considered for classification. This may not be realistic, as normally, these units should be labelled as pertaining to a rest class or silence, but it would have made it more difficult to compare units because the number of classes was not the same. In order to ease the understanding of the labelling process, it is illustrated by an example: Given the turn "jetzt *gehd g'radeaus stopp stopp" with durations and labels as in Table 4.8, labels for the various units are derived as shown in Table 4.9.

In the SmartKom database, labels were derived by simple majority voting. If the relative majority of a fixed-length unit pertained to silence, the unit was not used for classification. Words shorter

4.3. Features

Unit	Label sequence					
0.5s	N [0.5–1]	E [1–1.5]	E [1.5–2]	E [2–2.5]	E [2.5–3]	E [3–3.5]
1.0s	N [0–1]	E [1–2]	E [2–3]			
2.0s	N [0–2]					
VAD	E [0.49–2.63]	E [2.66–3.03]				
word	N [0.49–0.75]	N [0.86–1]	E [1.12–1.92]	E [2.04-2.44]	E [2.56–2.93]	
word ±1	N [0.49–1]	N [0.49–1.92]	E [0.86–2.44]	E [1.12–2.93]	E [2.04–2.93]	
chunk	N [0.49–2.44]	E [1.12–2.93]	E [2.04–2.93]			
turn	E [0–3.3]					

Table 4.9: Label mapping in the Aibo database from word based labels (see Table 4.8) onto the different units. Durations are given as intervals in seconds below the label.

than 0.1 seconds were also discarded.

Two further remarks concern all three databases: if a fixed length unit at the end of a turn does not have full length, it is not used. Furthermore, a word in context at the beginning of a turn consists of the first and the second word, likewise the last word in context consists of the last and the second to last word.

4.3 Features

Common features for speech emotion recognition are based on short-term acoustic observations like pitch or energy, as presented in Section 2.3.2. Since the specific values of these measures are usually not too expressive *per se*, but rather their change over time, the modeling of the temporal behaviour is crucial to the success of the task. Basically, there are two approaches to do this, which depend on the type of classifier that is used. Learning algorithms like HMMs model temporal changes by considering sequences of feature vectors, looking especially at the transitions between the vectors. Thus, a classification unit consists of a series of feature vectors and obtains one label by the classifier. Standard classifiers, however, assign one label to each feature vector.

As a result, time needs to be encoded in the features themself, usually by (optional) transformations of the basic values and applying (statistical) functions like mean calculation, that map a series of values onto a single value.

The latter approach is the one followed here. Of course, there is a huge number of possibilities how to transform value sequences to single values. Since emotional features are investigated extensively here, the goal is to calculate a multitude of possibly relevant features starting from the basic feature types. However, high-dimensional input does not only slow down classification, but can also deteriorate it if too many similar features that are dependent of each other are used. For this reason, the most important features of the initially calculated set can be chosen here by means of (combinations of) feature selection strategies: information gain, a correlation-based algorithm and sequential forward floating feature selection.

In the following sections, first feature extraction as used for the experiments described in the next chapter is described. This includes the calculation of the basic feature types as well as the actual features that were derived from each of them. Subsequently, the feature selection methods are presented.

4.3.1 Feature extraction

The strategy for feature extraction was inspired by the work of Oudeyer [173]. There, time series for pitch, intensity, low-passed and high-passed intensity as well as 10 MFCCs, were calculated for each signal chunk. Then, three additional series were derived from these basic time series looking only at the minima, at the maxima or at the distances between local extrema of the 10 Hz smoothed curve of the original series. For each of the four resulting series for each measure, mean, minimum, maximum, difference between minimum and maximum, variance, median, first quartile, third quartile, interquartile range and the mean of the absolute value of the local derivative were computed, which amount to ten statistical values. Thus, in total 200 features were used.

Here, further basic feature types are investigated, in particular pitch, energy, 12 MFCCs, the frequency spectrum and voice quality measures. Furthermore, the derivation of series from the basic series is extended. Since also derivatives of the basic series are considered, the last statistic, the mean of the absolute value of the local derivative, is dropped in contrast to Oudeyer's approach. Additionally, features related to voicing and global features such as duration, pauses, speaking rate, jitter and shimmer are integrated.

In the following, it will be described how these basic feature types were calculated and which features exactly were derived from them. A detailed description of the feature types and how they relate to emotions has been provided in Section 2.3.2. Note that the final features are categorised here according to the basic feature type they were derived from. This is not necessarily a phonetically valid categorisation — for example Batliner et al. [14] denote features related to the position of pitch on the time axis as durational features — but rather a practical categorisation.

Pitch

Pitch, or fundamental frequency, is the acoustic correlative of the perceived tone height. The automatic estimation of pitch is a non-trivial task. Sources for errors are the distinction of voiced and unvoiced segments, and within voiced segments, the pitch detection can be overshadowed by effects of vocal tract resonance and short-term perturbations in the speech signal [49]. Gross errors are mainly octave jumps when other harmonics have high energy which are then easily taken for the fundamental frequency, but also local errors occur in the determination of the exact Hertz values. Depending on the task, the latter may be negligible.

Here, the pitch algorithm described by Boersma [28] is used, whose high accuracy is generally accepted and which is part of the popular phonetics software PRAAT [29]. Thereto the speech segment is divided into frames of 80 ms length at a rate of 10 ms. Each frame is first windowed by a Gaussian window, then possible pitch values are calculated from the maxima of the auto-correlated signal. The possibility of an unvoiced frame is as well added to the list of candidate values. Each candidate has a strength associated that is based on a voicing and silence threshold for the unvoiced candidate and the auto-correlation value for voiced candidates. With dynamic programming, an optimal path through the candidates of all frames is searched, using a cost function that takes into account a cost for voiced to unvoiced transitions and an octave jump cost related to the log quotient of both candidate values for voiced to voiced transitions. This guarantees higher robustness against the earlier mentioned sources of errors compared to algorithms that find pitch values only locally, though it does not eliminate them fully. Besides, the accuracy of the algorithm increases with the length of the superordinate speech segment which however forbids an incremental pitch detection. For performance reasons, the algorithm was re-implemented here with a lesser depth when interpolating the frequency values of the maxima of the sampled auto-correlation to continuous resolution compared to its implementation in the original software (PRAAT). The allowed pitch range was restricted to 75–600 Hz for Berlin and SmartKom, and to 100–800 Hz for Aibo as it contains children's speech.

Pitch is very prone to inter-speaker differences, especially gender differences, so that "high pitch" can mean 200 Hz for one speaker and 300 Hz for another, and even higher for children. Different approaches are examined to remedy this. The first step into this direction is to logarithmise the pitch values, as this makes the pitch variation for male and female more similar [126]. An actual normalisation is obtained by subtracting the median from the logarithmised pitch values. Additionally, the "raw" pitch mean, median, first and third quartile values are normalised following Zhang et al. [268] by minimum and maximum pitch of the respective segment according to the following formula (exemplarily here for mean)

$$mean_{norm} = \frac{mean - min}{max - min} \qquad (4.1)$$

A further approach to the compensation of gender differences is investigated in Section 7.1. However, though the validity of unnormalised raw pitch values is questionable, the usefulness of normalised values is not less challenged here. Anyway, features modeling the dynamic behaviour of pitch, so for example related to the temporal distance between local extrema or relative magnitude of extrema, are assumed to be more important than the specific (raw or normalised) values of pitch. Evidence on this is given in the next chapter.

In order to obtain different views on the data, the above described series of raw values, log values and median-subtracted log pitch values are further transformed into the series of the local maxima, the local minima as well as the difference, distance and slope between adjacent local extrema. These transformations are illustrated by Figure 4.5. Furthermore, first and second derivation are obtained. From the resulting 22 pitch series, the standard statistic measures are calculated.

Further features are the position of the overall pitch maximum, which approximates the main accent in linguistically motivated segments, and the position of the overall pitch minimum. As indicators for pitch contours, the number of minima, maxima, falling and rising values are obtained. All these values are normalised by the number of pitch values in the segment, ending up with 208 pitch related features in total. Table 4.10 summarises all pitch features once again.

Energy

Signal energy corresponds to the perceived loudness of a sound. It is obtained using the ESMERALDA environment for speech recognition [78] where it is calculated for frames of 16 ms length at a rate of 10 ms. The mean adjusted and logarithmised signal energy SE is then calculated from each frame by

$$SE = \log \left(\frac{\sum_{i=0}^{N} s_i^2}{N} - \left(\frac{\sum_{i=0}^{N} s_i}{N} \right)^2 \right) \qquad (4.2)$$

where s_i is the amplitude value at time i of a frame of N samples length. Afterwards, the energy is normalised to the 95 % quantile of the previous frames.

4.3. Features

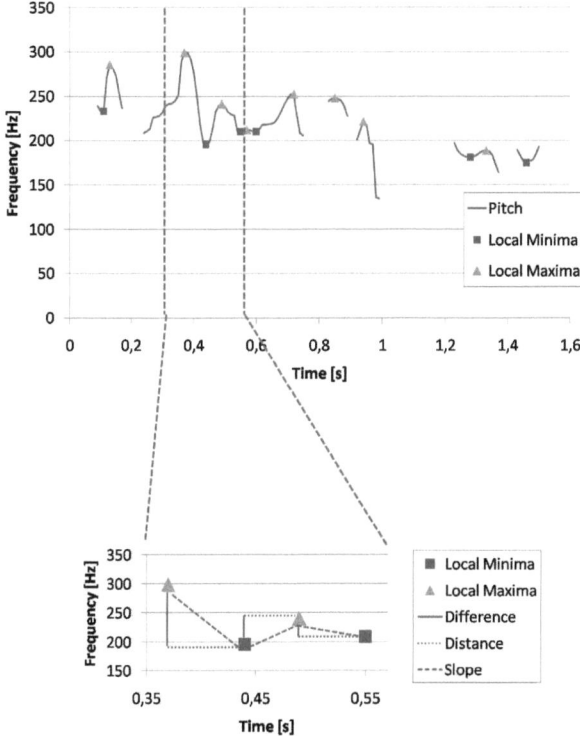

Figure 4.5: Transformation of time value series using pitch as example: local maxima, local minima (above); frequency distance, temporal distance and slope between adjacent local extrema (below).

Like for pitch, the series of only the local maxima and only the local minima are derived from the energy curve, as well as difference, distance and slope between adjacent local extrema. First and second order derivation together with the series of their local maxima and local minima are further added to the number of 12 resulting energy related value series, from which again the standard statistic functions are calculated.

The position of the global maximum and the number of local maxima, both normalised by the number of frames in the segment, are also joined to the feature vector, which finally contains 110 energy related features, as shown in Table 4.11.

Transformation	absolute pitch	logarithmised pitch	median subtracted log pitch
basic	S	S	S
local minima	S	S	S
local maxima	S	S	S
difference between local extrema	S	S	S
slope between local extrema	S	S	S
distance between local extrema	S	—	—
first derivation	S	S	S
second derivation	S	S	S
normalised by global minimum/maximum	mean, median, 1st quartile, 3rd quartile		
position	global minimum, maximum		
number	local minima/maxima falling /rising pitch frames		

Table 4.10: *Pitch features*: Transformations of the absolute, the logarithmised, and the median subtracted logarithmised pitch values. S indicates whether global statistics have been calculated.

Transformation	f	f'	f''
basic	S	S	S
local minima	S	S	S
local maxima	S	S	S
diff. between local extrema	S	—	—
slope between local extrema	S	—	—
dist. between local extrema	S	—	—
position	global max	—	—
number	local max	—	—

Table 4.11: *Energy features:* transformations of the basic series (f), first (f') and second derivation (f'') with global statistics (S) calculated, as well as further features.

MFCC

Mel-frequency cepstral coefficients (MFCCs) encode a compact representation of the frequency spectrum. They are calculated by ESMERALDA at the same frame length and rate as signal

4.3. Features

Transformation	f	f'	f''
basic (1–12, avg)	S	S	S
local minima (1–12, avg)	S	S	S
local maxima (1–12, avg)	S	S	S

Table 4.12: *MFCC features:* transformations of the basic series (f), first (f') and second (f'') derivation with global statistics from coefficients 1–12 and averaged sum.

energy according to the general description in Section 2.3.2. ESMERALDA additionally performs an adaptation to the microphone channel.

Adding the first and second derivatives of every coefficient yields 36 MFCC time series for every signal segment. From each series, the local maxima and minima series are also derived. Furthermore, a condensed representation — the average over all 12 coefficients for each basic, first and second derivation — is contrasted to the single features. This gives in total 1053 MFCC related features, as summarised in Table 4.12.

Durational features

Durational features are all features that relate to timing issues. Much of this information is encoded on the global unit level, not in time series, and some features described earlier in the sections on pitch resp. energy, for instance positional features such as the position of the pitch maximum/minimum or energy maximum, also model durational aspects. Three aspects of duration are represented explicitly in the full feature vector by four features:

1. Segment length, measured in seconds. This is a value that may not make sense in some contexts but is very useful in others. For example, the length of individual words is often not distinctive for a specific emotion but depends more on the type of word (e. g. function word, content word). On the other hand, length can be a very characteristic feature on utterance level, especially for acted emotions where utterance lengths are often comparable as the same utterance is spoken several times, and for instance boredom tends to be spoken very slowly.

2. Pause: This is grossly approximated by the ratio of unvoiced pitch frames to the total number of frames in the segment. Furthermore, the same voice activity detection algorithms as used for the pause detection in audio segmentation (see Section 4.2) was applied to each emotion segment and the proportion of non-speech was calculated. In the case of VAD units it may not make sense at first glance to apply this algorithm possibly twice to the

Basis	Feature
length	segment length
pause	unvoiced proportion
	non-speech proportion
speaking rate	zero-crossings rate

Table 4.13: Explicit *duration features*.

same speech signal. However, the threshold for voice activity is determined dynamically and adaptive to the energy in the specific context. As the context for segmentation into emotion units is longer than the context within an emotion unit, this usually yields a new speech/non-speech segmentation.

3. Speaking rate: A first approximation of speaking rate is already contained in energy features measuring the distances between local maxima. Additionally, the zero-crossings rate of the amplitude is roughly related to the speaking rate. There exist more sophisticated speaking rate measures than these two, however, they were preferred here for their fast and straight-forward calculation.

The four explicit duration features that are not derived from any of the other basic feature types can be found in Table 4.13.

Spectral analysis

In order to gather spectral information, the acoustic signal is broken down by Fourier transformation (FFT) into a series of short-term spectra of 16 ms length at a rate of 10 ms. Since especially information on the slope of the spectrum was regarded as important, for each short-term spectrum, the distance between the 10th and the 90th percentile, the slope between weakest and strongest frequency, as well as two linear regression coefficients a and b to model the energy E with the frequency spectrum f by ordinary least-square estimation are calculated:

$$E = a - bf \tag{4.3}$$

with

$$a = \overline{E} - b\overline{f} \tag{4.4}$$

$$b = \frac{\sum_{i=1}^{n}(f_i - \overline{f})(E_i - \overline{E})}{\sum_{i=1}^{n}(f_i - \overline{f})^2} \tag{4.5}$$

4.3. Features

Transformation	Features
centre of gravity	S
distance between 10 and 90 % frequency quantile	S
slope between strongest and weakest frequency	S
linear regression, coefficient a	S
linear regression, coefficient b	S

Table 4.14: *Spectral features:* features based on global statistics of transformations of short-term spectra.

where f_i is the ith frequency of the spectrum, E_i the energy of f_i in the spectrum, $\overline{f}$ the mean frequency and $\overline{E}$ the mean energy.

Furthermore, the centre of gravity (CG) of the spectrum is obtained according to the formula

$$CG = \frac{\sum f_i \cdot E_i}{\sum E_i} \qquad (4.6)$$

The centre of gravity parametrises the spectral balance between high and low frequencies for a signal segment [236].

Each of these five values yielded a new 1-dimensional time series, from which the standard statistics were derived (see Table 4.14).

Voicing features

The length and distribution of phonetically voiced and unvoiced segments, as obtained from the pitch calculation, in a speech signal is related to certain voice characteristics that may give hints on the emotional state of the speaker. For example a chopped speaking style may be reflected by the distribution of voiced and unvoiced segments. Therefore, the lengths of both the voiced and the unvoiced segments in an emotion unit are used to create new value series. Applying the standard statistic measures yields for instance the mean length of voiced segments in the unit. Furthermore, the number of voiced segments normalised by the number of pitch frames in the unit is added. Table 4.15 shows the full list of voicing features.

Voice quality

Voice quality refers to the different types of phonation, for instance a harsh voice may reflect anger. The harmonics-to-noise ratio (HNR) as well as the glottal pulses are used as voice quality

Basis	Features
length of voiced segments	$\mathcal{S}$
length of unvoiced segments	$\mathcal{S}$
voiced segments	number

Table 4.15: *Voicing features:* Features based on unvoiced/voiced decisions of pitch frames.

Basis	Features
HNR	$\mathcal{S}$
glottal pulses	number
	jitter
	shimmer

Table 4.16: *Voice quality features:* based on Harmonics-to-Noise ratio (HNR) and glottal pulses.

features here. HNR is obtained from the pitch algorithm described in Section 4.3.1 with a Hanning window instead of a Gaussian window, and the window length being twice as long. The calculation is based on the implementation in the PRAAT software for each frame as follows:

$$HNR = 10\log_{10}\frac{r}{1-r} \tag{4.7}$$

where r is the strength of the fundamental frequency in the frame. This yields a series of HNR values over an emotion unit from which the standard statistic functions are derived.

Furthermore, jitter and shimmer of the glottal pulses of the whole segment (compare Section 2.3.2) which correspond to the variability in distance and amplitude of the glottal pulses respectively, as well as the number of glottal pulses normalised by the segment length in seconds are added to the feature set (see Table 4.16).

Summary

The exact numbers for each feature type are summarised in Table 4.17. As can be seen, MFCC features outnumber the others by far, but this is only because every coefficient is represented individually which produces a large number of features.

Altogether, the features accumulate to a total of 1451. Although some of the features have only approximative character, their advantage is that they can be computed very fast, which is important in respect to the intended use of real-time feature extraction.

4.3. Features

Feature type	Number of features
pitch	208
energy	110
MFCC	1053
duration	4
spectral properties	45
voicing related features	19
voice quality	12
Σ	1451

Table 4.17: Number of features in each feature type.

At this point, also a systematic nomenclature of the features should be introduced which starts with the basic feature type, then lists transformations of the basic value series in the order of their application, and finally specifies statistical functions, all separated by "_". The abbreviations that are used can be found in Table 4.18. The mean of the local minima of the logarithmised pitch values would thus be encoded as `pitch_log_mins_mean`.

4.3.2 Feature selection

The feature set as described in the last section contains a lot of features, many of them probably redundant or not relevant, at least for particular tasks. As already indicated in Section 2.3.2 feature selection can have several benefits, for the interpretation of features as well as for the further proceeding. Here, three purposes are pursued by feature selection. Firstly, a selection of the extracted features should give hints on which types of features are relevant and how much, both for individual features and subsets of features. Then, for the emotion recognition system described later in Chapter 6 feature selection is beneficial for efficiency reasons, as a smaller set with comparable results is preferred over a larger set, because training as well as classification times are shorter. Thirdly, in practise a feature selection can actually increase performance, because with the learning algorithms used here, an addition of bad, redundant or correlated features may even deteriorate accuracy. On small training data sets, the effect of overfitting may occur. Furthermore, feature sets should be optimised for the respective application scenario, since it is assumed that good feature sets are very different depending on the data type.

Here, three different approaches to feature selection and evaluation will be applied that have already been shortly described in Section 2.3.2. For a start, features are ranked according to their information gain in order to evaluate each feature individually. Then, a method is examined that removes correlated features (CFS), and finally, sequential forward floating feature selection (SFFS) with classifier performance as selection criterion is used to optimise the classification

	Description	Abbreviation
Feature categories	pitch	pitch
	energy	energy
	MFCCs	mfcc
	duration	dur
	short-term frequency spectrum	spectral
	voicing related features	voicing
	voice quality	voiceQual
Transformations of multidimensional data	average	avg
	centre of gravity	cog
	range of 10 % percentile and 90 % percentile	prange
	slope between minimum and maximum	slope
	linear regression, coefficient a	linRegA
	linear regression, coefficient b	linRegB
	Harmonics-to-Noise ratio	hnr
Transformations of time series	local maxima	maxs
	local minima	mins
	difference between adjacent local extrema	x_diff
	distance between adjacent local extrema	x_dist
	slope between adjacent local extrema	x_slope
	1st derivation	d
	2nd derivation	dd
	logarithmised	log
	logarithmised and median subtracted	log_median
	length of voiced segments	voiced
	length of unvoiced segments	unvoiced
Functions	normalisation	norm
	position	pos
	number	num
Statistics	mean	mean
	maximum	max
	minimum	min
	range	range
	variance	var
	median	median
	1st quartile	q1
	3rd quartile	q3
	interquartile range	qrange

Table 4.18: Denotation of features.

4.3. Features

result. In order to restrict the search space, two combinations of the strategies are also evaluated. These are information gain ranking prior to CFS, as well as CFS followed by SFFS.

Information gain feature ranking

The information gained from a specific feature to predict an emotion gives evidence on its usefulness. It is measured by the gain in entropy $H()$ of that feature with respect to the emotion class and is obtained from

$$IG(Emotion, Feature) = H(Emotion) - H(Emotion|Feature) \tag{4.8}$$

In order to rank features according to their information gain, the data mining toolkit Weka [255] was used.

Correlation-based feature subset evaluation

In contrast to ranking features individually by information gain, correlation-based feature subset selection (CFS, [98]) evaluates sets of features taken from the original set. The goal is to find a subset where the correlation of each feature with the class is maximised, while the correlation of the features among each other is low. This strategy is especially beneficial for the Naïve Bayes classifier which performs badly when features are highly correlated since it assumes features to be independent for simplification reasons.

Again, the Weka toolkit was used to evaluate feature subsets with CFS in combination with a Best-First search to find suitable subsets.

Sequential forward floating search

In order to find a good feature subset with sequential forward floating search (SFFS, [185]), subset selection starts with an empty set. Then, sequentially that feature is added from the full feature set which gives best evaluation scores. Evaluation criterion is the mean accuracy per class obtained from the Naïve Bayes classifier obtained from two-fold speaker independent cross-validation. After each feature addition, sequentially features can be eliminated from the current set as long as the score is higher or equal. The maximal subset size is restricted here to 200, but as can be seen later in Section 5.3.6, the best sets found are considerably smaller.

Since usually lots of subset evaluations are needed in order to find an optimal set, this search method can in practise only be run with a learning algorithm that is fast in training and classification. For this reason, only Naïve Bayes was used for this purpose. However, the resulting set is thus optimised towards this classifier and not necessarily well suited for others. For the implementation of SFFS, the code in the electronic annex of [224] was adapted.

4.4 Classification

Classifiers are needed for three different purposes here: first, for the evaluation of units and features (Sections 5.2–5.3), second, for an experiment on the comparison of classifiers (Section 5.4), and last, for integration into the stand-alone emotion recognition system of Chapter 6.

Starting with the last point, the implemented algorithms are Naïve Bayes and Support Vector Machines (SVM). As already indicated in Section 3.3, Support Vector Machines have proved to be very competitive and are used by a large number of approaches. The Naïve Bayes classifier is fast to train, especially in high-dimensional input spaces, and though it is a very simple classifier, it still gives good results [148, 158, 180]. For this reason, it is used exclusively for experiments on units and features here. The algorithms and actual implementations of SVM and Naïve Bayes are described later in this section. For further information the reader is referred to the vast body of literature on pattern recognition and machine learning, which often deals with these two popular classifiers (e. g. [26, 68, 156]).

Finally, for the experiment on classifiers, a selection of popular algorithms from Weka is compared. Since the focus of this book lies on feature calculation and emotion units, no extensive testing of classifiers is conducted here and the majority of classifiers has not been reimplemented or altered. The algorithms are in detail:

- **0-R:** The 0-R classifier always classifies into the majority class. This classification scheme has no practical importance, however, it is a useful baseline algorithm: a good classifier should be at least better than this one. Mean accuracy per class of 0-R corresponds to chance accuracy. When classes are unbalanced as in Aibo and SmartKom, it may be even difficult for other classifiers to outperform 0-R's overall accuracy.

- **Naïve Bayes:** The Weka implementation of Naïve Bayes is almost identical to the one presented later in this section and gives only very slight and insignificant differences in classification rates.

- **SVM:** The LibSVM [43] implementation of Support Vector Machines (SVM) that is integrated into the stand-alone emotion recognition system of Chapter 6 and will be described later is also available in Weka. Features are normalised prior to training and classification.

4.4. Classification

- **MLP:** The Multi-Layer Perceptron (MLP) [26] is a Neural Network with an output layer of neurons, but also hidden layers that are connected with each other and the output layer. The weights of the neurons can be learnt with the backpropagation algorithm to match the training patterns. The MLP is a sophisticated classifier that has been shown to work well on a number of problems. However, depending on the complexity of the network, training as well as testing can take very long.

- **3-NN:** The Nearest-Neighbour classifier [2] classifies new instances according to the class of the k (here: $k = 3$) most similar instances found in the training database. It is a simple well-known algorithm that obviously requires no training time, though dependent on the size of the training set, classification can be time consuming.

- **Random Forest:** A Random Forest [30] classifier is a combination of Random Tree classifiers that depend at each node on a certain number of randomly selected features. Tree algorithms are relatively seldom used for emotion recognition, but have in some cases proved to be very accurate [21].

- **RIPPER:** Rule-based classifiers are scarcely found in the literature on emotion recognition. For the sake of completeness, the RIPPER (Repeated Incremental Pruning to Produce Error Reduction) [51] classifier is included here as an example for rule-based classification.

Now, the SVM and Naïve Bayes classifiers are described in detail.

4.4.1 Support Vector Machines

Support vector machines (SVM) belong to the group of linear learning algorithms, but they overcome some of the limitations of regular linear classifiers. The idea behind SVM is to find a hyperplane between the instances of two classes in such a way that the shortest distance between the instances and the hyperplane is maximised. Thus, a *maximum margin hyperplane* is defined on the basis of so called support vectors, which are training instances situated at the class boundaries (Figure 4.6). The class y of a test instance $\vec{x}$ is then assigned by the side of the hyperplane it is located at:

$$y = \text{sgn}(b + \sum_{i=1}^{N} \alpha_i c_i \vec{s}_i \vec{x}) \tag{4.9}$$

Here, $\vec{s}_i$ is one of N support vectors, c_i is the class value of s_i which is either 1 for class 1 or -1 for class 2, and b and α_i are coefficients to be determined during training [255].

Chapter 4. Databases and methods for speech emotion recognition

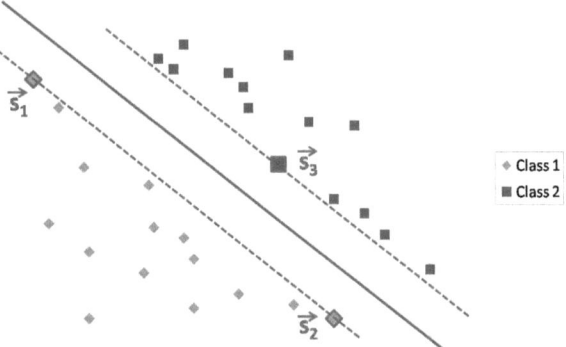

Figure 4.6: Support vectors $\vec{s_1}$, $\vec{s_2}$ and $\vec{s_3}$ for a SVM classifier maximise the distance between two classes. The solid blue line indicates the maximum margin hyperplane.

An advantage of SVM is that it can also solve linearly not separable class problems by a transformation into a higher-dimensional space. That way, class boundaries are non-linear in the original space, but linear in the transformed space. In order to achieve this, non-linear functions are applied to the product $\vec{s_i}\vec{x}$ of the test instance and the support vector in Equation 4.9. These functions are called kernel functions. Possible kernel functions are a polynomial kernel $(\vec{s}\vec{x})^n$, or a radial basis function kernel $\exp^{-(\vec{s}\vec{x})^2}$.

The drawback of this transformation into a higher-dimensional space is that the number of coefficients to be trained increases. So SVMs in general need a lot of training material to build a reliable classifier that can generalise to unseen instances, otherwise the model might overfit the data. Furthermore, the time it takes to train a SVM classifier is relatively long.

Note further that SVM primarily treats only two-class problems, but it can be extended to multi-class problems by splitting the original problem into a set of two-class problems.

In the experiments described in the next chapter, the libsvm implementation [43] of SVM, a generally accepted library, is used. A linear kernel is applied because it is faster to train and empirically proved to be better when the majority of instances belongs to only one class, which applies often to spontaneous emotion classification, in particular to the Aibo and the SmartKom databases. Before classification, features are normalised by their maximum and minimum values in the training set for this classifier.

4.4.2 Naïve Bayes

Naïve Bayes is a simple classifier based on the Bayes Theorem which states:

$$P(E_i|f_1,\ldots,f_n) = \frac{P(E_i)\prod_{j=1}^{n}P(f_j|E_i)}{P(f_1,\ldots,f_n)} \quad (4.10)$$

In other words, this means that the probability of the emotion E_i given an observed feature vector $(f_1,\ldots,f_n)$ of dimension n depends on the *a-priori* probability $P(E_i)$ of the emotion, multiplied by the product of the probability of each feature f_i given the emotion, divided by the *a-priori* probability of the feature vector. As classification result, the emotion E_i from a set of N emotions $E_1,\ldots,E_N$ that maximises Equation 4.10 is chosen. This is simplifying in so far (and hence the name *Naïve* Bayes), as the Bayes Theorem assumes the features to be independent from each other. In reality, and especially in the approach taken here, where a multitude of possibly redundant and interdependent features is calculated, this is usually not true. However, Naïve Bayes has still proved to be quite successful in a variety of tasks [255, p. 91].

Parameters for the probability distributions $P(E_i)$ and $P(f_j|E_i)$ are gained from the annotated training material. For practical purposes, the denominator in equation 4.10, $P(f_1,\ldots,f_n)$, can be omitted as it is constant with respect to the emotion class. Furthermore, for the implementation of the algorithm here, the logarithmised probability $\log P(E_i|f_1,\ldots,f_n)$ is computed, which transforms the products of equation 4.10 into sums, to avoid floating point exceptions caused by very small numbers that emerge from multiplying very often (here up to 1451 times) only numbers smaller than 1. Since the real probability values are of no interest here, but rather the relation of the probabilities of different emotion classes for a given feature vector, this does not affect the validity of the result.

$P(E_i)$, and $P(f_j|E_i)$ are modelled by discrete probabilities if the f_j have discrete values. If the f_j can take a continuous range of values, they are usually, and here in particular, assumed to be normally distributed:

$$P(f_j|E_i) = \frac{1}{\sigma_j\sqrt{2\pi}}e^{\left(-\frac{(f_j-\mu_j)^2}{2\sigma_j^2}\right)} \quad (4.11)$$

where μ_j and σ_j are the mean and standard deviation of the jth component of all feature vectors annotated as class E_i in the training material. The constant term $\sqrt{2\pi}$ is again omitted in the implementation.

4.5 Summary

This chapter presented databases and methodology for speech emotion recognition. The Berlin database of emotional speech, the FAU Aibo Emotion Corpus and the SmartKom database were introduced. Among these the Berlin database contains acted emotions, whereas the other two databases contain spontaneous or elicited emotions. Several non-linguistic and linguistically motivated units that can possibly be used for emotion recognition from speech were presented, including units with fixed length, units segmented by voice activity detection, words, words in context, speech segments delimited by pauses obtained from automatic speech recognition — possibly supported by manual labelling —, utterances and turns. For feature extraction, an approach computing global statistics from basic feature types for each unit is chosen. The calculation of the basic feature types pitch, energy, MFCCs, duration, spectral and voicing information, as well as voice quality was described. Finally, the classification algorithms for a classifier comparison experiment were presented, among these Naïve Bayes and SVM in more detail, because they are also used for further experiments in this book. Thus, all prerequisites are now provided to conduct the experiments in the next chapter.

Chapter 5
Experimental results

The previous chapter introduced methodology for suitable segmentation units, features and classifiers for emotion recognition from speech. This methodology will now be evaluated by experiments, particularly with respect to a compromise between fast and accurate algorithms for online recognition. The following questions are investigated:

1. *Which emotion units are suitable in which scenario?*

2. *Which features are useful, seen individually and in the context of subsets?*
   What are the advantages/disadvantages of feature subsets selected by various strategies?
   This includes within feature type investigations, as well as contrasting feature types, statistical functions or other groups of features.

3. *Which classifiers are advantageous?*

All these questions are interdependent. For example, good features may vary for different segmentation units or classifiers. Therefore, first suitable segmentation units will be assessed with a standard feature selection method (CFS) and classifier (Naïve Bayes). Then, relevant features of each database will be evaluated for the most suitable unit with the Naïve Bayes classifier. Last, classifier performance will be discussed. Prior to the description of the experiments, however, the evaluation measures used will be discussed.

5.1 Evaluation measures

System performance is usually measured by recognition accuracy. This can be in terms of the overall accuracy OA:

$$OA = \frac{\#\ correctly\ classified\ instances}{\#\ total\ instances} \quad (5.1)$$

which is the proportion of correctly classified instances to the overall number of test instances, commonly given in percent. Another possibility is to use the averaged accuracy AA[1] for each class, which is related to the mean precision in information theory:

$$AA = \sum_{i=1}^{N} \frac{1}{N} \frac{\#\ instances\ correctly\ classified\ as\ class\ i}{\#\ total\ instances\ in\ class\ i} \quad (5.2)$$

where N is the number of classes. While the overall accuracy is usually the primary measure of interest, it can be misleading in tasks with an unbalanced class distribution. If the number of instances in the classes is very unequal, a high overall accuracy can be achieved by simply classifying into the majority class. For this reason, it is useful to look at the averaged accuracy as well. Since two of the tree databases used here have a highly unbalanced class distribution (Aibo and SmartKom), the primary measure to optimise here will always be averaged accuracy, as for approximately equal class numbers as in Berlin, accuracy and precision are equivalent. F-Measure, which is the harmonic mean of OA and AA, would be a possibility to combine both in one measure, but it is abstained here from using the F-Measure because it is less intuitive. Furthermore, it gives OA and AA equal importance while AA should be emphasised more here, for the reasons given before.

When feature sets with only few features are compared, recognition rates can be so low, around or below chance level, that they are not meaningful. It may then be more reliable to compare the sets in terms of the information gained from the individual features. Therefore, in these cases two additional measures will be used, the mean information gain value and the mean rank according to the information gain of all features in a set for each database.

In order to measure the confidence of a result, the 95 % confidence interval estimate for the true error will be used according to the following formula based on Mitchell [156, chap. 5.2.2]:

$$acc_T = z_t \sqrt{\frac{acc_T(1 - acc_T)}{N}} \quad (5.3)$$

where the constant z_t is defined as $z_t = 1.96$ for 95 % confidence, acc_T is the accuracy (OA or AA) on the test set T of a particular learning scheme and N is the number of instances in T. In the following discussions, confidence intervals will not be given explicitly, but remarks on significance always relate to Equation 5.3. Of course, different confidence intervals are applied to each database. Under certain circumstances significantly worse results may still be more useful, if they are better in other respects.

---

[1]Among other names that can be found in the literature to denote AA are class-wise recognition rate[21] or unweighted accuracy[213].

5.2. Emotion units

Unit	Total	Joy	Anger	Fear	Disgust	Boredom	Sadness	Neutral
fixed length 0.5s	2487	298	607	223	236	402	387	334
fixed length 1s	1111	130	268	96	110	183	179	145
fixed length 2s	543	64	133	56	48	85	79	78
automatic pause segmentation by VAD	498	57	128	54	46	68	84	61
word	4827	634	1242	546	355	782	514	754
word in context (± 1 word)	4827	634	1242	546	355	782	514	754
utterance	493	64	127	55	38	79	52	78

Table 5.1: Numbers of instances per emotion unit in Berlin: total and per class.

Unit	Total	Motherese	Neutral	Emphatic	Anger
fixed length 0.5s	13683	1366	6974	2905	2438
fixed length 1.0s	8184	835	3884	1903	1562
fixed length 2.0s	4244	497	1842	1046	859
automatic pause segmentation by VAD	6121	552	2830	1542	1197
word	17618	1432	11547	2472	2167
word in context (± 1 word)	17618	1432	11547	2472	2167
manual syntactic/prosodic boundary detection (chunks)	6413	664	3254	1397	1098
turn	3995	487	1307	1334	867

Table 5.2: Numbers of instances per emotion unit in Aibo: total and per class.

5.2 Emotion units

In Section 4.2, the need to find appropriate units in speech for emotion recognition has already been motivated: suitable units should be short enough to have no change of emotion within, long enough to reliably calculate features based on statistical functions, well-defined and consistent to the labelling scheme. In the following, results from a systematic comparison of various different units as listed previously in Table 4.7 is reported, because a study of this scale is missing so far in the literature.

Unit	Total	Positive	Neutral	Negative
fixed length 0.5s	19483	713	15840	2930
fixed length 1.0s	9238	332	7500	1406
fixed length 2.0s	4203	152	3390	661
automatic pause segmentation by VAD	3256	124	2765	367
word	13222	487	11581	1154
word in context ($\pm$ 1 word)	13222	487	11581	1154
pause segmentation by ASR	1831	70	1594	167
turn	1816	70	1579	167

Table 5.3: Numbers of instances per emotion unit in SmartKom: total and per class.

First of all, the number of instances, total and per class, are given for each unit and database in Tables 5.1 to 5.3. The first four units in each table do not require linguistic knowledge, thus are especially suitable for online speech emotion recognition. The other units do need linguistic information obtained from either an automatic speech recogniser or a human, and are in the literature usually considered to be more suitable for emotion recognition. As can be seen, the distribution of the number of instances per class does not change much among the units of a database. In the Aibo database, the proportion of neutral instances decreases with the length of the unit. This reflects the strategy mapping labels from words to other units that reduces the influence of neutral for longer units.

Figure 5.1 shows the average length of each unit. Of course, the length correlates with the number of instances: the longer the unit, the lower the number of instances. Words are shortest in Berlin, and VAD based units are shorter in SmartKom and Aibo as in Berlin. The reason for that is that Berlin contains read speech: the shorter word length can be explained by a higher speaking rate as speakers do not have to plan what to say and by the limited vocabulary of the 10 sentences which does not contain extraordinarily long words. Furthermore, when reading one makes fewer pauses than when speaking freely and spontaneously, so that there are less breaks in the voice activity, thus VAD based units are longer in Berlin than in Aibo or SmartKom. The speech in SmartKom is especially characterised by pondering so it is no surprise that here, VAD units are shortest. It can further be observed that VAD units are shorter than utterances or chunks (manually or by ASR), so they seem to be rather one segmental level lower. Comparing automatic with linguistic units with respect to length, 1.0s approximately matches the word in context of ± 1 word, and 2.0s approximates utterances or manual chunking. A word is even shorter than 0.5s.

Table 5.4 shows recognition results for the different segmentation units for the three databases.

5.2. Emotion units

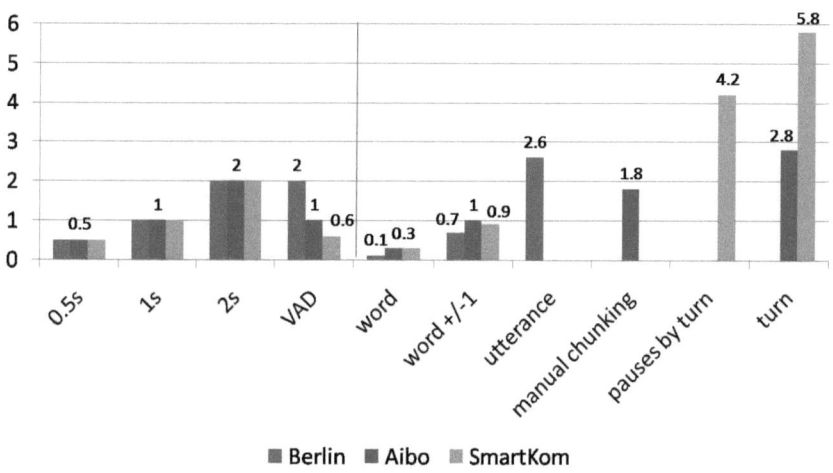

Figure 5.1: Average duration of units in seconds for the Berlin, Aibo and SmartKom databases.

For the Berlin database, the difference in results between the units is most dramatically: the best unit (utterances) is almost twice as good as the worst (words). This may be due to the very short average word length: 0.1s is obviously too short for global statistics features. A dynamic classification approach might give better results here. In the SmartKom database, words also score worse than longer units, though the difference is not as big. In contrast, results for words and chunks on the Aibo corpus are very similar, but here it is important to notice that the labelling was based on words. With regard to the question whether turns are too long because they may often contain several emotions, results indicate that this effect is not huge as they score quite good in both Aibo and SmartKom. VAD units on average come off best which argues in favour of not overly long units. Even though this unit is rather targeted at non-prompted speech as in Aibo or SmartKom, VAD units score worse only than utterances and 2.0s segments in the Berlin database. So they apparently do not give bad results on prompted speech either. For this reason, VAD is chosen as unit in the experiments on features and classifiers in the following sections.

Concluding, the best type of unit is different in each database. Apart from the characteristics of the contained speech (read, spontaneous), this is probably due to the labelling, which is always based on only one unit, and different in each database. In Berlin, this variance is most obvious.

Unit		Berlin	Aibo	Smart-Kom
fixed length 0.5s	AA	44.4	47.5	43.9
	OA	47.6	44.4	49.9
fixed length 1s	AA	57.6	48.7	44.0
	OA	59.7	45.6	50.8
fixed length 2s	AA	64.9	48.8	42.4
	OA	67.0	45.3	52.1
automatic pause segmentation by VAD	AA	60.0	**51.0**	**48.5**
	OA	60.8	**47.6**	**64.7**
word	AA	38.8	**51.0**	44.3
	OA	38.8	**47.6**	54.3
word in context ($\pm$ 1 word)	AA	51.6	**50.7**	45.1
	OA	53.0	45.5	56.0
manual syntactic/prosodic boundary detection (chunks)	AA	—	50.3	—
	OA		40.7	
pause segmentation by ASR (chunks)	AA	—	—	45.1
	OA			58.8
utterance	AA	**73.4**	—	—
	OA	**73.2**		
turn	AA	—	49.3	46.1
	OA		**47.2**	60.1

Table 5.4: Comparison of segmentation levels: AA and OA in % from Naïve Bayes classifier are given. Best and insignificantly worse results for each database in bold.

5.3 Feature evaluation

The central role of good features for emotion recognition has been motivated before. Now, the feature set described in the last chapter is evaluated in several aspects. First, insights on suitable features are obtained from an information gain ranking. Then, two of the seven feature types, pitch and MFCC, will be examined closer. For pitch, the benefits of normalisation will be discussed, for MFCCs, whether features derived from the average of all coefficients perform equally well as features for each single coefficient, which reduces the overall number of features. The next topics are the significance of the different feature types and of statistical functions, while the evaluation of feature subsets and feature selection strategies finishes this section. As said before, each database is analysed with automatic voice activity detection as unit.

5.3. Feature evaluation

Rank	Berlin	Value
1	pitch_d_qrange	0.6999
2	pitch_x_diff_q3	0.6243
3	spectral_cog_median	0.5997
4	mfcc_d_11_var	0.5988
5	pitch_x_diff_qrange	0.5926
6	pitch_x_diff_mean	0.5883
7	pitch_q3	0.5869
8	pitch_log_q3	0.5869
9	spectral_cog_q1	0.5788
10	pitch_dd_qrange	0.5781
no IG (#)	392	

Table 5.5: 10 best features from information gain ranking, as well as number of features with no information gain for the Berlin database.

Rank	Aibo	Value
1	energy_range	0.1233
2	spectral_slope_q1	0.1194
3	spectral_linRegA_var	0.1168
4	spectral_slope_var	0.1141
5	energy_max	0.1088
6	spectral_slope_qrange	0.1078
7	energy_maxs_max	0.1074
8	spectral_slope_mean	0.1067
9	spectral_linRegA_mean	0.1052
10	spectral_slope_median	0.1051
no IG (#)	108	

Table 5.6: 10 best features from information gain ranking, as well as number of features with no information gain for the Aibo database.

5.3.1 Individual feature ranking

In order to evaluate single features, the information gain for all features with respect to emotion classes was calculated in all databases. The information gain of a feature tells about its individual ability to predict certain emotional classes. However, for classification, a feature set composed of the best ranked features is not necessarily a good set because the information contained can be redundant. Still, an information gain ranking shows which acoustic characteristic are especially important for emotion recognition in reference to the given databases.

Tables 5.5 to 5.7 show the 10 best features for the Berlin, Aibo and SmartKom databases ac-

Rank	SmartKom	Value
1	mfcc_d_2_var	0.0689
2	mfcc_d_2_qrange	0.0561
3	mfcc_d_2_maxs_var	0.0552
4	mfcc_d_2_range	0.0544
5	mfcc_d_2_max	0.0501
6	energy_d_qrange	0.0498
7	energy_d_mins_mean	0.0497
8	mfcc_d_2_maxs_max	0.0495
9	energy_slope_mean	0.0493
10	energy_d_var	0.0486
no IG (#)	264	

Table 5.7: 10 best features from information gain ranking, as well as number of features with no information gain for the SmartKom database.

cording to their information gain. The most important feature types are quite obviously pitch for Berlin, spectral information and energy for Aibo, and MFCCs and energy for SmartKom. In the latter case, important features can even be limited to the derivation of the second MFCC coefficient and to energy derivation and slope. Thus, timing seems to be especially important here.

The information gain values are by far the highest for the Berlin database, and lowest for the SmartKom database. This is consistent to how the difficulty of the databases in respect to emotion recognition can be estimated, with the Berlin database containing the most, and the SmartKom database the least emotional speech.

Overall, not too many features had no information gain at all, which allows the preliminary conclusion that the feature set used in the experiments here is generally suitable for the task. There were 40 features that added no information in all three databases, among them 35 features derived from MFCCs, four from pitch and one from energy. These seem to be the least relevant features. Good features, however, vary a lot among databases, and there are no features shared among the three databases for the ten highest ranked features.

The distribution on features types of the 100 best ranked features can be seen in Figure 5.2. Of course, the proportions of the feature types cannot be equated in general with their importance, as types with large numbers such as MFCCs obviously appear more frequently. The distribution is most balanced for the Aibo corpus; for the other databases one feature type predominates. Also, the number of feature types included in the best 100 features is highest for Aibo. This suggests that this database contains very heterogeneous information. Voicing features cannot be found among the 100 best ranked features. However, this alone is no criterion for complete exclusion.

5.3. Feature evaluation

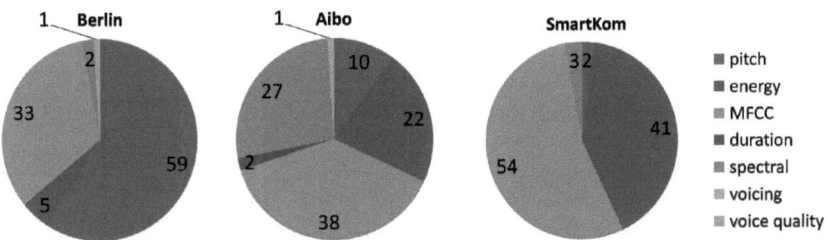

Figure 5.2: Distribution on feature types of the 100 best ranked features according to their information gain for the Berlin, Aibo and SmartKom databases.

5.3.2 Intra-feature type comparisons

Prior to comparisons between feature types and looking for relevant features within feature types, pitch and MFCC features will be examined closer. For pitch, the benefits of normalisation methods will be investigated. For MFCCs, a compact representation of all coefficients will be contrasted to using all single coefficients. Final answers to these questions, however, will have to wait until the discussion of automatically selected features in Section 5.3.5.

Pitch

Absolute pitch values are strongly dependent on speaker types. Men have a mean pitch of about 80–100 Hz, the mean pitch of women is about twice as high, and children's voices have a mean pitch around 400 Hz, depending on their age [96]. Therefore, it is difficult to tell from a measured mean pitch value whether it is increased or decreased by affective influences as it must always be seen relative to the standard value of the gender or age group. One possibility is to normalise pitch values according to a reference value (e. g. minimum or maximum pitch). Here, however, for the calculation of a feature vector, only information should be used that is available in that acoustic segment the feature vector stands for, so that classification is possible without further, especially no hand-crafted knowledge. So if the reference value is from the same segment, information can be lost compared to the unnormalised value, since an already increased/decreased reference value may scale an actually increased/decreased pitch value to a normal value.

In order to investigate the question whether normalisation is worth the effort under these circumstances, a comparison of the normalisation techniques described in 4.3.1 is now presented by means of two experiments. First, those features derived from raw pitch, logarithmised pitch, median subtracted logarithmised pitch, and all three together are compared. Secondly, mean, median, first quartile and third quartile of raw, logarithmised, median subtracted logarithmised

Database		all	raw	log	log median subtracted
Berlin	AA	**39.5**	33.2	35.0	**42.7**
	OA	38.4	32.5	33.9	**43.4**
Aibo	AA	**31.4**	**30.7**	30.1	**31.8**
	OA	**27.1**	**27.9**	25.4	**28.1**
SmartKom	AA	33.8	32.0	34.3	**37.7**
	OA	56.3	55.2	58.4	**74.6**

Table 5.8: Different pitch transformations to compensate for speaker differences: all transformations, raw, logarithmised, and logarithmised and median subtracted. AA/OA in % from Naïve Bayes classifier are given, best and insignificantly worse results in bold.

Database		all	raw	log	log median subtracted
Berlin	mean IG	0.2702	**0.3595**	0.242	0.2092
	mean IG rank	407	**217**	463	540
Aibo	mean IG	0.027	**0.031**	0.0285	0.0216
	mean IG rank	677	**595**	654	782
SmartKom	mean IG	0.0129	**0.0134**	0.0132	0.012
	mean IG rank	748	**729**	741	775

Table 5.9: Different pitch transformations to compensate for speaker differences: all transformations, no, logarithmised, logarithmised and median subtracted. Mean information gain value and mean information gain ranking is given, best results in bold.

and minimum/maximum normalised pitch are contrasted. The experiments are evaluated with respect to classification results (overall accuracy (OA) and averaged class accuracy (AA) obtained from Naïve Bayes) as well as mean information gain of the features and their average rank in the information gain ranking.

Tables 5.8 and 5.9 show results for the first experiment. Recognition rates are low, except for Berlin around or only slightly above chance level. However, this is not a problem in general, as better results can be expected by the full classification later with more features and the evaluation of the experiment also relies on the information gain.

Both tables show very clear, though contradicting tendencies: in terms of recognition rates, the logarithmised median subtracted pitch performs always best or among the best while the information gain is by far the highest for raw pitch. Apparently, the information contained in raw pitch features is high, but redundant. Pitch that is only logarithmised, however, scores worst. Furthermore, it is not necessary to use all pitch features as results for all pitch features together

5.3. Feature evaluation

Database		raw	log	median subtracted log	min/max normalised
Berlin	AA	25.4	22.8	22.2	20.9
	OA	30.1	28.9	25.7	**29.3**
Aibo	AA	33.4	27.1	26.9	25.3
	OA	**47.5**	37.1	42.4	45.9
SmartKom	AA	35.8	**34.4**	**34.6**	**34.2**
	OA	**83.5**	**84.3**	83.2	**84.5**

Table 5.10: Mean, median, first quartile, 3rd quartile of different pitch normalisations to compensate for speaker differences: no, logarithmised, logarithmised median subtracted, min/max normalised. AA/OA in % from Naïve Bayes classifier is given, best or insignificantly worse results in bold.

Database		raw	log	median subtracted log	min/max normalised
Berlin	mean IG	0.5298	**0.5331**	0.1101	0.1063
	mean IG rank	**22**	**22**	760	860
Aibo	mean IG	0.0756	**0.0758**	0.008	0.0021
	mean IG rank	**52**	**52**	1142	1332
SmartKom	mean IG	**0.0155**	**0.0155**	0.0082	0.0089
	mean IG rank	**626**	**624**	878	999

Table 5.11: Mean, median, first quartile, 3rd quartile of different pitch normalisations to compensate for speaker differences: no, logarithmised, logarithmised median subtracted, min/max normalised. Mean information gain value and mean information gain ranking is given, best result in bold.

do not exceed those of the single transformations, both in recognition rate and information gain.

The second pitch normalisation experiment gives further evidence in favour of raw pitch which tends to have best recognition rates (though often not significantly) and, together with logarithmised pitch, highest information gain. Regarding the bad results for median subtracted logarithmised pitch it must be noted that one of the four values, the median, does not contribute in this case. The minimum/maximum normalised pitch proved not to be useful.

Summing up both experiments, it is arguable whether to normalise pitch or not. The most important pitch features for emotions seem to be those that describe rather relative changes than absolute values. For these features, normalisation is irrelevant. In any case, it is not necessary to use all pitch features as this leads always to lower performance. However, results obtained here are probably dependent on the segmentation unit.

Database		all	sum	single coefficients
Berlin	AA	**52.6**	**51.5**	38.3
	OA	**54.4**	**53.4**	36.8
Aibo	AA	**45.6**	**44.9**	40.0
	OA	**43.5**	**43.0**	37.5
SmartKom	AA	**44.1**	**44.7**	42.9
	OA	**61.1**	**61.5**	59.5

Table 5.12: Comparison of different representations of MFCCs: AA/OA in % from Naïve Bayes classifier is given, best or insignificantly worse results in bold.

Database		all	sum	single coefficients
Berlin	mean IG	0.1273	0.1257	**0.1462**
	mean IG rank	777	785	**679**
Aibo	mean IG	0.0212	0.0204	**0.0309**
	mean IG rank	799	818	**563**
SmartKom	mean IG	0.0138	0.0138	**0.0143**
	mean IG rank	760	764	**711**

Table 5.13: Comparison of different representations of MFCCs: Mean information gain value and mean information gain ranking is given, best result in bold.

MFCCs

A further experiment contrasts the average of all 12 MFCC coefficients with features obtained from each coefficient individually and with both the averaged and individual representation. The same evaluation measures as for pitch are employed: overall accuracy, averaged class accuracy, mean information gain, mean information gain ranking.

As can be seen in Table 5.12 recognition rates are well above chance level for all databases so they can be considered meaningful. Single coefficients are always better than the averaged representation here; however, the less emotional the data and the harder the task is, the lower is the difference. The performance increase obtained from all compared to the individual features is negligible and never significant which suggests that using both feature sets is unnecessary.

Interestingly, the information gain evaluation shows an opposing tendency and is in favour of the averaged representation. However, this is probably an artifact caused by a large number of single coefficients features having a low information gain, but still not deteriorating the classifier.

Thus, this evaluation lets conclude that if a low number of features is desirable, the averaged MFCC representation is a good alternative, especially for natural data, but higher accuracies can

Berlin	pitch	energy	MFCC	duration	spectral	voicing	voice quality
joy	38.6	12.3	42.1	5.3	15.8	**47.4**	10.5
neutral	**67.2**	34.4	**68.8**	55.7	60.7	6.6	13.1
anger	51.6	71.1	64.8	72.7	**77.3**	16.4	**78.1**
fear	**40.7**	11.1	**40.7**	1.9	20.4	29.6	3.7
disgust	21.7	**65.2**	43.5	6.5	21.7	13.0	15.2
sadness	26.2	36.9	**63.1**	40.5	46.4	16.7	34.5
boredom	**51.5**	32.4	**54.4**	23.5	20.6	17.6	20.6
AA	42.5	37.6	**53.9**	29.4	37.6	21.1	25.1
OA	43.8	41.8	**56.4**	37.0	44.0	20.1	33.3

Table 5.14: Feature type comparison for the Berlin database. Recognition rates of individual classes for each feature type as well as averaged (AA) and overall (OA) recognition rate in % from Naïve Bayes classifier is given, best or insignificantly worse results for each class in bold.

be obtained with each coefficient represented individually.

5.3.3 Inter-feature type comparison

A central question to speech emotion recognition is which types of features are most suitable for the task. It is assumed that these will differ for different data types. In the following, this question shall be investigated for pitch, MFCC, energy, duration, spectral, voice quality and voicing related features. Furthermore, it will be explored whether certain feature types are especially suitable for the recognition of particular classes. One problem with this experiment here is that the number of features is very unequal for different types (see Table 4.17). A large number can be positive for a feature type, as the chance of catching meaningful properties is higher, or negative, if redundant features interfere with each other. In order to make the feature set sizes a bit more equal and to restrict the sets to meaningful and discriminative features, a correlation based feature subset selection (Section 4.3.2) was carried out for each type. In the following, recognition results obtained from each feature type after correlation analysis will be discussed for each database and class.

Table 5.14 shows the results obtained for the Berlin database. Anger, neutral, disgust and sadness achieve high accuracies while joy and fear seem difficult to distinguish from other classes. Anger can be detected very accurately by all feature types except for voicing and pitch, by the latter, however, with at least medium accuracy. Neutral is recognised well by pitch, MFCC, duration and spectral features, but achieves low accuracies with the other feature types. For disgust, energy features contribute most, whereas for sadness, MFCC features achieve the highest accuracy.

Aibo	pitch	energy	MFCC	duration	spectral	voicing	voice quality
angry	74.2	42.5	61.3	22.1	34.0	26.8	**79.7**
emphatic	27.9	37.0	**49.5**	32.8	33.6	29.3	14.6
neutral	26.8	29.1	44.9	**77.5**	28.3	73.7	12.2
motherese	6.5	63.8	45.3	0.0	**74.5**	5.3	18.7
AA	33.9	43.1	**50.3**	33.1	42.6	33.8	31.3
OA	34.5	36.8	**49.3**	**48.4**	34.9	47.2	26.6

Table 5.15: Feature type comparison for the Aibo database. Recognition rates of individual classes for each feature type as well as averaged (AA) and overall (OA) recognition rate in % from Naïve Bayes classifier is given, best or insignificantly worse results for each class in bold.

Boredom is discriminated moderately well by pitch and MFCC features. Voicing features are the best indicator for joy, pitch and MFCC for sadness, though for both classes, only low accuracies can be achieved. Looking not at the classes but at the feature types, it can be observed that pitch detects neutral better than other classes, while energy is a good indicator for anger and disgust, so rather for negative emotions with high activation, but not for other classes. MFCCs have the broadest aptitude and are best for neutral, anger and sadness. Duration features are mainly good at detecting anger, spectral features at detecting neutral and anger. Voicing features seem to have discriminating ability only for joy, and voice quality for anger. With regard to the recognition rates for all classes, only MFCCs classify correctly in more than half of the cases, though all feature types classify above chance level. Duration, voicing and voice quality feature are, however, considerably worse than the other feature types. Obviously, MFCCs have the best generalising power though they do not perform best in each class. A positive result is that each feature type contributes to the recognition accuracy, though for most classes, single types stand out, while most perform bad.

In the Aibo database (see Table 5.15), the classes angry, neutral and motherese can be recognised very well, only emphatic is difficult to detect. Voice quality, pitch and MFCC features are relevant for anger; for emphatic, only MFCCs give useful results. Neutral is best discriminated by duration and voicing features which in turn have considerably lower scores for the other classes. However, due to the unbalanced class distribution in the Aibo database, it is hard to tell whether these features are especially suited to recognise neutral voices or whether they just classify in the most frequent class. Motherese is recognised best by spectral and energy features. Again looking at the feature types, pitch, MFCCs and voice quality detect anger well, energy and spectral motherese, duration and voicing neutral. Each feature type excels in only one class. Overall, again MFCCs are best (again with about half of the instances classified correctly), followed by energy and spectral features.

5.3. Feature evaluation

SmartKom	pitch	energy	MFCC	duration	spectral	voicing	voice quality
positive	4.8	8.1	12.1	0.0	**26.6**	14.5	0.0
neutral	86.9	68.5	65.3	95.9	49.5	72.3	**96.8**
negative	19.1	57.0	58.3	14.2	**68.7**	23.2	6.3
AA	36.9	44.5	45.2	36.7	**48.3**	36.6	34.4
OA	76.1	64.9	62.5	**83.0**	50.8	64.5	**83.0**

Table 5.16: Feature type comparison for the SmartKom database. Recognition rates of individual classes for each feature type as well as averaged (AA) and overall (OA) recognition rate in % from Naïve Bayes classifier is given, best or insignificantly worse results for each class in bold.

The problem of unbalanced class distribution is even more serious in the SmartKom database (see Table 5.16). Especially the difference in recognition rate for the most and least frequent classes, neutral and positive, is extreme. Results for neutral and the overall recognition rate are therefore not overly meaningful. For positive emotions, spectral features are by far the best, but still below chance level. Spectral features, and to a lesser extent also MFCC and energy features, are most important for negative emotions. The importance of spectral features is noticeable. Again, MFCCs show the best performance over all classes.

Comparing all three databases, MFCC features generally prove to be the most descriptive type of features. However, it is hard to say whether this is due to the quality of the features or just to their high number (even after correlation analysis). Furthermore, each feature type contributes at least at one point so it is not wise to drop any type completely. Neither is it possible to make a general statement valid across data types which feature types are especially suited for certain emotions. For example, voice quality is important for anger in the Berlin and Aibo databases, but not for negative in SmartKom. Apparently, however, the less emotional the data is, the higher is the importance of MFCCs. If classification always relied on that feature type that recognises a particular class best, that means if the fusion scheme was ideal, even a higher result could be obtained by a multi-level classification split into feature types than with all types together (see Table 5.25 below). Of course, relevant features and feature types do not only depend on the emotional classes that are considered; for other databases, units or classifiers, different features may be relevant than were found here.

5.3.4 Reducing the number of statistical measures

The goal of the following two experiments is to look at the statistical measures that are applied when generating features automatically from the acoustic time series as presented in Section

Database		Mean	Median	Min.	1st q.	Max.	3rd q.	Range	Interq.	Var.
Berlin	AA	57.3	56.2	42.9	56.6	43.6	56.0	40.8	56.3	46.0
	OA	57.4	58.0	45.6	57.0	45.6	57.0	44.2	56.2	48.8
Aibo	AA	45.7	43.5	43.9	44.6	45.8	42.3	41.5	44.8	43.9
	OA	46.1	46.1	38.6	46.2	41.8	46.3	36.0	47.8	40.2
SmartKom	AA	45.5	45.2	42.5	44.9	44.4	46.5	42.9	47.8	43.2
	OA	69.3	68.8	60.4	69.9	60.9	67.7	57.6	67.2	46.0

Table 5.17: Individual evaluation of statistical measures: Comparison of mean/median, minimum/first quartile, maximum/third quartile, range/interquartile range/variance of time series: AA and OA in % from Naïve Bayes classifier is given, best or insignificantly worse results for each group in bold.

4.3.1 of the last chapter and see whether some of them are redundant, thus can be left out. For this purpose, first each measure was analysed individually, then a group analysis was carried out.

When looking at the nine statistics used throughout this book — mean, minimum, maximum, range, variance, median, 1st quartile, 3rd quartile, interquartile range — it is apparent that they fall into groups of similar measures. These groups are mean/median, minimum/first quartile, maximum/third quartile, and lastly variance/range/interquartile range as dispersion measures. One measure in each group is a quartile measure which are especially robust towards outliers. In the first experiment it will be examined which measure in each group is the best. Subsequently, it will be examined whether an equally good or even better result can be achieved by an appropriate subset than with all nine measures. This analysis considers only those features from all time series across all feature types that result from systematic feature generation. Features such as jitter, shimmer or number of voiced frames were excluded.

Classification results obtained from the Naïve Bayes classifier for all nine measures individually are given in Table 5.17. Results for mean and median are very similar. Mean is more often slightly, but not significantly better than median. Apart from that, the quartile measures outperform their counterparts, except for AA of maximum value and $3rd$ quartile in Aibo. Variance mostly gives intermediate results between the absolute range and the interquartile range. In this experiment, the difference between AA and OA in SmartKom is especially large. As already mentioned, the effect of a large difference between AA and OA appears with unbalanced class distributions. Though this difference also exists for Aibo, the effect is not as huge, because the class distribution of SmartKom is considerably more unbalanced, but it might be also because of the different labeling strategies based on speech only or on video that the most frequent class, the neutral class, is especially general in the SmartKom database and easily subsumes other classes as well.

These results suggest the analysis of the following four groups in the next experiment:

5.3. Feature evaluation

Database		ALL	MQQQ	MMMR	MeanQQQ
Berlin	AA	55.1	**60.2**	48.9	**61.2**
	OA	56.6	**60.6**	51.0	**61.9**
Aibo	AA	**47.8**	45.0	**46.5**	45.5
	OA	**46.1**	**47.3**	41.9	**47.3**
SmartKom	AA	47.0	**48.2**	45.0	**48.2**
	OA	61.0	**66.5**	60.4	**66.6**

Table 5.18: Group evaluation of statistical measures: Comparison of all 9 statistics (ALL) vs. median-$1st$ quartile-$3rd$ quartile-interquartile range (MQQQ) vs. mean-maximum-minimum-range (MMMR) vs. mean-$1st$ quartile-$3rd$ quartile-interquartile range (MeanQQQ): AA and OA in % from Naïve Bayes classifier are given, best or insignificantly worse results of each condition in bold.

1. *ALL:* all nine measures as reference,

2. *MQQQ:* four quartile measures,

3. *MMMR:* four non-quartile measures (mean, minimum, maximum, range),

4. *MeanQQQ:* the best of each group (mean, first quartile, third quartile, interquartile range).

As Table 5.18 shows, MeanQQQ achieves best results but the difference to MQQQ is only marginal and not significant. ALL yields highest class-wise accuracy for the Aibo database. MMMR is by far worse than the other groupings. Thus, it seems favourable to restrict the full set and to use either MeanQQQ or MQQQ, with a slight advantage in favour of MeanQQQ.

5.3.5 Automatically selected features

It is difficult to predict from the evaluation of individual features or feature types how they perform in a feature set together with other features, as they can contribute supplementary or overlapping information. Techniques for automatically selecting feature subsets therefore can yield quite different results of which features are relevant. For this reason now results of an experiment are presented where features of subsets selected by different algorithms are analysed. The algorithms were explained in detail in Section 4.3.2. The selection techniques included:

1. *CFS:* correlation analysis by correlation-based features subset selection (CFS),

2. *IG+CFS:* CFS on features with an information gain above average on the training set,

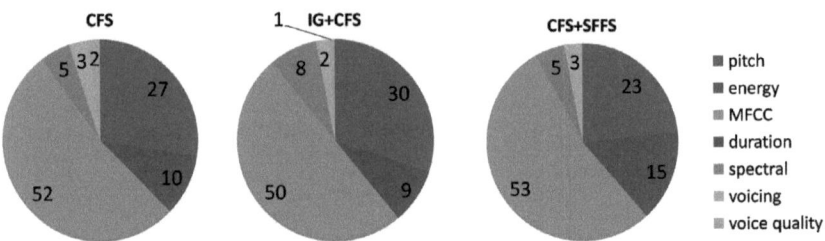

Figure 5.3: Distribution on feature types in % of the three subset selection strategies for Berlin.

3. *CFS+SFFS:* a sequential floating forward selection (SFFS) on the features selected by CFS. The evaluation criterion of the subsets was averaged class recognition accuracy (AA) by Naïve Bayes.

The preceding step of information gain selection and CFS in 2. and 3. is supposed to speed up the selection by a restriction of the search space. Only selected features are analysed, recognition performance is discussed in the next section.

The distribution on feature types is especially interesting in comparison to the information gain ranking (see Section 5.3.1). In the Berlin database (Table 5.3), the influence of energy and MFCCs increases and the influence of pitch decreases compared to the information gain ranking. For the subset selection strategy IG+SFFS the influence of pitch is still highest, which is natural as features were preselected by information gain. Results for the subset selection confirm the negligible influence of duration and voice quality for this particular database. Voicing features now can be found in the subsets, and the impact of spectral features is also higher than in the information gain ranking.

In the Aibo database (Table 5.4), more MFCC features and less spectral features are selected compared to the information gain ranking. Again, the diversity of feature types is higher than for the other databases: all seven feature types are selected by each of the selection strategies. The information gain ranking for the SmartKom database contained only few feature types. Subset selection yields a much more diverse range of features, with all types found by CFS, and all but one found by IG+CFS and CFS+SFFS (Table 5.5).

Besides these observations, general tendencies are similar for information gain ranking and subset selection. Furthermore, it is noticeable that, across subset selection strategies, the distribution on feature types is always similar for each database. Though this may partly be due to the fact that CFS is involved at some point in every strategy, it makes results more universally valid. Generally, however, the high proportion of MFCC features stands out, which is between one half and

5.3. Feature evaluation

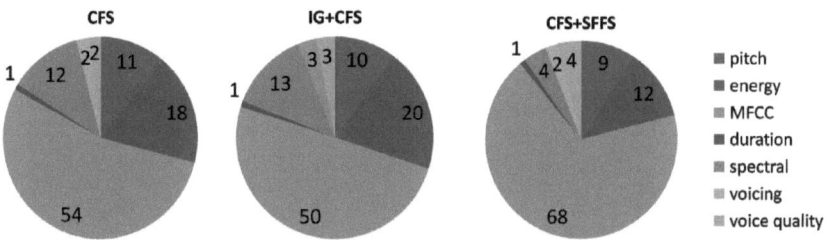

Figure 5.4: Distribution on feature types in % of the three subset selection strategies for Aibo.

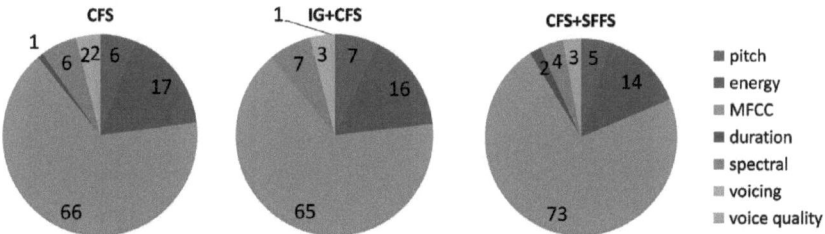

Figure 5.5: Distribution on feature types in % of the three subset selection strategies for SmartKom.

three quarters of the features. The outcome that the proportion of MFCC is highest in SmartKom confirms again that the less emotional the speech is, the more important MFCCs are.

When analysing the number of features per type, however, one has to keep in mind their proportion in the full feature set. For example, it is not surprising that duration does not reach a proportion higher than 2 %. The proportions of the types in the selected subsets correspond roughly to the proportions in the full set (see Figure 5.6). They are even rather higher for the types with low numbers. This indicates that the more features are generated from one type, the less new information is added by individual features.

Only few features are selected by all strategies from a database. These are mfcc_d_3_-mins_mean for the Berlin database, mfcc_4_mean, mfcc_4_q1, mfcc_4_maxs_mean, mfcc_d_2_mean and mfcc_d_6_q3 for the Aibo database, and none for SmartKom. The relevance of these features in this context is thus obvious. Their information gain value is likewise high above average.

Of equal interest as those features that occur in the selected subsets are those that do not, as this information can be used to possibly exclude features from the extraction process. From a point of view of efficiency it is, however, not necessary to exclude single features of series, but rather

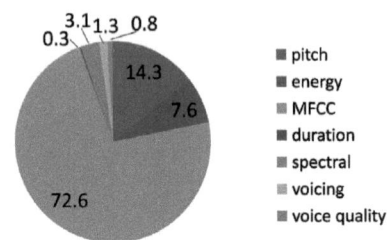

Figure 5.6: Distribution on feature types in % of the full feature set.

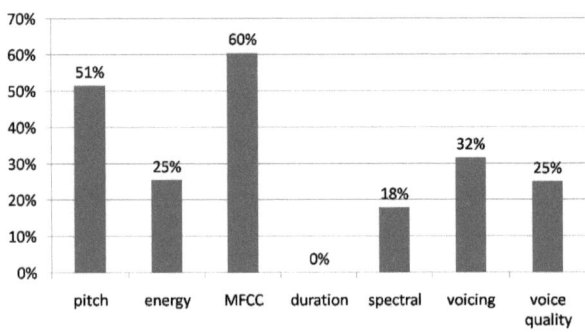

Figure 5.7: Proportion of discarded features in each feature type, totalled over all strategies and databases.

whole series, types, or features not belonging to a series. However, it never occurred that all features from one series were not selected.

Altogether, 789 features were never included in any subset which is about half of the full feature set. Figure 5.7 shows the proportion of omitted features per feature type and Figure 5.8 shows the proportions of the feature types in all discarded features. Obviously, feature types with many features lose percentally more features than those with few features. On the one hand, as said before, this is not surprising as less new information may be expected. On the other hand, this possibly speaks against the generation of very many features from one type rather than adding new types. No feature type was completely discarded, which proves once more that all types are relevant for emotion recognition.

Overall, 107 pitch features were discarded. The feature `pitch_num_rising` was never selected and thus can be dropped in the future. None of the four normalised features `pitch_norm` were selected. This is consistent with the previous analysis of pitch normalisation in section

5.3. Feature evaluation

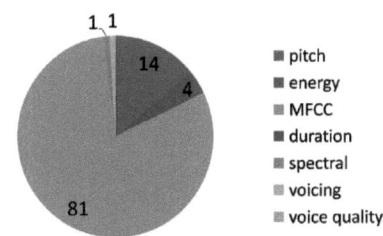

Figure 5.8: Proportion of feature types in discarded features in %, totalled over all strategies and databases.

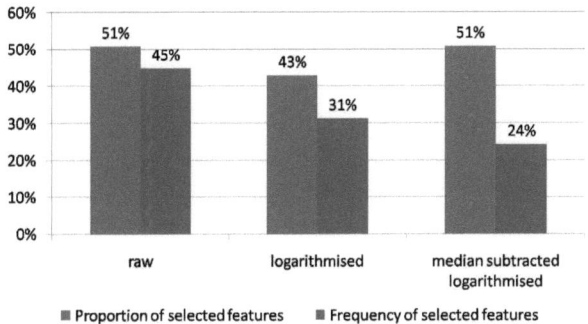

Figure 5.9: Proportion and frequency of selected features for raw, logarithmised and median subtracted logarithmised pitch, totalled over all strategies, databases and units.

5.3.2 where normalised pitch features proved inferior, so also the normalised pitch features can be dropped. Furthermore, the question whether raw, logarithmised or median subtracted logarithmised pitch is best that has also been discussed in Section 5.3.2 can now be concluded. Figure 5.9 shows the proportion of selected features of all raw, logarithmised and median subtracted logarithmised pitch features, respectively, which tells how diverse the selection in this type was, and the frequency of selection as percentage of all selected raw, logarithmised and median subtracted logarithmised pitch features. Apparently, though a diversity of features is used from median subtracted logarithmised pitch features, overall they are selected relatively seldom, especially in comparison to raw pitch. This results makes it hard to decide between raw and median subtracted logarithmised pitch as highest recognition accuracy still holds for the latter, so it seems wise to keep both. Logarithmised pitch, however, can be omitted. A further remarkable result is that the basic series and the first derivation are especially important as almost all of those features are selected at some point, while more than half of the features in the series of maxima and of minima are omitted.

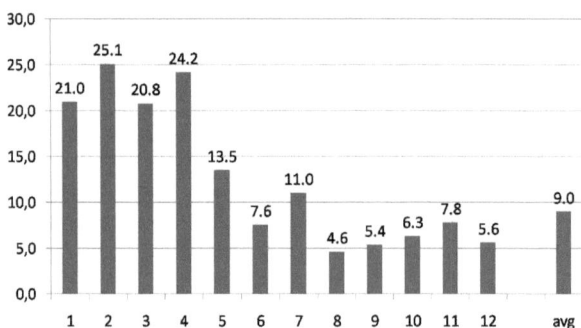

Figure 5.10: Mean number of selected features for each single MFCC coefficient and for the average of all coefficients per database split.

From the energy features, 28 features were never selected, a considerably lower proportion than from pitch, and it is not possible to leave out any features, because at least four feature were selected in every series. Most features were discarded from the series energy_dist, energy_d_maxs and energy_dd_maxs, least from energy, energy_d, energy_dd and energy_maxs.

More than half of the MFCC features (636 of 1053) were discarded. Thus, as suspected, MFCCs have the highest proportion of redundant features. An analysis of the number of selected features for each coefficient (Figure 5.10) shows that the first four coefficients are significantly more important than the higher ones, with coefficient 2 being the most, and 8 the least important. So it seems not useful to consider even higher coefficients than the 12th. The number of selected features from the average of all coefficients is similar to those of the high coefficients. This is a further argument to the discussion in 5.3.2, that it is essential to consider all coefficients individually.

From the remaining feature types, only few features were never selected. Only dur_length was discarded from the durational features. The length of a segment with voice activity apparently has nothing to do with the occurring emotions. The least important spectral features seem to be derived from spectral_cog, those of the voicing features from voicing_voicedLength Finally, voiceQual_num_pulses is a deselected voice quality feature not belonging to any series and can thus be omitted.

5.3.6 Feature subsets

In this section, recognition performance and size of feature sets selected by different strategies shall be discussed. On the one hand, of course high recognition accuracy is the ultimate goal and that feature selection strategy that most often yields highest accuracy is preferable. However, on the other hand, a low number of features is desirable in terms of speed, and furthermore a high accuracy achieved by a high number of features may be due to overfitting and thus not yield similar results on unseen test data. Three groups with overall 10 feature sets will be compared in the following: a group of "simple" selection strategies, a group of subset selection strategies on the full feature set and finally, a group of subset selection strategies on a restricted feature set. In detail, the following simple feature sets will be compared:

- **All:** the full feature set as described in Section 4.3.1 as reference set.

- **Manual:** a subset selected manually from the full set based on experience. This serves to compare the approach of automatic generation of a large number of features on the basis of acoustic functions followed in this book with knowledge-based approaches with small hand-crafted feature sets. The features contained in this manual set are listed in Table 5.19.

- **InfoGain100:** the best 100 features ranked according to their information gain (see Section 5.3.1). This is a very fast selection strategy as every feature needs only to be evaluated individually, not in context, and that yields a reasonable set size. But assumedly, this selection contains a lot of redundant features.

The selection strategies of Section 5.3.5 will now also be evaluated in terms of recognition accuracy. These are:

- **CFS:** features selected by correlation-based subset selection (CFS).

- **IG+CFS:** features with an information gain above average and subsequently selected by CFS.

- **CFS+SFFS:** features are selected by CFS, and the resulting set is further limited to the most relevant features according to Sequential Floating Forward Search (SFFS).

Furthermore, based on the findings of the experiments described in Sections 5.3.1 to 5.3.5, a restriction of the full feature set is proposed here, where features are omitted that did not prove to be relevant across databases. The knowledge on the suitable restriction of this set is based on both training and test splits, thus it is not independent. However, as it is obtained from three very different databases chances are high that results are generally valid. The set itself as well as after further automatic selection shall be evaluated:

- **Restriction:** In detail, the following features are omitted:
  - all median, maximum, minimum, range and variance features
  - all logarithmised pitch features
  - all normalised pitch features
  - all averaged MFCC features
  - `pitch_num_rising`, `dur_length` and `voiceQual_num_pulses`.

  This new feature set has a size of 582 features. With a considerably lower number of features, it should still yield similar accuracies as the full feature set, according to the previous experiments.

- **Restriction+IG0:** In a first database-dependent step, the previous set can be further restricted by leaving out all features with an information gain of 0 on the training database, as these features are not expected to contribute to the classification.

- **Restriction+IG0+CFS:** In a second stage, a CFS can be performed on the remaining features.

- **Restriction+IG0+CFS+SFFS:** In the third and last stage, SFFS can be performed on the CFS selected features to reach a very low number of features.

Tables 5.20 to 5.22 show the recognition results for the 10 feature sets. The discussion of the results in the following refers only to AA as criterion. Obviously, it is not only faster, but also more accurate not to use all features. The manually selected set performs worst of all. Of course, it can be argued that a bad performance is due to a bad manual selection in this case and not in general to manual selection. But the set should be representative for an average manually selected set as found in the literature. The full and the information gain based selected set perform a little better, but still significantly worse than the other sets.

The subset selection strategies on the full feature set generally perform very well, differences in classification performance are only slight and hardly significant. Two-stage selection reduces the number of features, but also often deteriorates results a little. CFS always achieves best or non-significantly worse results.

The best result for each database is obtained from (subsets of) the restricted set, though all from different strategies. The most robust strategy overall seems to be CFS whose rank of accuracy averaged over all three databases is best compared to the other schemes (see Table 5.23). Sequential feature selection (SFFS) shows to be successful in the Aibo database, but seems not favourable for SmartKom. Possibly, the feature set becomes too small. This holds equally for

5.3. Feature evaluation

Type	Series	Features
pitch	x_dist	mean, max, min, var
	log_median_maxs	mean, max, min, var
	log_median_d	mean, max, min, var
	log_median_dd	mean, max, min, var
	pos	max
energy	-	mean, max, min, var
	dist	mean, max, min, var
	pos	max
	d	mean, max, min, var
	dd	mean, max, min, var
	num	maxs
mfcc	avg	mean, max, min, var
	d_avg	mean, max, min, var
	dd_avg	mean, max, min, var
duration	-	length
	num	unvoiced
	-	speechProp
	-	zeroCrossings
spectral	cog	mean
	prange	mean
	slope	mean
	linRegB	mean
	linRegA	mean
voicing	voicedLength	median
voice quality	hnr	mean
	num	pulses
	-	jitter
	-	shimmer

Table 5.19: Manually selected feature set based on experience.

Task		All %	#	Manual %	#	InfoGain100 %	#
Berlin	AA	**55.6**		38.8		45.3	
	OA	**57.2**		40.2		48.4	
Aibo	AA	47.6		43.8		**48.0**	
	OA	45.9	1451	36.6	61	42.7	100
SmartKom	AA	47.3		46.4		**48.4**	
	OA	61.3		**66.4**		58.8	

Table 5.20: Comparison of "simple" feature sets: AA and OA in % from Naïve Bayes classifier, and number of features (#) are given, best or insignificantly worse accuracies in bold.

the Berlin database: while it seems favourable for Berlin to keep relatively many features, results on Aibo rather improve by reducing the number of features (Tables 5.21 and 5.22). Regarding

Task		CFS		IG+CFS		CFS+SFFS	
		%	#	%	#	%	#
Berlin	AA	**60.0**	128	**58.8**	100	**57.1**	60
	OA	**60.8**	101 -	**59.6**	76 -	**59.0**	37 -
Aibo	AA	**51.0**	173	**50.9**	151	**51.0**	61
	OA	47.6	168 -	47.7	133 -	**51.4**	43 -
SmartKom	AA	**48.5**	115	**48.6**	97	44.4	43
	OA	64.6	100 -	63.7	81 -	**67.2**	35 -

Table 5.21: Comparison of feature subsets selected from the full feature set: AA and OA in % from Naïve Bayes classifier, and number of features (#) are given, best or insignificantly worse accuracies in bold.

Task		Restr.		Restr.+IG0		Restr.+IG0-+CFS		Restr.+IG0-+CFS+SFFS	
		%	#	%	#	%	#	%	#
Berlin	AA	**61.5**		**59.9**	419	**59.8**	94	55.1	49
	OA	**62.8**		**60.6**	376 -	**60.0**	76 -	56.6	35 -
Aibo	AA	46.3		46.7	536	**50.8**	111	**51.3**	52
	OA	48.2	582	48.5	514 -	50.3	97 -	**52.3**	29 -
SmartKom	AA	49.0		**50.8**	412	**49.5**	95	44.4	46
	OA	66.3		63.9	356 -	67.1	83 -	**70.7**	33 -

Table 5.22: Comparison of feature subsets selected from the restricted feature set: AA and OA in % from Naïve Bayes classifier, and number of features (#) are given, best or insignificantly worse accuracies in bold.

SmartKom it is very interesting to observe that the information gain seems to be very meaningful: across all three tables of results (5.20 to 5.22) schemes with information gain based selection score best.

From these results it can be concluded that in order to obtain high accuracy, it is most advantageous to do automatic feature subset selection. The generally best method is to put a large number of features into the selection process and to remove correlated features. However, a prior restriction of the full feature set yields in most cases for practical purposes equal recognition rates with at the same time lower numbers of features and selection times. The relation between selection and classification times of all strategies, exemplarily for one training/test split of the Berlin databases with 394 instances in the training split and 104 instances in the test split is shown in Table 5.24. Obviously, differences in the selection time are substantial, especially when considering that Berlin is a very small database. For the other two databases, times are severalfold higher. Classification times also exhibit great differences, selection leads to at least halving the time. The two lowest values are indeed achieved by the longest selection times. For

5.3. Feature evaluation

Rank	Selection Strategy
1	CFS
2	Restr.+IG0+CFS
3	Restr.+IG0
4	IG+CFS
	Restr.
6	CFS+SFFS
7	Restr.+IG0+CFS+SFFS
8	all
	IG100
10	manual

Table 5.23: Ranking of selection strategies based on AA in Tables 5.20 to 5.22.

Selection Strategy	Selection time [min]	Classification time [ms]
All	0	153
Manual	0	10
InfoGain 100	0:02	15
CFS	1:59	17
IG+CFS	0:29	15
CFS+SFFS	16:09	9
Restr.	0	65
Restr.+IG0	0:01	45
Restr.+IG0+CFS	0:09	10
Restr.+IG0+CFS+SFFS	8:02	7

Table 5.24: Selection time of different feature selection strategies on one training split of the Berlin database, and classification time on the corresponding test set.

Naïve Bayes, classification of 104 instances takes less than 200 ms even for the full set; for many other algorithms, however, the differences in classification time would be higher, as will be shown in the next section.

During recognition, the most costly in terms of time is not classification but feature extraction. Unfortunately, however, it is often not possible to save time here by reducing the number of features, because the most time-consuming step is the calculation of the raw acoustic measures; in comparison, calculating statistical functions is negligible. So as long as not a whole feature type is eliminated, not much time-saving is possible in feature extraction.

Concluding, although CFS leads in general to the best accuracy and a very low number of features, at medium selection time, it may be decided anew before each application design whether accuracy, selection or classification time is given precedence, or what compromise of all three is sought.

5.4 Classifiers

The main focus of this book lies on analysing suitable emotion units and features, not classifiers. Therefore, no extensive comparison of classifiers as in approaches with emphasis on emotion classification is carried out here. Since emotion recognition is a general classification problem, any data-mining or pattern recognition approaches can be applied. However, recent approaches often explore multi-layer classification [136, 148, 261], that is, the original classification problem is divided into several easier problems, e. g. two-class problems. In order to still evaluate some classifiers with special regard to online recognition, the standard data-mining software Weka is used to compare some common classification algorithms on the most successful unit (voice activity detection) and feature set (CFS on the full feature set) as evaluated in the previous sections for the three databases. The algorithms are 0-R, Naïve Bayes, Support Vector Machines (SVM), Multi-Layer Perceptron (MLP), Nearest-Neighbour (3NN), Random Forest and Repeated Incremental Pruning to Produce Error Reduction (RIPPER) and have been described in detail previously in Section 4.4. Among these, 0-R, Naïve Bayes and 3-NN are naïve classifiers, while SVM and MLP can be regarded as more sophisticated functions. Except where stated explicitly, standard Weka configurations were used because the search for optimal parameters usually means a high adaptation to the training or test situation, even when a hold-out set is used. It appears, however, that these parameter configurations are often not general enough to work well on new databases, situations or even just new test sets. Here, a method should be found that yields good "out of the box" performance under a variety of conditions without extensive parameter tuning.

The results in Table 5.25 show that the overall accuracy is always highest for SVM. With regard to the averaged accuracy for Berlin, SVM, and also MLP, again work best. Naïve Bayes is a little worse, but achieves by far the best AA for Aibo and SmartKom. For SmartKom, Naïve Bayes is actually the only algorithm that outperforms 0-R considerably. The overall accuracy of 0-R for Aibo and SmartKom is, due to the unbalanced class distribution, very competitive. For Smart-Kom, even no other scheme yields significantly better results, but a trend can be observed that the better AA is, the worse OA. Once more this can be explained by the difficulty of this database for emotion recognition and emphasises the use of AA as evaluation criterion. The schemes 3-NN, Random Forest and RIPPER work more or less well, but always worse than Naïve Bayes, SVM or MLP. Thus, measured by AA, Naïve Bayes excels over the other algorithms.

In Table 5.26 times needed to train a classifier and test a set of instances are presented for the seven algorithms. Again, this analysis was carried out on one split of the Berlin database with 394 training and 104 test instances. 115 features were selected by CFS for this split. Weka is

5.4. Classifiers

Database		0-R	Naïve Bayes	SVM	MLP	3-NN	Random Forest	RIPPER
Berlin	AA	14.3	**59.5**	**63.5**	**62.1**	53.5	50.1	41.1
	OA	25.7	60.4	**66.5**	64.3	56.6	55.0	45.4
Aibo	AA	25.0	**51.1**	46.8	46.2	43.4	43.2	42.5
	OA	46.2	47.7	**58.0**	53.1	51.1	54.5	55.4
SmartKom	AA	33.3	**48.5**	33.5	39.4	38.1	37.1	36.1
	OA	**84.9**	64.6	**85.0**	78.8	81.5	**84.5**	82.5

Table 5.25: Comparison of classifiers: AA and OA in % are given, best or insignificantly worse results in bold.

Classifier	Training time [s]	Classification time [ms]
0-R	0.11	0
Naïve Bayes	0.15	84
SVM	0.96	451
MLP	162.95	168
3-NN	0.07	272
Random Forest	0.44	89
RIPPER	2.53	39

Table 5.26: Comparison of training and test times of the classifiers on one training/test split of the Berlin database.

a very practical testbed for data mining, however, it is not very fast due to various reasons. For example, the Naïve Bayes classifier of Weka is considerably slower than the one implemented in the framework for this book (cf. Table 5.24), mainly because it is implemented in C instead of Java, but also because there is less overhead from the overall framework and a simpler, but quicker solution to ensure precision of floating point exceptions is used. Classification times are given as the extra time needed compared to 0-R. Generally, the magnitude of the differences between the times should be considered rather than the absolute times, as these are very database and feature set size dependent. Table 5.26 clarifies once again the superiority of Naïve Bayes over SVM and MLP as fastest and most robust classifier.

In conclusion, similar or even better results with other classifiers and schemes, or other parameter configurations, have been reported in the literature on the evaluated databases, e.g. 96.5 % for Berlin by Schuller and Rigoll [204], 68.9 % AA for Aibo by Steidl [225] and 48.5 % for SmartKom by Batliner et al. [16], but results are not fully comparable, because for instance Schuller and Rigoll use, as is done in many other work on the Berlin database, speaker-dependent 10-fold stratified cross-validation as evaluation strategy, which may yield higher accuracy, but is a weaker predictor with respect to unknown speakers. Steidl obtained results on syntactic chunks and from a combination of acoustic and linguistic features. Furthermore, only chunks containing at least one of the highly prototypical AMEN words (see Section 4.1.2) were used, while here, the full speech data of turns containing at least one AMEN word was included. Finally, Batliner et al. used a different subset of the SmartKom corpus, the PUBLIC subcorpus. Thus, the evaluation here showed that Naïve Bayes is a fast classifier that yields good results under a variety of conditions.

5.5 Conclusion

In this chapter, various strategies for segmentation, feature extraction and classification have been investigated. The questions posed at the beginning of this chapter could all be answered satisfactorily. These were:

1. *Which emotion units are suitable in which scenario?*
    In search of an automatic segmentation and word-independent unit, VAD based units compared very well to traditional units in all three databases. There was a tendency for read, acted speech (Berlin) to prefer long units while for other speech types medium-sized units were best.

2. *Which features are useful, seen individually and in the context of subsets?*
    This question proved to be very database dependent. While for read, acted speech, pitch features were dominant, the less emotional the data was, the higher was the importance of MFCC and spectral features. Thus, it can be concluded that acted speech is no good substitute for real emotions when exploring features, as results can be very different. This finding strengthens the need to focus as much as possible on natural emotions in research. Evaluating each class individually, MFCCs also proved to be the most generally successful feature type across databases.
    What are the advantages/disadvantages of feature subsets selected by various strategies?
    Though best results for each database can be obtained by specific methods, a general method selecting features with low correlation from a large feature set (CFS) proved to be most robust across databases.

3. *Which classifiers are advantageous?*
    While with more prototypical data (Berlin), Support Vector Machines (SVM) and Multi-Layer Perceptrons (MLP) that are traditionally known as very accurate classifiers in speech emotion recognition performed slightly better, Naïve Bayes, a very simple classifier, yielded best results for more natural data, and is considerably faster at the same time.

New contributions gained from the experiments presented in this chapter include that no such comprehensive and systematic comparison of units for emotion recognition from speech has

5.5. Conclusion

been conducted so far. It showed that non-linguistic units may also have very good performance, though so far, rather the opposite has been implicitly assumed, as there is almost no work using such units. This positive result holds at least under the specific conditions (e. g. databases, features, classifier, evaluation strategies) under which experiments were conducted here. In particular, to the best of knowledge, VAD based units have not yet been examined.

With regard to features, it became apparent, that pitch features are important, but not as strongly as very early work assumed; this finding is conform to other more recent work. A further result that has not been elaborated so clearly so far or contradicts established assumptions is that pitch normalisation has, if at all, only a minor effect. Moreover, the generative approach of calculating many features combined with automatic feature selection has proved here, similar to Schuller [203], as more advantageous compared to a smaller hand-crafted feature set, even though this latter is preferred by most other authors. However, MFCC features take on an oversized role here. As they are very general and actually intended to filter out non-linguistic influences in speech, there is probably still more potential in the search for good feature types. When evaluating the general usefulness of the feature set used here, also a comparison for the Aibo corpus with the feature sets of the CEICES initiative suggests itself. For example, in [21], where a subset of the features used here and the Naïve Bayes classifier were directly compared with approaches of other institutions, other sites achieved higher accuracies (between 54.8 and 56.6 % compared to 52.3 % with the approach taken here). However, all of them included linguistic features from a manually revised word transcription, so that the influence of the quality of the acoustic features is not clear. The only other approach that did not use linguistic features achieved only 46.6 % accuracy, though with a very limited feature set. Furthermore, evaluation strategy (two-fold cross-validation by schools) as well as units (turns) differed compared to the accuracy of 51.1 % obtained in this book. Schuller et al. [209], who did not compare among institutions but pooled features from all, again achieved better results than here, probably because even more features and types were given to the selection process; however, results were again obtained from a different unit (syntactic chunks).

A further new insight gained in this chapter is revealed by the classifier comparison which also contradicts the established trend that SVM is the most successful classifier. This holds in particular for non-acted data.

Therefore, moving on to online speech emotion recognition in the next chapter, selected methodologies are voice activity detection for segmenting speech into emotion units, correlation based feature subset selection on the full feature set to obtain a limited size feature set, and Naïve Bayes as a robust and fast classification algorithm.

Chapter 6

EMOVOICE — Real-time speech emotion recognition

The two previous chapters presented methods for speech emotion recognition and experiments to evaluate them in view of real-time processing. This chapter now presents a framework called EMOVOICE that integrates gained insights into a comprehensive toolkit for online and offline speech emotion recognition. The module for online recognition is a standalone application which can easily be linked to other applications that make use of information on the emotional state of a user.

As has been already mentioned in Section 3.5, there exist only very few fully implemented systems for online speech emotion recognition so far, none of them in serious commercial products. Consequently, this is still a novel and not fully explored topic, the major impediment of current systems being their low accuracy. However, the availability of such a system, even with relatively low accuracy, may boost development of affective applications, giving in turn insights to refine recognition system to produce higher accuracy.

The primary requirements for online emotion recognition are that it should be 1) fast, 2) robust and 3) as correct as possible. Therefore, the following points have to be considered:

- Audio segmentation is faster and more consistent the less knowledge is used. Furthermore, it should work incrementally.

- Feature extraction may, of course, not include any manual knowledge. It also has to be compatible to the audio segmentation. For example, it may not rely on word length or information, if no automatic word recognition is available.

- Classification should be fast and robust, as well. If no online retraining or adaptation of the classifier is necessary, feature selection and training of the classifier do not need to run in real-time, however, this depends on the particular application.

- During runtime, occurring emotions are no closed set as in a pre-recorded database. Thus, only those emotions the application is intended to react to can be defined beforehand. An online system needs to find a solution how to cope with other emotions.

This chapter first explains the architecture and modules of EMOVOICE. Furthermore, the topic of data acquisition for online recognition is considered. In order to demonstrate the utilisability of EMOVOICE, a number of applications and projects that were linked with EMOVOICE are presented. Moreover, differences in the expression of emotions under realistic conditions in applications and under fixed conditions in an emotional speech database are discussed. Finally, by means of three of these applications, studies of EMOVOICE are described that assess user evaluation of the system.

6.1 Architecture

EMOVOICE consists of a set of command line tools developed for Linux, but can also be run non-natively on Windows systems with the Linux emulator Cygwin[1]. It is implemented in C and partly based upon the ESMERALDA environment for speech recognition [78]. As Figure 6.1 illustrates, four groups of tools can be distinguished: tools for audio processing, for feature processing, tools related to classifier building and tools for full online and offline systems. The tools are built stepwise upon each other.

Thereby, the tool `audio/segment` can segment audio signals at a fixed frame rate and shift, according to a given annotation, or by automatically detecting segments with voice activity. The expected input format are raw, i.e. uncompressed, audio samples at a rate of 16 kHz. `features/extract` extracts acoustic features in two versions. Version 2.0 is the one described earlier in Section 4.3, while version 1.0 is a previous version extracting 1316 acoustic features based on pitch, energy, MFCCs, duration, spectrum and voice quality. It does not contain logarithmised pitch features, spectral slope or spectral linear regressive features, and only HNR based voice quality features.

`classification/train` and `system/train` both train a Naïve Bayes or Support Vector Machine classifier (for implementation details see Section 4.4), and `classification/classify`, `system/classify` both classify new instances with classifiers built by the training

---
[1] http://www.cygwin.com

6.1. Architecture

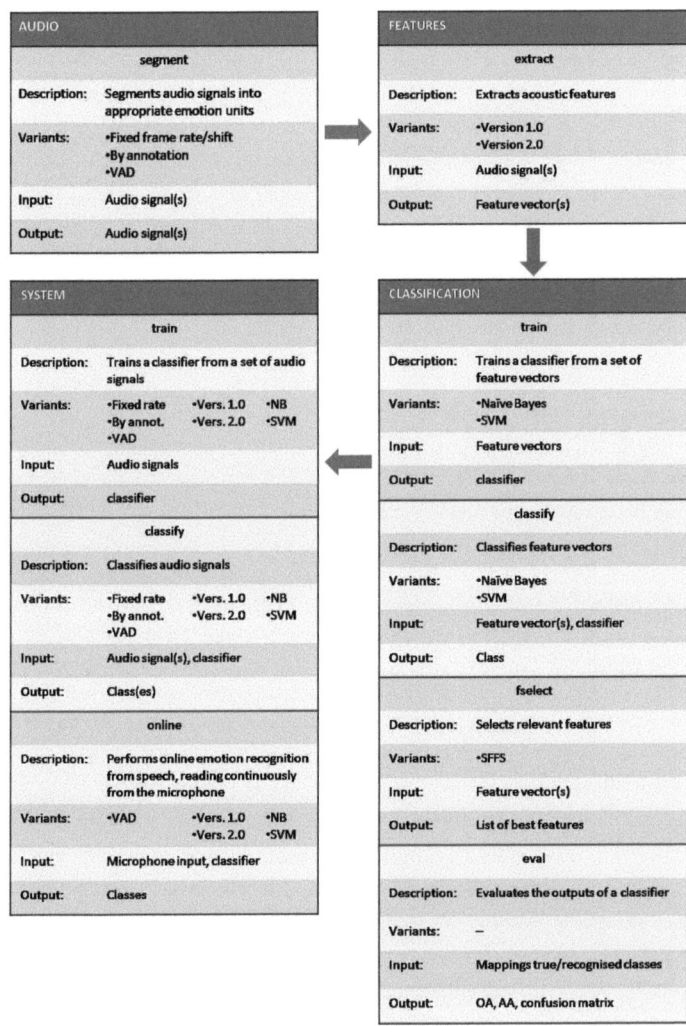

Figure 6.1: Overview of tools in EMOVOICE.

tools. The `classification` and `system` versions differ in that the former operate on feature vectors, while the latter are full systems processing audio files. All four tools may use all features in the set, but can also be given a list of features for restricting the set. This list can be obtained in various ways, for example by empirical knowledge, by feature selection algorithms from Weka [255] or by the tool `classification/fselect` that selects relevant features with Sequential Floating Forward Feature Search. At least one pair of training and evaluation split of feature vectors is needed (if more are given, they are cross-validated) and a classification algorithm (Naïve Bayes or SVM) has to be specified. This tool is located in the `classification` group because feature extraction as well as a classifier are needed to perform the search. If a reference annotation is available, classification outputs can be evaluated with `classification/eval` that outputs the overall recognition accuracy (OA), the recognition accuracy averaged over classes (AA), a confusion matrix and some statistics of the test data. Finally, `system/online`, also called `emo_online`, continuously reads audio input from a microphone, incrementally finds segments of voice activity, extracts features from them and classifies them, and outputs the results as soon as it is available.

Since `emo_online` is the key tool of the framework, it is described in more detail now. It works in three threads, as shown in Figure 6.2:

1. In the *signal recording* thread, signal chunks of 16 ms length at a rate of 10 ms are continuously buffered and provided to the next thread.

2. The *voice activity detection* thread analyses for each incoming chunk whether it contains speech, and incrementally adds voiced chunks until a threshold number of successive nonvoice chunk is detected. Once a voiced segment is completed in doing so, it is provided to the last thread.

3. In the last thread, *feature extraction and classification* are performed on the voiced segments. Results are outputted to the console or to a socket.

Obviously, classification results are obtained here continuously during talking, there is no "push-to-talk". The output is either the most probable class or all classes with their confidence scores. Thereby, audio stream segmentation by voice activity detection permits continuous and language-independent processing, without the necessity of other time-consuming steps such as speech recognition. This kind of segmentation is especially suited for spontaneous spoken language and it was shown in the previous chapter that it yields meaningful emotion units. In contrast, when reading speakers usually do not make long enough pauses, even between text sections that differ in terms of content, and emotions. However, in EMOVOICE, there is also the option to set a maximum interval for the output of a classification result if no pause has occurred before. For this interval, 2–3 seconds turned out to be a suitable duration.

The adequacy of the feature extraction has likewise been demonstrated in the previous chapter. Furthermore, it is fast enough for real-time processing. Extracting features for an audio segment of 1 second length takes about 0.4 seconds. The two classification algorithms that are currently integrated in EMOVOICE (Naïve Bayes and SVM) both have advantages and disadvantages in

6.1. Architecture

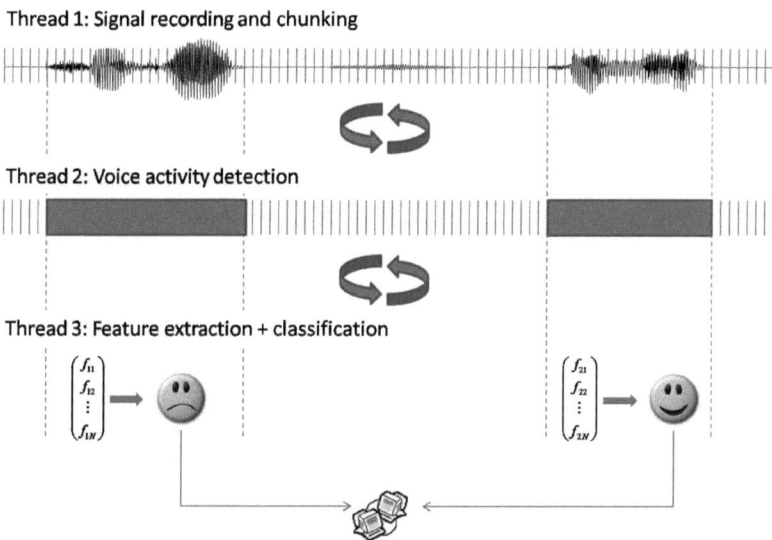

Figure 6.2: Overview of emo_online, the online speech emotion recognition module of EMOVOICE.

view of real-time processing. The Naïve Bayes classifier is very fast, even for high-dimensional feature vectors, but was shown in previous work to have slightly lower classification rates than the SVM classifier which is a very common algorithm used in offline emotion recognition. Empirically, however, Naïve Bayes is relatively robust against mismatching training and test conditions. SVM is slow for high-dimensional data, but in combination with feature selection and thereby a reduction of the number of features to less than 100, SVM results can also be obtained in real-time.

The task of emo_online is simply to recognise emotions which usually makes no sense *per se*, but only if there is another module or application interpreting or reacting to this information. As the output of emo_online can be transmitted over a socket, linking with external applications is straight-forward. A sample of applications that EMOVOICE has been connected to so far is presented in Section 6.3. In order to ease the use of EMOVOICE for software developers unfamiliar with speech emotion recognition in general but who want to integrate affective user speech in their application, a set of graphical user interfaces exists that make it very simple to record a speech database and to build a classifier (see Figure 6.3). Thus, application developers do not need to care about implementation details of EMOVOICE. Database creation is further supported by a recording script which is the topic of the next chapter.

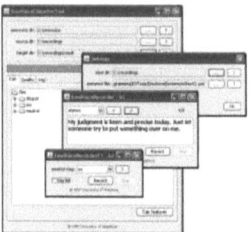

Figure 6.3: Graphical user interfaces supporting speech database creation and classifier building.

Recently, EMOVOICE has been integrated as toolbox into Smart Sensor Integration (SSI)[2], a framework for multimodal sensor fusion and multimodal emotion recognition in real-time by the University of Augsburg [251]. Since November 2009, it can be downloaded freely in this form under the terms of the Gnu Public License v3.0 as open-source software after prior registration[3].

6.2 Data acquisition

As mentioned before, statistical classifiers need training data. Thus, while EMOVOICE can technically be integrated into arbitrary applications, the classifier needs to be trained with suitable data to give reasonable results. What could be a suitable corpus for a real-time emotion recognition system? There are no general purpose databases for emotion recognition, for several reasons. For a general database, first, an "emotion inventory" would be needed, from that, similar to a phoneme inventory for speech recognition, other emotions could be composed. However, such an inventory does not exist. Mehrabian [153]'s PAD (**P**leasure, **A**rousal, **D**ominance) model could possibly provide an approximation to this, by either building regression models from continuous labels, or by training discrete areas in the model and then interpolating between these areas to model others. Still, environmental factors (microphone, background noise, etc.), speaker groups (general vs. selected speakers, adults vs. children, etc.) and languages in train and test data would not necessarily match. This is a general problem for speech emotion recognition systems integrated into applications because state-of-the-art technology is not flexible enough to cope with different environmental factors. Existing databases are likewise only suited for their specific conditions. In particular, specific non-prototypical emotions that are usually limited to the application context will rarely be found in existing databases. Thus, application specific training databases have to be recorded.

Given this insight, a second point to consider with respect to data acquisition is that if speech

---
[2]http://mm-werkstatt.informatik.uni-augsburg.de/ssi.html
[3]http://mm-werkstatt.informatik.uni-augsburg.de/EmoVoice.html

emotion recognition is integrated into many applications, creating a database for each application involves lots of effort, in terms of time and manpower, and cannot be carried out any more by the speech emotion recognition system developers. If application developers are to record databases, availability of time and knowledge are reduced. From experiences gained for example in the EU project CALLAS[4] where artistic showcases interpreting multimodal affective input are developed (see the next section), it was observed that it is not possible to record as many hours of thoroughly labelled emotional speech data for each application as is usually used for offline analysis, not only because the primary goal is software development and not extensive data collection but also because of a general problem for applied speech emotion recognition under realistic conditions: Though it would be best to record large amounts of data from users interacting with the application, and use them as training data, this is often not possible, mainly because there is no test data yet, but also because it is too time consuming, especially to annotate the data, or not feasible to do by non-experts. For integrated speech emotion recognition systems, application developers need to be able to create databases in a simple and fast fashion on their own. Furthermore, applications are conceivable where users create their own speaker dependent recognition systems whose accuracies can be expected to be considerably higher than that of a general recognition system. Even if the quality of these databases is not as high as of those created by experts, they will be better suited for their purposes.

For these reasons, a work flow was designed for the application developers to record their own training database adjusted to their application and the easy-to-use interface for recording and training an emotional speech corpus, as presented in the previous section and in Figure 6.1, was integrated into EMOVOICE. The interface offers the possibility to present stimuli that are similar to those occurring in the applications. The emotion label then results from the stimulus and labelling afterwards is not necessary. The interface lets developers decide on the emotions they want to recognise (though they might not yet know which emotions actually occur, see above), on the language, they can provide as similar as possible background noises and select suitable speakers. One successful method used for emotion elicitation was inspired by the Velten mood induction technique [237] as used by Wilting et al. [254] where subjects had to read out loud a set of emotional sentences that should set them into the desired emotional state. A predefined set of such sentences is provided with EMOVOICE for the four quadrants in a two-dimensional emotional space (positive-active, positive-passive, negative-active, negative-passive) as well as neutral which could be mapped for example on the emotions joy, satisfaction, anger and frustration (and neutral). Examples for the 200 sentences (40 per emotion) can be found in Figure 6.4. However, developers making use of the system are encouraged to change sentences according to the emotional experiences of the recorded persons, or base them on the topics of their application.

---

[4]http:www.callas-newmedia.eu

positive-active	negative-active
I feel amazingly good today! It would really take something to stop me now! You won't believe it, I got the new job!	This is so unfair! That's dangerous what you're doing, stop it! You really get on my nerves.

positive-passive	negative-passive
I think my life is beautiful. I like listening to flowing water in the mountains. My life is completely under control.	I feel rather sluggish now. It often seems no matter how hard I try, things still go wrong. I just can't make up my mind.

neutral
Bibliography notes should appear at the end of the paper. The museum is at the end of the road. The Greater Munich area is home to over 5 million people.

Figure 6.4: Examples for emotional stimuli sentences inspired by the Velten mood induction technique [237].

The interface allows to quickly build a customised classifier, but there also arise problems from the recordings being made by non-experts. The Velten method is in principle a very suitable method, but especially when conducted by non-experts it cannot be guaranteed that speakers really immerse in the respective emotions. Though the goal is usually the recognition of non-acted emotions, of course, this method does not yield truly natural emotions; instead, they could rather be called semi-acted. However, even if the recorded emotions may not be fully spontaneous because the sentences are read, they represent a hard and realistic problem because the speakers are usually no professional actors and do not produce full-blown or prototypical emotions as professional actors would do. Listening tests on a database recorded with EMOVOICE for an Italian artistic showcase revealed that it was often hard for humans who could not speak Italian to detect the target emotion.

By giving over the recording process into the hands of the application developers, the recognition system developer is no longer able to control the adherence to the standards for recording, for example if indeed similar settings were provided. Furthermore, the amount of data is usually small. For these reasons, there is a discrepancy between training and test data, which is likely to occur in real-time systems. Of course, this can seriously affect recognition accuracy. What adds further is that conditions in general are very difficult in some applications as they are not exclusively centred around the requirements of the speech emotion recognition system and may produce for example background music as well. Especially voices in the background negatively affect the

6.2. Data acquisition

recognition rate as the system cannot distinguish which voice it should recognise emotions from.

In order to assess the suitability of the work flow, two data sets created with this method were analysed. The first data set was obtained from 29 students (8 females, 21 males) between 20 and 28 years who created the recordings as part of an exercise to a lecture. The sentence set was the predefined set described above, but with only 20 sentences per emotion, and in German, though there were also 10 non-native speakers among them. Students could do the recordings at home, so the audio quality and equipment were not controlled, but all students were told to use a head-set microphone. Offline speaker-dependent accuracies in 10-fold cross-validation for all 4 classes varied — not surprisingly — a lot among speakers and ranged from 24 % to 74 %, with an average of 55 %. This great variation is to a good extent due to the uncontrolled audio recordings which led to very different audio and emotion qualities but this makes the setting especially realistic with regard to how people cope with the technology on their own.

From all test persons, 10 German native speakers (5 female, 5 male) whose speaker-dependent accuracy was not below 40 % and where audio quality was satisfactory were selected to train a multiple-speaker classifier that could be used as a general classifier in many applications responding to emotional states in the recorded set. This resulted in a recognition accuracy of 41 %, obtained again in 10-fold cross-validation. All results were obtained with the Naïve Bayes classifier on the full feature set (no selection) and though the figures may not sound high overall, they are well above chance level. Especially in the speaker-independent evaluation, the use of different microphones is responsible to a great extent for low recognition rates. For good results in a realistic setting and online recognition, only 2 or 3 of these classes should be used anyway. As an example, recognition rates between 60 % and 70 % can be obtained for the multiple-speaker system when leaving two classes out. Again note that all recognition accuracies were obtained offline, though speech data and recording conditions were expected to match online conditions closely. A systematic evaluation of online recognition accuracy has not been done yet, but is empirically 10–20 % lower than the offline accuracy if applied in a scenario similar to the recording conditions.

It took the speakers about 10–20 minutes to record the 80 sentences. For a good speaker dependent system, however, it is recommended to have at least 40 sentences per emotion.

The speakers of the second data set were recorded for showcases of the CALLAS project. The four male speakers read English sentences for three emotional classes (positive-active, neutral, negative-passive). Two of them were non-native speakers and the class distribution of the 1346 sentences was approximately balanced. Not all speakers read the same amount of sentences. Again, reported recognition accuracies were obtained with the Naïve Bayes classifier offline. Speaker dependent accuracies in 10-fold cross-validation ranged from 54.5 % to 65.4 %. When evaluating all speakers together, again in 10-fold cross-validation, accuracy was lower with 49.5 %.

Thus, from the analysis of both data sets it can be concluded that even if the results obtained from the work flow may not be perfect, it does yield useful results, so that it is a good alternative if no suitable pre-recorded and annotated databases exist.

6.3 Sample applications and prototypes

Of course, knowing the emotion expressed by one's own voice is not very useful *per se*, but only in the context of an application making use of the affective information. However, for fully natural low-intensity emotions in online recognition, only low accuracies can be expected. At the current state of the art, rather applications should be considered where expressive speech comes natural, e.g. games, voice training or artistic expressions of emotion.

The integration of `emo_online` with other applications is simple, as the result of the emotion recognition can be continuously transmitted over a socket connection to that application. Therefore, EMOVOICE has been successfully integrated in a number of applications or existing architectures. So far, there exist a number of prototypes and applications that use EMOVOICE and that have been developed internally or at external institutions, either in cooperation or independently. The applications will be described in the following and fall into two groups: conversational applications, where conversations with an artificial character or robot are analysed with respect to the affect conveyed in the user's voice causing changes in the behaviour of the artificial companion or where direct feedback of the emotionality of the user's voice is given, and artistic applications, that should appeal to the human sense of aesthetics or provide artists with new ways to express themselves emotionally and that have mainly been developed in the context of the CALLAS project. User studies have been conducted only on some of the applications and will be presented later in this chapter.

In the presented applications and prototypes, four different languages, German, English, Italian and Finnish, were used. This shows that the methodology of EMOVOICE is language-independent.

6.3.1 Conversational applications

The six conversational applications are intended to support affective conversations. In two of them (Barthoc jr. and Greta, see Figure 6.5), EMOVOICE was integrated into existing architectures to see whether affective behaviour makes a robot or virtual agent more believable. Barthoc

6.3. Sample applications and prototypes

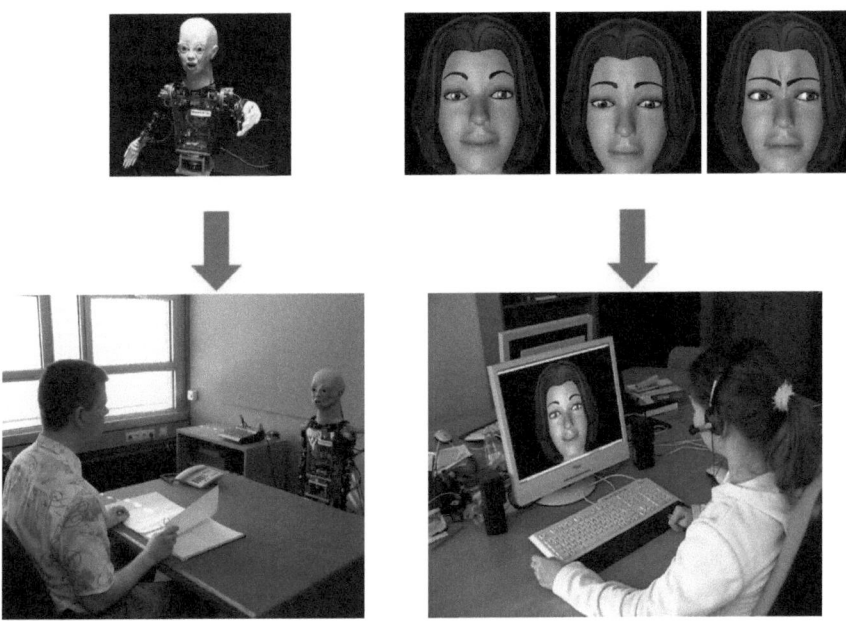

Figure 6.5: The humanoid robot head Barthoc jr. (left) and the virtual agent Greta (right) as empathic listeners mirroring the user's emotional state with their facial expressions.

jr. [95] is a humanoid child robot head of the University of Bielefeld, that is capable of very detailed and human-like facial expressions. In the scenario, users read the fairy tale "Rotkäppchen" (English: "Little Red Riding Hood") and the robot mimicked the recognised emotions with its facial expressions. Hegel et al. [102] showed in a user study a preference of the emotionally reacting robot over a robot without emotion recognition. This evaluation study is described in more detail in Section 6.5.1.

Greta [61] is a virtual agent, whose facial expressions can, like Barthoc jr., be changed at runtime. It was integrated at the University of Augsburg with EMOVOICE in an empathic listener scenario, where the user can talk freely with the agent and Greta mirrors the user's emotional state in her face. Furthermore, from time to time she gives emotionally coloured small-talk feedback, thus showing empathy with the user [247].

Three further applications, EmoEmma, the virtual Karaoke singers and the Affective Interactive Narrative installation, are entertainment applications where the flow of the application is influenced by affective information conveyed in the voice (see Figure 6.6). EmoEmma [42] is an interactive storytelling system based on Gustave Flaubert's novel "Madame Bovary", and has been

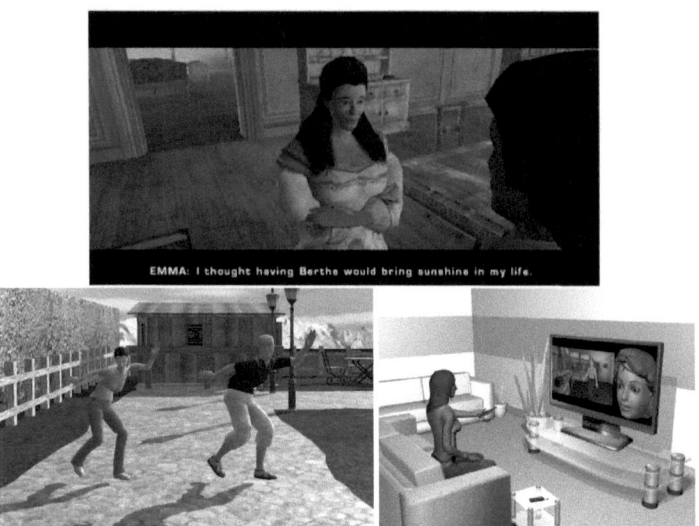

Figure 6.6: EmoEmma (top), karaoke singers (bottom left) and Affective Interactive Narrative installation (bottom right): agent behaviour is, among others, controlled by the affect conveyed in the voice of the user.

developed at Teesside University, UK, within the EU Network of Excellence IRIS[5] (**I**ntegrating **R**esearch in **I**nteractive **S**torytelling) which is concerned with the development of novel technologies for interactive storytelling. Recognition of affect is one of the novel techniques to be integrated into virtual storytelling environments. In EmoEmma, users can influence the outcome of the story by acting as one of the characters, Rodolphe, who wants to seduce Emma, the main character of the novel, and the interaction mode is restricted to the emotional tone of their voice.

Rehm et al. [188] implemented a karaoke system where virtual characters dance during the user's karaoke performance. The user can control the expressiveness of the characters' dance movements by singing and gestures. Singing is analysed with EMOVOICE in terms of activation, while gestures can be performed with the Nintendo® Wii Remote controller, which has an inbuilt motion sensor, and are analysed with WiiGLE[6] (Wii-based Gesture Learning Environment), a toolbox for feature extraction and classification of acceleration-based gesture sensor data. By means of this approach, the users' situated arousal and personal style can be expressed and communicated to the outside world in an immersive 3D environment.

In the Affective Interactive Narrative installation from the CALLAS project, a virtual character

---

[5] http://iris.scm.tees.ac.uk
[6] http://mm-werkstatt.informatik.uni-augsburg.de/project_details.php?id=46

6.3. Sample applications and prototypes

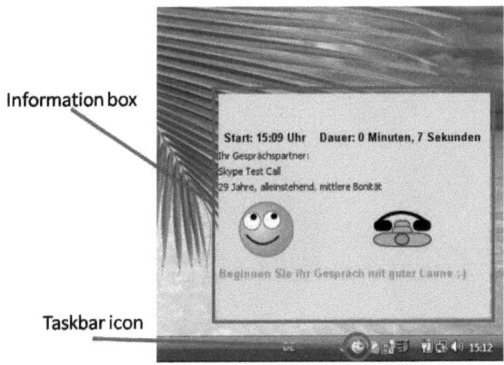

Figure 6.7: EmoSkype, an add-on to the internet voice messaging software Skype™, gives feedback on how a user acts on his/her phone conversation partner.

(again Greta) watches a (horror) movie and reacts to the emotions conveyed in the scenes and by a human spectator [44]. Furthermore, the narrative tension of the generated story can be strengthened or weakened depending on whether positive or negative feedback is given. Emotions are detected from acoustic and from word information as recognised by a multi-keyword spotting system.

Finally, EmoSkype, developed in a student project at the University of Augsburg, is designed as a an add-on to Skype™[7], an internet voice and instant messaging software. It analyses the voice of a user during talking and gives objective feedback on the conveyed emotions. This should bring users insights on how they act on their conversation partner and allow them to adapt their voice in order to transmit the desired emotional tone. The feedback is displayed in a small box with further information on the call and the callee, and/or as a corresponding icon, realised with smileys, in the taskbar, as shown in Figure 6.7. EmoSkype is primarily intended to support call centre employees in the banking sector.

6.3.2 Artistic applications

Other applications integrated with EMOVOICE are of artistic nature and have the goal of visualising emotions or allowing users to express themselves emotionally. One of them is an animated kaleidoscope [220] that changes according to a speaker's emotions. Colours, speed and forms of the animations are specific to each emotion, as can be seen in Figure 6.8.

Within CALLAS (**C**onveying **A**ffectivity in **L**eading-edge **L**iving **A**daptive **S**ystems), an In-

---
[7]http://skype.com

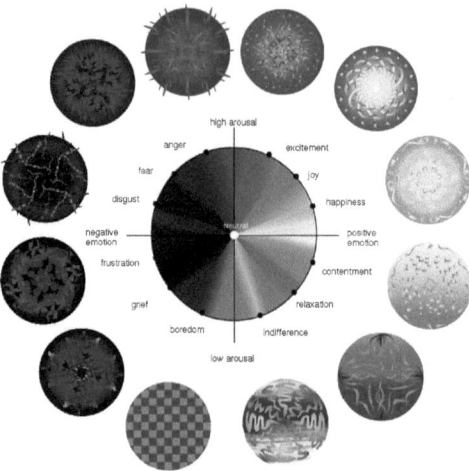

Figure 6.8: An animated kaleidoscope to visualise online recognised emotional states.

tegrated Project funded by the EU, showcases of interactive art are being developed that respond to the multimodal emotional input of performers and spectators in real-time. Some of them are intended to be used primarily by professional actors, and it is assumed and encouraged that users express themselves with strong, possibly exaggerated and acted emotions. For this reason, these scenarios are ideally suited for the current state of the art in emotion recognition technology.

The following showcases in CALLAS, illustrated in Figure 6.9, make use of EMOVOICE to detect emotions from the user's voice or employ parts of EMOVOICE to analyse acoustic features of emotional speech input.

- *E-Tree:* E-Tree [86] by Teesside University, UK, is an Augmented Reality art installation of a virtual tree that grows, shrinks, changes colours, etc. by interpreting affective multimodal input from video, keywords and emotional voice tone.

- *Galassie:* Galassie [118] by Studio Azzurro[8], Italy, creates stylized shapes similar to galaxies for each present user. The visual appearance of the galaxies depends on the user's emotional state which EMOVOICE detects from the user's voice.

- *PuppetWall:* In the PuppetWall showcase [141] by Helsinki University of Technology (TKK), Finland, a user may influence a 2D graphics by the movements of physical puppets and the emotional tone of his or her voice. In contrast to the other showcases where the

---

[8]http://www.studioazzurro.com

6.3. Sample applications and prototypes 135

system responds to emotional states, PuppetWall is controlled by acoustic features of the user's voice.

- *Interactive Opera:* Interactive Opera by Digital Video[9], Italy, is a live performance for children recreating characters and sceneries of famous compositions from W.A. Mozart, Giacomo Puccini, Giuseppe Verdi and many others. The children may influence the outcome of the story by expressing emotions using facial expressions and their voices that are mapped onto the characters.

- *MusicKiosk:* MusicKiosk [140] by XIM[10], UK, is an interactive museum installation that presents music instruments to young people in an innovative way enabling them to control music by expressing their feelings.

- *ElectroEmotion:* ElectroEmotion [142] by TKK is an affective, interactive installation for public spaces that mainly served to collect a multimodal corpus of emotion data. In this showcase, users are directly requested to express different kinds of emotions which are visualised to provide the users with feedback.

Most showcases are fully implemented and have been used already by real users, partly in user studies (E-Tree, ElectroEmotion), but also under realistic conditions. For example, Galassie has been performed in July 2008 at Teatro Arcimboldi in Milan, Italy, and E-Tree has been presented to users at the EC's ICT (Information and Communication Technologies) event 2008.

In all cases, EMOVOICE was used to analyse the users' vocal emotions in real-time while they were interacting with the installations. Some showcases were completely controlled by the user's emotional state. That is, there was no analysis of the semantic content. In most cases, the user's emotional state was reflected by the system's display. For example, in the E-Tree installation there was a direct mapping between the user's emotional state and the colour and size of the tree. In the Interactive Opera, the system did not simply mirror the user's emotional state. Instead a more sophisticated reasoning process was required to determine the output of an appropriate system response. Some showcases, such as the MusicKiosk and Interactive Opera, were specifically designed as multi-user applications.

---

[9]http://www.toonz.com
[10]http://www.xim.co.uk
[11]The pictures are courtesy of University of Teesside, Studio Azzurro, Helsinki University of Technology (TKK), Digital Video and XIM Ltd respectively. The copyright remains with these organisations.

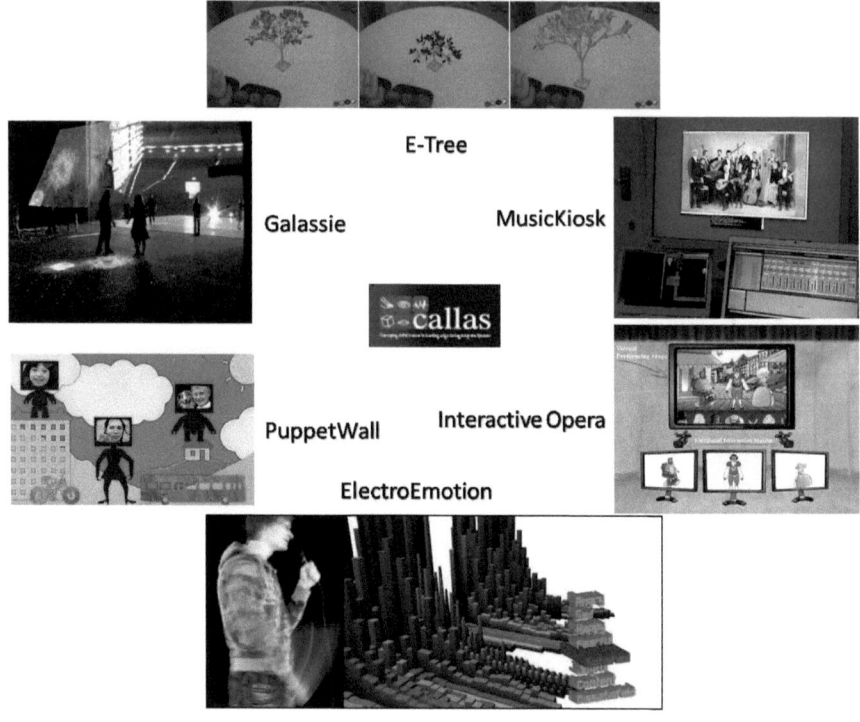

Figure 6.9: Showcases of interactive art in the CALLAS project making use of EMOVOICE.[11]

6.4 Emotion expressions under realistic conditions

In work on offline emotion recognition (see Chapter 3), usually, a corpus of emotional speech is collected and annotated with emotional states using either emotion categories or emotion dimensions. Typically, the ground truth is given by a majority vote of the labellers and ambiguous cases are often discarded. Thus, all occurring emotions are known.

With online recognition, the situation is more complicated, as normally, occurring emotions cannot be restricted, and if it is possible, it is still not guaranteed the user adheres to this demand. Nonetheless, all emotions have to be reacted to in some way. In the following, therefore, the expression of emotions under realistic conditions in applications based on EMOVOICE is addressed and what has to be considered in view of the problems that arise.

Emotions expressed by the users in the various applications presented in the previous section are very varied. They range from rather prototypical emotions in E-Tree, where users explore

6.4. Emotion expressions under realistic conditions

which emotional expressions can make the tree respond, to absolutely unprototypical and unpredictable expressions e. g. of spectators in Galassie or users of EmoSkype. Except for Barthoc jr. and ElectroEmotion, where emotions were specified by the conductor of the experiment, allowed emotions cannot be imposed on the users. Furthermore, everybody has their own individual interpretation of emotions and expresses them differently. For example, for Galassie, a classifier for three emotional states (positive/high-arousal, neutral, negative/low-arousal) was trained. In this showcase, the users were intended to control the system via their emotional states as expressed by speech. When analysing the showcase Jacucci et al. [118] identified, however, fourteen different emotion states based on reported user experiences: interest, transport, ludic pleasure, amazement, involvement, creation, serenity, freedom, confusion, irritation, indifference, frustration, boredom, distressed. Interest, transport and ludic pleasure were reported most frequently, that is by 50 % of the users. Of course, some of these emotions can be subsumed under the classes positive/high-arousal, neutral and negative/low-arousal, but not all, and additionally, it is not possible with these general terms to respond to the user very specifically. Most of all, it could not be known beforehand that exactly these emotions will occur. This example illustrates that it cannot be predicted how users interact with affective applications and that emotional expression is individual, in particular its strength. It is only possible to define — based on the application — which emotions the system will react to. Furthermore, in order to be able to frequently react to the user's affect appropriately, it is not sufficient to focus on prototypical or standard Ekmanian emotions.

A number of further factors contribute to non-standard expressions of emotions in the presented applications: some have a limited, pre-selected user group, for example EmoSkype could be conceived as a personalised application, and Interactive Opera addresses only children. For others, in turn, potential users cannot be restricted. Languages comprise English, by native and non-native speakers, German, Italian, and Finnish. Background noises also vary a lot among and within applications. For instance, E-Tree has been performed in quiet office environments and at exhibitions. In Galassie, Interactive Opera and PuppetWall, the background noise level is high and the voice of the speaker to be analysed competes with other voices in the background, or, as in EmoSkype, EmoEmma or Greta as empathic listener, with the voice output of the human or virtual conversation partner. For Barthoc jr. and the kaleidoscope, on the contrary, a quiet office environment can be assumed. Though it is recommended that every speaker wears a headset microphone, this is not feasible in some circumstances.

Emotions in the artistic CALLAS showcases or in entertainment applications such as EmoEmma or the karaoke singers often are rather exaggerated, which might ease recognition. However, expectations of users are very high. In Galassie, users expected the system to be as sensitive as humans, or even more, to their emotional state and to understand even very subtle emotions. This is of course an expectation that cannot be met with current technology. The same expectations probably also have users of EmoSkype and there, a further aggravating factor is that emotions are presumably not very intense. But also the other demands go beyond those encountered at the offline analysis of existing emotional speech databases as done by previous and many current work on speech emotion recognition and require new strategies.

The primary strategy that is applied with EMOVOICE to cope with the diversity of emotions is to train a limited set of general emotion classes based on pleasure and arousal in a dimensional emotion model, for example the PAD model. For instance, five emotion classes (positive/high-arousal, positive/low-arousal, neutral, negative/low-arousal, and negative/high-arousal) were trained for EmoEmma which should then subsume the actually expressed emotions at runtime. In both the E-Tree and EmoEmma scenarios, the classes are then mapped again onto points in the PAD space. In E-Tree, other modalities also provide PAD values which allows accommodation of non-prototypical emotions by multimodal fusion of PAD-based emotional representations. Furthermore, a decay is introduced by combining the overall score with previous values to make changes in the tree's appearance smoother and interaction more natural [87]. A problem with emotions trained with the help of the EMOVOICE workflow described in Section 6.2 is, however, that often rather prototypical, full-blown emotions are elicited. The more subjects during recording of the training database can be made to immerse in the respective emotions, for example by situational or personal stimuli, the better the quality of the classifier will be.

Another possibility to cope with non-prototypical data is to concentrate on a few important and specific categories and to add a "garbage" class for all other occurring emotions. This garbage class should then be very general as it has to include very different kinds of emotional expressions. This strategy has not been applied with EMOVOICE yet, though a similar objective was pursued in EmoEmma, where a "noise" class was trained with undesired environment noises, thus adapting to the background environment. A further possibility to deal with a garbage class is multi-level classification by first differentiating between relevant emotions and garbage, and to analyse then which of the relevant emotions actually occurred.

Thus, the major problems occurring with online emotion expressions are described and first strategies to cope with them are identified. However, this topic is not yet concluded and still poses great challenges for the future.

6.5 Evaluation studies

Offline systems are usually evaluated in terms of their recognition accuracy on a test database. A classifier that should be used in an online system can of course also be evaluated offline in the same way. In order to evaluate it at run-time, however, further issues need to be considered: a first question is what should be evaluated, the subjective or objective experience. The subjective evaluation can be better or worse than the objective evaluation. Especially in artistic installations, mainly the subjective experience of the user is of interest and evaluated, i.e. if the user has the impression that the system is responsive. This may diverge from the objective accuracy of the system, though the latter is often difficult to determine, as first a ground truth has to be established. This can be done by annotating test data after run-time though this may be too late and thus not applicable for many purposes. Other methods are physiological measurements as a ground truth (E-Tree) or video observations (ElectroEmotion). In general, the objective recognition rates of online systems must be expected to be lower than in offline analysis. However, because the range of occurring emotions cannot be predicted, it may not always be possible to assign an emotional state to a class present in the system, or only if a garbage class exists. Finally, it has to be decided whether to evaluate a system's ability to recognise emotions over time (E-Tree) or whether to evaluate the concept of automated emotion recognition as a whole (EmoEmma). In the first case, the system's results need to be compared with ground truth data at particular points in time. In the second case, a posteriori evaluation of the system usually concentrating on user experience is performed. Furthermore, in multimodal systems, the influence of single modalities on the subjective evaluation can often not be separated from the performance of the whole system.

In order to give an impression of the performance of EMOVOICE, the results of evaluation studies of Barthoc jr., E-Tree and EmoEmma, conducted by the respective system developers, are described shortly in the following.

6.5.1 Barthoc jr.

As described before, the humanoid robot head Barthoc jr. (see Figure 6.5) is capable of very realistic facial expressions. In particular, it can display five basic emotions. After displaying an emotional expression, the head moves back into a neutral expression before displaying the next emotion.

The mimic control interface (MiCo) of Barthoc jr. was integrated with EMOVOICE through the XML-based Communication Framework XCF [258] in order for the robot to be able to mimic the emotions conveyed in a user's voice with its facial expressions. A user study [102] was conducted to see how users accept an emotionally responsive robot and if they find interaction more natural or not. A further goal was to evaluate their impressions of the accuracy of EMOVOICE. Subjects were asked to sit in front of the robot and read out loud excerpts of the fairy tale "Rotkäppchen" (English: "Little Red Riding Hood"), acting as if they were reading it to a child. For each excerpt, a suitable emotion was suggested for the subjects to convey. The emotions included happiness, fear and neutral. The robot mirrored the emotions recognised by EMOVOICE with his face. As neutral was also the standard facial expression that the robot showed while the participant was still reading, a short head movement was executed to characterise it as a reaction to the user's utterance. After each sentence, participants were instructed to pause and observe Barthoc jr.'s reactions.

Overall, 28 test persons (13 females and 15 males) between 18 and 35 years old took part in the experiment. 17 subjects interacted with the emotionally responsive robot as described above. In the interaction with the remaining 11 subjects, Barthoc jr. always showed a neutral expression, with only the neutral head movement as confirmation to a fully read utterance. Comparisons of the two groups were intended to reveal whether emotional feedback was preferred by the participants or not. Directly after the experiment, which lasted about five minutes on average, participants were given a questionnaire that consisted of three groups of questions. With the first group of questions, the appropriateness of Barthoc jr.'s reactions with respect to the social situation was assessed. Participants rated on separate 5-point scales with 0 as worst and 4 as best evaluation the degree as to 1) Barthoc jr.'s facial expressions overall fit the situation, 2) whether Barthoc jr. recognised the emotional aspects of the story, and 3) whether Barthoc jr.'s response came close to a human counterpart. In all three ratings, the mimicry condition scored significantly better than the neutral condition, though both remained in the area between 1 and 2.

In the second block of questions users rated again on a 5-point rating scale the degree as to which individual facial expressions occurred too infrequently, just right, or too frequently. In general, emotions in the mimicry condition were rated as occurring too frequently, while the opposite was found for the neutral condition. However, this difference was only slightly significant.

The last question assessed the appropriateness of the timing of Barthoc jr.'s response. The average rating on a 5-point scale (-2 = too early, 0 = just right, +2 = too late) was 0.4 and 0.1 for the mimicry and the neutral condition, respectively, indicating that the timing of Barthoc jr.'s responses was quite good, but might appear more natural if Barthoc jr. responded a bit quicker.

Concluding, it can be said that the emotionally responsive robot was evaluated better than the neutral robot by the users, showing that an emotional robot is accepted better and is more believable, and that in general, users had the impression that EMOVOICE often recognised the correct emotion. Probably, however, users evaluated EMOVOICE's performance integrated into the robot more favourable than they would have if presented with the pure recognition results.

6.5.2 E-Tree

As presented earlier in Section 6.3.2, E-Tree is a multimodal Augmented Reality (AR) system of interactive art shown on a large screen. Speed of growth or shrinkage, colour and branching

6.5. Evaluation studies

of the tree are determined by affective input. Modalities include speech emotion recognition by EMOVOICE, multi-keyword spotting, where predefined sequences of words were recognised and assigned to an affective category, as well as video features for detecting and tracking facial geometries and optical flow within a video stream. Results of each modality are mapped into the PAD space. For example EMOVOICE was trained to recognise the classes positive-active, neutral and negative-passive that can be easily mapped onto PAD vectors with a dominance value of 0 in all three cases. The overall PAD vector is obtained by summing the vectors of all modalities. In order to smooth transitions between successive vectors, the current vector is always combined with previous results, where those that had occurred more recently have higher influence. The fusion model is described in detail in [87]. Unfortunately, keyword spotting was used almost never, due to several reasons including low detection and occurrence rates of the limited vocabulary and bugs in the fusion system.

Two user studies were conducted, both with the goal of evaluating the multimodal fusion system and whether E-Tree was an engaging interactive installation. 10 subjects participated in the first study [86], while the second was conducted with 16 test persons. Subjects acted in pairs to ease conversation. All pairs each had two runs of interaction with E-tree, which took about 5 minutes overall. In the second set of tests, additionally skin conductivity was measured to obtain a ground truth for arousal. Since a positive linear correlation of 0.79 was observed between skin conductivity and the values for arousal summed over all modalities, it is probable that at least the arousal dimension was recognised quite accurately of the multimodal system. It is difficult, however, to infer the accuracy of EMOVOICE from this, as it only contributed 11 % to the recognition of arousal. This is a general problem with multimodal and in particular real-time systems, that the influence of a single modality cannot be measured isolated. The contribution of EMOVOICE to all three PAD dimensions was 21 % on average. It is peculiar that the contribution to pleasure was much higher than that to arousal, though usually, acoustic features are better suited for the recognition of arousal. This could be due, however, to an exceptionally high relative influence of the video features on the recognition of arousal, instead to an absolute low contribution of the acoustic features. The contribution to dominance was 0 as it was kept constant in the classes recognised by EMOVOICE.

After the interaction, subjects were given a questionnaire (individually, not in pairs) with four semantic differential questions on a scale between 1 and 5 where 1 indicated the most negative opinion and 5 the most positive. In the first study, the questions concerned the users' interest in the installation, how realistic they found the tree's appearance, if it was responsive to their actions and how representative it was of their own emotions. As can be seen in Figure 6.10, the overall evaluation was quite positive showing that participants found the interaction engaging and novel, and felt they could affect the tree's behaviour. The relatively low score of the representativeness of the users' own emotions may partly result from low accuracy of the multimodal recognition

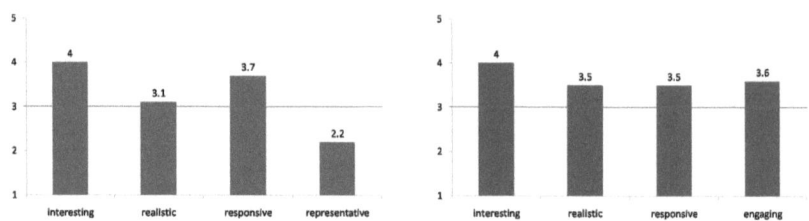

Figure 6.10: Questionnaire results of the first (left) and second (right) E-Tree user study.

components, though it is probably mainly due to that users did not intend to communicate their own actual emotional state to the tree, but just any emotions, including acted ones. For the second users study, the question regarding representativeness was therefore dropped in favour of a question about the engagement of the installation. Again, a generally positive overall response was received (see Figure 6.10). The higher evaluation of realism might reflect the improved graphics and tree behaviour in this second study.

Thus, the multimodal setting of E-Tree was well received by the users and recognition accuracy was seemingly good. EMOVOICE's share of this, however, cannot be specified exactly.

6.5.3 EmoEmma

The interactive storytelling system EmoEmma has been introduced previously in Section 6.3.1. As with Barthoc jr., interaction is restricted here solely to acoustic emotion processing by EMOVOICE which was trained to recognise the classes negative-active, negative-passive, neutral, positive-active and positive-passive. The story planning of the system changed according to the output of EMOVOICE. Word information was not used in the interaction, as in order to immerse deeply into the story, the user should be enabled to talk naturally and without restrictions of vocabulary. For a high accuracy, however, a speech recognition system would have required a limited vocabulary. Thus, the system relied only on the emotional tone of the voice for interaction.

EmoEmma was evaluated in a study with 14 users [42] with the aim to validate the overall concept of the system and assess user engagement. Subjects interacted with the system by taking over the part of one of the characters, Rodolphe, and were told that the main character Emma would react to the emotional content of their responses. However, they did not know to which aspects of affect Emma was reacting to, in particular, they did not know that the meaning of their utterances was not processed. Users were not restricted to answering Emma's question in the interaction, but could address Emma at any time. They could react negatively or positively to

6.5. Evaluation studies

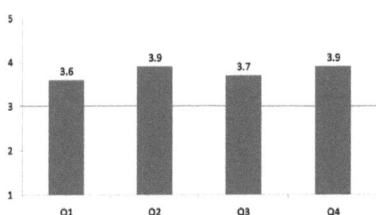

Figure 6.11: Averaged answers to the evaluation study of EmoEmma.

Emma, or choose not to react at all which also altered the planning of the story. The influence of the user's emotion on the development of the story was not obvious, as a reaction might occur immediately, with a delay or not at all. Each interaction took about three minutes and the end of the story was either negative, that is Emma left in despair, or positive when she finally engaged with Rodolphe. Both endings occurred approximately equally often. The story took longer if the user showed contradicting emotions in succession. However, it could also be the case that this was not intended by the user, but was due to the error rate of EMOVOICE, and users tried to compensate it by repeating utterances in the desired emotion until it was recognised correctly. In any case, the engagement level was quite high which is reflected by the high number of utterances (on average 7.4 per interaction) and by the length of these utterances (on average 7.5 words per utterance, with many longer than 10 words).

After the interaction, subjects were given a questionnaire with the following four questions:

Q1. I had the feeling that Emma understood what I was saying.

Q2. I had the feeling that Emma was responding emotionally to what I was saying.

Q3. I had the feeling that Emma was expressing emotions.

Q4. Emma's speech reflected the changes in the story.

Results to these questions are shown in Figure 6.11. Obviously, the test users had a very positive impression of the installation and perceived Emma as a believable character that responded appropriately to their interaction. These results can be taken as evidence for the effectiveness of EMOVOICE. Since it was the only mode of interaction, especially the positive evaluation of Emma's responsiveness is a direct result of the speech emotion recognition system.

On the one hand, the limitation of the emotion recognition to five categories (which actually is a relatively high number for the current state of the art) restricts the interactive story as the original novel of course contains a plethora of emotions. On the other hand, from the perspective of interactive storytelling and other digital entertainment systems, emotion recognition is a very favourable mode of interaction as it represents a more feasible alternative to large-scale natural language processing.

6.6 Conclusion

Based on the insights of the previous chapters, the framework EMOVOICE could be presented in this chapter, that allows for real-time emotion recognition from acoustic features of speech, can easily be integrated into other applications and provides tools for feature extraction and classifier training, as well as for the creation of training databases. In particular, the following aspects are integrated:

- Voice activity detection is used as an incremental and consistent speech segmentation method, that does not require an automatic speech recognition system.
- The acoustic feature extraction is completely automatic, effective and fast enough.
- Classification with Naïve Bayes is fast and robust.
- The highly variable expression of emotions in online applications is met by the training of general emotion classes. The training of a rest class as additional instrument is available in the framework without difficulty, but has not been used yet.

Furthermore, the practical applicability of EMOVOICE could be demonstrated by means of several already implemented applications and showcases under various conditions as well as with the help of user studies. Particularly the user studies showed that there is a considerable interest and acceptance of emotionally aware interfaces. The major challenges for the future will be to achieve higher accuracy, but also to deal better with the non-prototypical expression of emotions which should not or cannot be restricted in online applications. This could mean finding better and more natural stimuli for creating the training speech database, but could also include retraining of the classifier with data collected at run-time. Hereby, it should still be possible to rely on labels that arise from the situational context, though a detailed manually revised annotation would probably lead to significantly better results.

Chapter 7

Multimodal emotion recognition

As was shown in the previous chapters, acoustic emotion recognition is possible, but accuracies are still far from perfect or from human performance, when it comes to natural data. This is not surprising, as humans in general employ more information than just voice tone to judge the emotional state of a conservation partner, for example also word information, facial expressions, context, their acquaintance with the person etc. Thus, the situation for an automatic speech emotion recogniser can be compared to a human trying to detect the emotional state of an - unknown! - conversation partner speaking a foreign language on the telephone. Humans would not succeed too well in this task and an automatic system cannot be expected to perform better - at least now and in the next decades. Rather, it should be given as much information at hand as humans have, or at least as much as possible. Agreement of multiple modalities makes decisions more confident, whereas conflicts between modalities may help to detect social masking of emotions or to yield higher accuracy by finding more reliable modalities in particular situations.

So, for multimodal analysis, the modalities have to be combined in some way to give a single result. In general, this can be done on the *feature level*, that is, a joint feature vector is computed for all participating modalities that can be used as input for any suitable classifier, or on the *decision level*, where the classification results of feature vectors of the individual modalities are combined [175]. In the latter case, a fusion scheme has to define the result in cases where the individual modalities give conflicting results. The simplest fusion scheme is majority voting, however, this does not consider the confidence of the single decisions as some modalities may be better suited for the recognition of certain emotions. For instance, Fagel [74] found the visual modality to convey more reliable information on valence, and speech to be better suited for the recognition of activation. Therefore, other schemes have been explored such as weighting by posterior class probabilities [36], fusion by an emotion-specific multi-ensemble approach [130], or weighting by reliability of modalities for certain emotions or situations obtained e.g. from an independent training set or from perception experiments.

A further problem arising from multimodal fusion is that often, different modalities have different segmentation levels. For example, units in speech are naturally defined by speech activity. Facial expressions are continuously available, except when the face is turned away from the camera. Also the segment duration that is necessary for analysis differs. In speech, a word of 200 msec may already contain comprehensive information on the emotional state, for biosignal, in contrast, time periods at least longer than one second are necessary. Finally, the sampling rate of different modalities varies. The choice of synchronisation always depends on the particular modalities and the scenario, so there is no single general solution to this problem.

Previous work on multimodal emotion recognition has been addressed already in Section 3.7. This chapters presents four studies combining either context information (gender), biosignals, words or facial expressions with acoustic information. The acoustic feature set is always the EMOVOICE feature set (see Section 4.3), though in most cases in previous versions as the studies were conducted within a period of several years. Of course, covering all participating modalities with high quality requires the use of special databases instead of only the Berlin, Aibo and SmartKom databases. The studies on biosignals, linguistic information and facial expressions were conducted as cooperations by colleagues of the Universities of Bielefeld and Augsburg, who specialise in the respective modalities.

7.1 Gender information

The different anatomies of men and women, for example the length of the vocal tract length and shape of the larynx, have direct influence on the magnitude of acoustic measures commonly used as feature types for speech emotion recognition. Especially pitch is gender-dependent, with approximately 160 Hz separating male from female pitch in a neutral emotional state and normal conversational tone. This threshold is used by Abdulla and Kasabov [1] for separating genders to improve automatic speech recognition. But also most other features are gender-dependent to varying degrees. If the recognition system ignores this issue a misclassification of utterances might be the consequence. For instance, highly aroused utterances of men might be confused with neutral utterances of women. This is a great disadvantage for an automatic system, particularly compared to human listeners who would easily distinguish these two cases, even if they cannot see their conversational partner.

One possibility to deal with this phenomenon is to normalise gender-dependent features. For example, mean pitch can be normalised in terms of minimum and maximum pitch (see Section 4.3.1) in the respective segment or by the mean pitch of neutral speech of the same speaker [35]. Still, gender-specific emotion recognisers perform better than those with both genders mixed [137]. Ververidis and Kotropoulos [239] showed that the combined performance of a male and a

7.1. Gender information

female emotion recogniser is better than that of a gender-independent recogniser and also many other works separate genders before emotion recognition [8, 105, 128, 133, 222, 261, 262]. Of course, in order to do so, one must know the gender of a speaker. Ververidis and Kotropoulos [239] assumed gender information to be given *a priori*, but in most (online) applications this is not the case, unless the user is queried beforehand.

Therefore, a scheme is proposed here that precedes the emotion recognition with an automatic gender detection module which decides on whether a recogniser trained with male or a female emotions is used for classification of the respective utterance. In contrast to other works, in particular [1], which use only pitch to separate genders, the same feature extraction and selection methods as for emotion recognition are used here to improve the accuracy of gender detection on emotional speech. Still, since automatic gender detection will not be 100 % correct, this method could have a negative effect on the overall classification accuracy. On the other hand, combining gender and emotion recognition could also lead to an even higher improvement compared to a gender-independent emotion recognition system than an emotion recognition system based on correct gender information. Evaluations to investigate this question were performed only on the Berlin and the SmartKom databases as they contain adult speech. In the following, first, the classification framework will be described in detail in Section 7.1.1. Then, results are discussed in terms of relevant features (Section 7.1.2) and classification results (Section 7.1.3).

7.1.1 Combined gender and emotion recognition

Automatic gender detection usually achieves a high accuracy with little effort, so it is straight forward to integrate gender detection and emotion recognition into a two-stage recogniser, which first predicts the gender of the speaker and then, depending on the outcome, uses a gender-specific emotion recogniser as illustrated in Figure 7.1. All three recognisers can be built in the same manner, here by selecting the most relevant features for the given task from a large acoustic feature set by Best-First search (equivalent to Sequential Floating Forward Selection (SFFS)) with the accuracy of the Naïve Bayes classifier as selection criterion. Then, Naïve Bayes was used for classification of the reduced feature vectors. Feature selection as well as classification were carried out with the data mining software Weka [255]. The acoustic feature set differed slightly from the one presented in Section 4.3, as it was a previous version. Base feature types included raw pitch, energy, MFCCs, the centre of gravity of the spectrum, duration and pause. Statistical values were derived from the pitch, energy, MFCCs and spectral series as well as transformations of them. Overall, 1289 acoustic features were used. As argued above, it may also be beneficial for gender detection to rely on more features than just pitch because gender detection in emotional speech is more difficult. Especially those features in the acoustic set that are gender dependent should also be suitable for the detection of the gender.

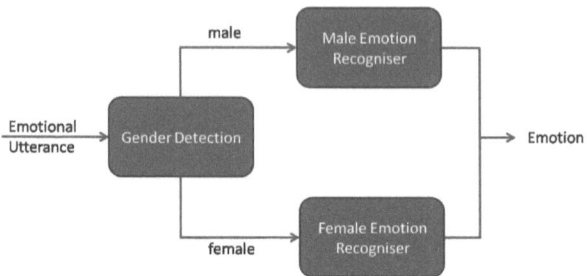

Figure 7.1: Combination of a gender detection system and two gender-specific emotion classifiers into a single emotion recognition system.

The Berlin database was evaluated by five-fold speaker-independent cross-validation as in the experiments in Chapter 5 with all seven classes (anger, joy, sadness, fear, disgust, boredom and neutral). Whole utterances were classified. For the SmartKom database, again only the dialogues from the mobile setting were used. This subset was split into a training set with 56 speakers (24 male and 32 female) and a test set with 14 speakers (7 male and 7 female) which is a 80/20 % splitting of the speakers. In contrast to the three-class task evaluated in Chapter 5, the original annotation of 12 emotional states was merged into a four-class problem applying again a scheme suggested by Batliner et al. [16]: neutral and unidentifiable utterances were mapped onto neutral, strong and weak joy and strong and weak surprise onto joy, strong and weak pondering/reflecting and strong and weak helplessness onto helplessness, and finally strong and weak anger onto anger. The distribution of emotions is 81 % neutral, 4 % joy, 10.5 % helplessness and 4.5 % anger, which is obviously very unbalanced and makes a good classification especially challenging. The units of emotional analysis were speech segments with no silent parts of more than 0.2 seconds based on voice activity detection. In both databases, only those utterances of the training set that were classified to the respective gender by the gender detection system were used for the training of the gender-specific emotion systems.

7.1.2 Relevant features

As described in the previous section, relevant features were selected by a best-first search through the feature space using the classification accuracy of a Naïve Bayes classifier on a test set as selection criterion. This always resulted in only a very small subset of the original 1289 features, but altogether, a wide range of features was selected in all tasks.

The selected features are discussed now, however, only classes of features are considered here, because a more in depth examination of single features is not practical. Since the number of

7.1. Gender information

Features	Berlin	SmartKom
Pitch	1	2
Energy	2	3
MFCC	17	7
Σ	20	12

Table 7.1: Relevant features for gender detection in the Berlin and SmartKom databases.

Feature types	gender-independent	male	female
Pitch	1	2	3
Energy	2	1	2
MFCC	17	7	15
Σ	20	10	20

Table 7.2: Relevant features for gender-independent, male and female emotion classification on the Berlin database.

features is very large and many features are highly correlated, it is not reasonable to make an assertion about a particular feature.

Relevant features for gender detection

The features used for gender detection in the two databases are listed in Table 7.1. Apparently, not only pitch-related features, but also MFCC and energy-related features are meaningful for gender detection, and in reverse also gender-dependent with respect to emotion recognition. In combination with other features, energy and MFCCs even play a more important role than pitch. Pitch, however, *is* the most discriminating feature when used alone.

Differences in relevant features for male and female emotions

The features selected for the classification of gender-independent, male and female emotions in the Berlin database are displayed in Table 7.2. It is notable that the energy features were all derived from the energy derivation series and that, compared to the features chosen for emotion recognition without gender information, few energy features are found. Almost half of the features in both male and female emotions were the first quartile or interquartile range of a feature series. The number of features was constrained by the number of instances in the least frequent class as represented in one of the five training sets and is therefore not meaningful in the case of the Berlin database.

Feature types	gender-independent	male	female
Pitch	1	3	1
Energy	3	1	1
MFCC	6	13	4
$\sum$	10	17	6

Table 7.3: Relevant features for gender-independent, male and female emotion classification on the SmartKom database.

The respective features for the SmartKom database are shown in Table 7.3. Numbers of features, which were not restricted for this database, are striking as for male emotions, almost three times as many features were selected. The number of features for the gender-independent classification lies in between. Again, a lot of features were the first quartile of a feature series.

Altogether, slightly more pitch-related features can be found in the gender-specific selected feature sets which confirms that pitch is more meaningful when gender effects are eliminated. Furthermore, no spectral or durational features were selected, neither for gender nor for emotion detection.

7.1.3 Results and discussion

In the following, results for gender detection with many acoustic features and with pitch only will be analysed. Furthermore, the combined gender and emotion detection system will be compared to an emotion recognition system without gender information and to one with information about the correct gender.

Gender detection

Table 7.4 shows the results for the gender detection on the two databases, 1) using only mean pitch as suggested in [137] and 2) after selection of the most relevant features from the original emotion recognition feature set of 1289 features. The optimised feature sets are in both cases significantly better compared to mean-pitch-only separation. The difference is higher for the Berlin database which contains a much higher proportion of emotional speech. It is therefore important not to use mean pitch only for gender detection in this kind of speech, and the hypothesis that opting for more features than only mean pitch when processing gender detection from emotional speech, as in this system, is confirmed.

7.1. Gender information   151

Database	mean pitch	optimised feature set
Berlin	69.4	90.3
SmartKom	87.6	91.9

Table 7.4: Accuracy in % for gender detection from mean pitch only and from the optimised feature set on the Berlin and SmartKom databases.

While emotion recognition is much harder for spontaneous than for acted speech, no such extreme difference could be observed for gender detection. This is not surprising, as gender differences are much more obvious and are hardly affected by audio quality. That the gender detection is even slightly better for spontaneous speech is presumably due to the larger number of training instances in the SmartKom database compared to the Berlin database and to the less emotional speech in it.

In the Berlin database, misclassified utterances were observed only for certain emotional categories: wrongly classified female utterances were found in disgusted, bored, sad and neutral emotional states, while wrongly classified male utterances were found in joy, fear and anger. For the SmartKom database, a similar observation could not be made.

Kotti and Kotropoulos [133] and Xiao et al. [261] reported higher accuracies for the same task on the Berlin database, Kotti and Kotropoulos [133] even achieved an accuracy of 100 %. However, both evaluations were not speaker-independent, though speaker-independence is considered here as essential in view of only ten speakers overall.

Emotion recognition

Table 7.5 shows the recognition results for emotion recognition without gender information, with gender information and with automatically detected gender information. Overall recognition accuracy (OA) and averaged class recognition accuracy (AA) are given. Combining gender and emotion recognition leads to an improvement of 0.6 % (Berlin database) respectively 6.7 % (SmartKom database) of the averaged classification rate AA compared to the gender-independent classification of emotions. At least in the case of the SmartKom database, this is a significant improvement, and the new system even outperformed the system with correct gender information. Gender detection should probably be interpreted here as a detection of male or female sounding voices rather than of male or female persons leading to a better partition of the data. In the Berlin database, emotions of utterances recognised as male were classified significantly worse than those recognised as female, causing an only slight improvement compared to the gender-independent case. Indeed, the rates for correct and recognised female emotions are very similar,

152   Chapter 7. Multimodal emotion recognition

Task		Berlin		SmartKom	
		OA	AA	OA	AA
Without gender information		81.1	79.2	75.1	34.4
With correct gender information	female	84.6	83.4	79.0	37.4
	male	87.9	80.0	75.4	38.9
	overall	86.0	83.5	76.7	38.0
With recognised gender information	female	84.9	83.9	81.4	41.2
	male	80.1	72.3	75.8	41.6
	overall	82.8	79.8	78.2	41.1

Table 7.5: Overall recognition rate (OA) and class-wise recognition rate (AA) in % for emotion detection using a gender-independent emotion recognizer, a gender-dependent emotion recognizer, and a combined gender and emotion recognizer in the Berlin and SmartKom databases.

while the rates for male emotions differ considerably.

These results disprove a possible objection against two consecutive classifiers, that they might perform worse than one classifier when the second classifier gets false input from the first classifier, and errors might sum up. The reasons for this are probably that the gender detection is very accurate, and that even if it fails, this is in cases which are "untypical" for the true gender and so can as well or even better be recognised by the emotion recogniser of the detected gender.

Though splitting the classification task into two is more time-consuming, time constraints can be neglected as classification can still be done in real-time when using a simple but fast algorithm like the Naïve Bayes classifier.

7.1.4 Conclusion

This section presented a new framework to improve emotion recognition from speech by making use of automatic gender detection. Starting from the fact that gender-specific emotion recognisers work more accurately than gender-independent ones, the basic emotion recognition system was extended by a preceding stage of gender detection that determines which gender-specific emotion recognition system should be used.

Furthermore, it could be shown that gender detection is more reliable if based not only on mean pitch, as usually proposed in the literature, but also on energy and MFCC features.

Tests were carried out on the Berlin database with acted and the SmartKom database with spontaneous emotions. Differences could be found in the relevant features for the classification of emotions in male and female voices. With two-stage emotion recognition an improvement of the recognition accuracy was achieved, which was even higher for the database with spontaneous emotions. For this database, gender separation does still not finally solve the problem of finding good discriminative features for emotion recognition, but it leads to a considerable improvement.

7.2 Biosignals

Emotions influence the physiological state of a person, causing the heart beating faster, sweating, or a faster breathing rate. Though humans cannot directly measure physiological changes, they may be able to observe the effects. For instance, a high pulse may cause a reddish face colour, a high respiratory rate can be heard or may manifest itself in breathy speech; sweating may be visible or sensible when shaking hands. These physiological signals can also be measured by sensors that are attached directly to the body. Wearing sensors may seem obstructive and not very user friendly, especially if they limit mobility because of cables or to assure safe signal measurement. On the other hand, there are also situations where wearing sensors is not disturbing, or not much, for example, when sitting in front of a desktop PC, when exercising particular sports where athletes wear pulse monitors anyway, or in a medical context. Furthermore, sensors are being refined continuously, enabling for example wireless data transmission, making sensors smaller and even disappear in the environment, e. g. the clothes, and also increasing their robustness.

Several studies have been conducted so far on using physiological signals for emotion recognition, among them [129, 160, 179]. Emotions are usually induced by exposure to visual or acoustic stimuli. Sensors include heart rate, skin conductivity, temperature, muscle activity, respiration rate, electromyogram and electrocardiogram. Reported recognition rates are quite high with 81 % [179], 83 % [160], and 70 % [129] for 8/6/4 classes and 1/29/3 subjects, respectively. Emotional characteristics are to a high extent subject-dependent [241], yielding a big discrepancy between single speaker and multiple speaker recognition accuracies.

Biosignals complement speech well for emotion recognition, as they are available continuously, so that emotions may not only recognised while the user is speaking. On the other hand, some biosignals are not useful at certain points in time, for example respiratory rate during speaking, or pulse rate changes during body movements, which may not be related to emotions. Another advantage of biosignals over speech is that it is harder for a user to deliberately manipulate them, thus making them less subject of social masking.

In this section, work published in [131] is presented. This includes first a Wizard-of-Oz experiment that was conducted to collect a corpus with spontaneous vocal and physiological affective data. The corpus is then used to evaluate both modalities individually and combined by three different fusion methods, i. e. at the feature level, at the decision level and by a hybrid integration scheme combining feature and decision level fusion.

7.2.1 Experiment for data collection

A modified version of the quiz "Who wants to be a millionaire?" was used as a testbed for the experiment. Questions along with options for answers were presented on a screen whose design was inspired by the corresponding quiz shows on German TV. In order to make sure that a sufficient amount of speech data was obtained, the subjects were not offered any letters as abbreviations for the single options (as is common in quiz shows on TV), but were forced to produce longer utterances. The user's current score was indicated as well as the amount of money she/he may win or lose depending on the correctness of the answer. All three test subjects were students — three males in their twenties, all native speakers of German, which was also the language for the experiment. Each of the sessions took about 45 minutes to complete. The subjects interacted with a virtual quiz master via free speech and were at the same time connected to four biosensors to record electromyogram (EMG), electrocardiogram (ECG), skin conductivity (SC) and respiration changes (RSP).

The virtual quiz master was controlled by a human wizard and led the user through four phases of the quiz to elicit emotions corresponding to the four quadrants of a two-dimensional arousal/valence emotion space: low arousal/positive valence, high arousal/positive valence, low arousal/negative valence, high arousal/negative valence.

In the first phase, users were offered a set of very easy questions leading to a slight increase of the score to elicit low arousal and positive valence. In the next phase, high arousal and positive valence were stimulated by extremely difficult questions but where each answering option was correct and lead to a high gain of money. During the third phase, the user was stressed by a mix of solvable and difficult questions that lead, however, not to a drastic loss of money. Furthermore, the agent provided boring information related to the topics addressed in the questions to evoke negative valence and low arousal. Finally, the user was made frustrated by unsolvable questions that he could only answer incorrectly and similar sounding answers that the simulated speech recognition system of the agent recognised incorrectly, resulting in a high loss of money and leading to high arousal and negative valence.

Elicited emotions can be regarded as quite natural, however, with only three subjects, the amount of data is small.

7.2.2 Recognition of emotions from speech and biosignals

In the following, the unimodal systems to recognise emotions from speech and biosignals are described shortly, as well as three different fusion methods.

For both speech and physiological signals, Fisher's linear discriminant function (LDF), a linear combination of components weighted by known prior probability, was used to classify four emotional states, i.e., positive/high, positive/low, negative/high, and negative/low. Then, sequential forward feature selection (SFS) was employed to obtain a new subset of features which contained the most emotion-relevant features maximising the performance of the classifier. In order to make the best out of the relatively small amount of available data, leave-one-out cross-validation was used to train and test all classifiers.

Speech

As already mentioned earlier, synchronisation of different signal types, in particular with different sampling rates, is non-trivial. Due to their lower sampling rate, the physiological signals need a longer analysis window than would be needed for the speech signal. Therefore, all samples associated to one questions were used as one classification unit. For speech, it would have been possible to analyse each signal segment with speech activity separately and then fuse all belonging to the same question. However, in order to keep conditions for biosignals and speech as similar as possible to enable better comparability, all signal segments with speech activity belonging to the same question were analysed together. As a consequence, about 60 speech segments per subject were obtained. Again a feature extraction version previous to the one presented in Section 4.3 was used which was identical to the version described in the previous section (7.1.1) except that the spectral features were not yet available, resulting in 1280 features overall. In order to remove redundant features, correlation-based feature subset selection [98] was applied to the acoustic feature set. This yielded new subsets of 15–20 dimensional feature vectors. Numbers vary as for every task (single/multiple subjects) different features were removed, but a clear tendency towards one or two pitch minima or maxima related features and the rest being MFCC related features could be observed.

Physiological signals

All segments of physiological signal were at first lowpass-filtered with pertinent cutoff-frequencies, which were empirically determined for each biosensor channel, in order to remove noisy samples. In the case of single-subject classification baselines of all four signals were calculated. Overall 26 features per segment were extracted, including typical statistics such as mean and

System	A	B	C	All
Speech only	68	**75**	76	52
Bio only	77	60	85	53
Feature fusion	**78**	**75**	**92**	**66**
Decision fusion	77	**75**	85	57
Hybrid fusion	77	**75**	88	60

Table 7.6: Uni- and bimodal recognition results for speech and physiological signals in % for single users and all users together. The best result in each column is printed in bold.

standard deviation as well as spectral/subband features from the periodic signals (ECG, RSP). Each segment varied between 10 to 115 seconds in length (on average 42 seconds). Finally, all feature vectors were normalised by standard deviation and mean.

Bimodal emotion recognition

Three different fusion approaches were implemented for bimodal emotion recognition. In feature level fusion, the features of both modalities were merged into a single vector and classified. In decision level fusion, the outputs of the two unimodal classifiers for speech and biosignals were combined using different schemes, for example posterior probability criteria as used in [36] or majority voting based on the recognition rates of each emotion from the unimodal classifiers. Finally, a new hybrid scheme of both feature and decision level fusion was employed, in which the output of feature level fusion was used as an additional input to the decision level fusion stage.

7.2.3 Results and discussion

The data was classified for the single subjects (users A, B, C) and for all subjects together since this was supposed to give a deeper insight how the bimodal systems could improve the results of unimodal emotion recognition. Table 7.6 shows the results of unimodal and bimodal classification for all four tasks. Obviously, the emotions of users A and C were more accurately recognised by using biosignals (77 % and 85 %) than by their voice (68 % and 76 %) whereas it was the inverse case for user B (75 % for voice and 60 % for biosignals).

Recognition accuracies for the unimodal systems vary not only between subjects, but also for the individual emotional states. For instance, classification of the physiological data shows a poor result of only 36 % for negative valence/low arousal while the speech system achieved 60 % for the same emotional state. In contrast, recognition accuracy of positive valence/low arousal was just 38 % for the speech system, but 58 % for the physiological system. Table 7.6 also shows that bimodal recognition accuracy was always equal or higher than unimodal accuracy. Best results were obtained for feature level fusion and led to an improvement of 13 % compared to the best unimodal system (biosignals in this case) when classifying all users. While very high results can be achieved in the single subject tasks (up to 92 %), the results for all subjects are, as expected, with accuracies between 52 and 66 % considerably lower.

7.2.4 Conclusion

This section presented the fusion of speech and biosignals for emotion recognition on data collected in a Wizard-of-Oz study. The analysis revealed differences in the discriminative abilities of the unimodal systems, with respect to particular classes and subjects, which is a strong argument for multimodal recognition. Thus, several fusion methods were evaluated and compared with the unimodal recognition methods. Indeed, the best results were obtained by feature level fusion. In this case, not only single user, but also multiple user emotion classification could be improved compared to the unimodal methods. Since the data was only labelled based on the assumption that the four phases of the experiment actually succeeded in eliciting the desired emotions, even higher accuracy might be achieved by individual labelling of each turn.

7.3 Linguistic information

An obvious source of affective information to combine with acoustic features is linguistic information. If a robust speech recogniser is available, linguistic features can directly be integrated with acoustic features, as the problem of alignment of different units does not exist. In this section, an experiment on a transcribed audio corpus is presented which has been published in [172]. The experiment is insofar hypothetical, as it assumes a perfect speech recogniser. In real conditions, a recogniser cannot be expected to work with very high accuracy on arbitrary speech. Rather, a keyword spotting approach would be applicable.

Studies integrating acoustic and linguistic information have been conducted for example by Schuller et al. [207] who fused acoustic features with linguistic Bag-of-Word features where word stems have an entry in the feature vector with the frequency of their occurrence in the respective utterance, and by Truong and Raaijmakers [232] who combined acoustic features with N-Grams of words and speech rate as number of words per seconds. Both studies achieved slight improvements over acoustic or linguistic features only based classification.

Class	neg/high	neg/low	pos/high	pos/low	neutral	Σ
#	176	103	24	148	123	574

Table 7.7: Distribution of turns in the SAL database on the 5 emotion classes negative valence/high arousal (neg/high), negative valence/low arousal (neg/low), positive valence/high arousal (pos/high), positive valence/low arousal (pos/low) and neutral.

The work described in this section differs from previous work in that three types of linguistic features are examined, namely lexical features that exploit the occurrence of a word, stylometric features that rely on formal characteristics of words such as occurring letters or the length, and finally deictic features from the occurrence of deictic words, which includes demonstratives, time/place references etc. Furthermore, it is discussed whether the consideration of a unit in context, here previous utterances, and whether discretising acoustic features can augment multimodal recognition accuracy or not. Fusion of acoustic and linguistic features is again done on the feature and on the decision level. In the following, first the database used for the experiment is presented. Then, the acoustic and linguistic feature sets are described. Last, results are presented and discussed.

7.3.1 The SAL database

The Sensitive Artificial Listener (SAL) database [66] from Queens University, Belfast, was chosen for the experiment because it contains spontaneous speech from a general vocabulary. Emotions were induced in the subjects in a Wizard-of-Oz experiment by communication with an artificial listener simulated by a human operator that could have four different personalities (optimistic, confrontational, pragmatic and depressed) to encourage the user to engage in corresponding emotional styles.

Dialogue turns were transcribed manually and emotions in the turns were annotated with Feeltrace [55] along the continuous emotion dimensions valence and arousal. In total, SAL contains 27 dialogues (672 turns). In order to map the continuous Feeltrace values onto discrete classes, each turn was assigned the majority vote among all annotators of the Feeltrace values at the end of the turn. Since Feeltrace requires real-time labelling and there is therefore a lag between actual time of occurrence and labelling, the annotation at the end of the turn can be considered as reliable for the turn. Only those 574 turns where majority voting was possible were used for analysis here. Table 7.7 shows the distribution of the turns on the classes negative valence/high arousal, negative valence/low arousal, positive valence/high arousal, positive valence/low arousal and neutral.

7.3. Linguistic information

7.3.2 Feature sets

In the following, the acoustic and linguistic feature sets will be described. The linguistic feature set contained three types of linguistic features: lexical, stylometric and deictic information. Features were calculated for each turn, and for each turn including the seven previous turns in a dialogue because long units are advantageous for the linguistic features, as the number of words in single turns is often little. The length of the context was limited to seven as this was empirically found to be a good value. The classifier used throughout the experiments was SVM from Weka.

Acoustic features

The acoustic feature set contained the 1316 features of the feature extraction version 1.0 of EMOVOICE based on pitch, signal energy, MFCCs, the short-term frequency spectrum, and the harmonics-to-noise ratio. It was analysed in two variants: with continuous feature values and with discretised values. Discretisation was initially intended to make the acoustic features more comparable to the discrete linguistic features, but proved to have beneficial effects on accuracy, as will be shown later. It partitioned the continuous value range of a feature into a finite number of intervals using Fayyad and Irani's Minimum Description Length method [75] as implemented in Weka.

Linguistic features

For each of the three types of linguistic features (lexical, stylometric and deictic) several feature sets were calculated and evaluated; then, the ten best sets were used for evaluation in the multimodal experiments. In detail, the sets were:

- 29 lexical feature sets. Each set was a word occurrence vector of the s/n most frequent words in the SAL database where $s = 2033$ is the number of words in the SAL vocabulary and $n \in [1..29]$.

- 31 stylometric feature sets containing features based on letters, word length, digrams, standard deviation of word length and sentence length in words, the latter represented as frequency vector.

- 63 deictic feature sets containing features based on demonstratives whether used as determiners or pronouns, time and place references, third person word forms as well as 526 stopwords obtained from Weka. Though stopwords are no deictic words they are also a

| | | | Discretised acoustic features | |
Feature set	turn	turn + context	turn	turn + context
acoustic	39.2	57.7	45.7	**66.0**
lexical	36.9	**61.7**	—	—
stylometric	38.6	**61.3**	—	—
deictic	30.4	**62.9**	—	—
feature level fusion	46.7	62.3	52.8	**67.5**
decision level fusion	43.0	64.2	45.9	**64.9**
optimal decision level fusion	*71.5*	*76.5*	*73.7*	***77.8***

Table 7.8: Results for acoustic, lexical, stylometric and deictic feature sets and their fusion on feature and decision level, with and without turn context or discretisation of acoustic features. Averaged class-wise accuracy is given in %, best results in bold.

categorisation of the function of a word and thus fit best into the deictic feature set compared to the lexical and stylometric sets. The deictic features were evaluated as frequency vector.

7.3.3 Results and discussion

For decision level fusion, majority voting of the results of all four feature sets (acoustic, lexical, stylometric and deictic) was performed. If no majority could be established, gradually those sets were left out that had achieved the lowest accuracy in unimodal recognition until either majority voting was possible or only one set remained. Of course, also more sophisticated fusion schemes could have been deployed, however, the goal of this study was only a first exploration of the potential of fusing the underlying linguistic and acoustic feature sets. Further investigations on fusion schemes may follow. For feature level fusion, all four feature sets were merged into one single set. Table 7.8 shows the result for all feature sets individually and together in decision level and feature level fusion, respectively. The results given for *optimal decision level fusion* are those values that could be obtained in the case of perfect fusion when at least one feature set would classify a particular instance correctly and this set would be chosen for classification. The difference between these values and the actually achieved accuracies shows how much improvement would be possible with a better fusion scheme, while the difference between 100 % and the optimal fusion results shows what could be gained by improvements of the unimodal recognition rates.

Obviously, multimodality, context and discretisation all increased accuracy. However, the difference between single sets and multimodal accuracy (by feature level fusion) was, due to the small data set size, only statistically significant if no context was considered. Furthermore, if context was considered neither fusion at the feature level nor at the decision level could be regarded as superior as both achieved about the same recognition results.

Using context, better results could be achieved for both acoustic as well as linguistic features This result may hold only for this particular database as such a high number of context turns might be problematic in cases where emotions change rapidly. The discretisation of acoustic features remarkably improved classification rates. After discretisation, acoustic features scored better than linguistic features even if context was considered. The high impact of discretisation is probably due to the small size of the database. However, it could be shown that the effect still holds up to a considerable size [246].

7.3.4 Conclusion

This section presented a study of feature and decision level fusion of acoustic and linguistic features. Discretised acoustic features turned out to outperform linguistic features, while fusion led to only slight improvements. The optimal decision level fusion accuracy showed that there is still room for improvement of both the unimodal feature sets as well as the fusion scheme in the future. Unimodal accuracies could probably be improved by feature selection as well as by optimising features or by adding more modalities, while the fusion scheme may yield higher results by weighting feature sets, based on data-driven or perceptually inspired criteria.

7.4 Facial expressions

Facial expressions are, together with speech, the most obvious means for human-human affect recognition. This is equally true in human-computer interaction, as microphone and camera are straight-forward to use with a PC. Regarding the camera, the setting has to make sure that the face is in the scope of the camera. Similar to silent periods in speech emotion recognition, of course, no emotion can be recognised if the face is not visible. In previous work, so far, speech and facial expressions were combined in the offline analysis of actors [36, 38] or spontaneous emotions databases [266]. Studies reached about 3–6 % absolute improvement of the best unimodal recognition rate which is not an immense.

This section describes an exploratory study of bimodal emotion recognition on the acted DaFEx database, which was presented in [186]. In comparison to previous work, though the analysis is done offline the system is in principal capable of online processing, and in particular, faces of talking persons are analysed. Furthermore, the unimodal subsystems differ those used from

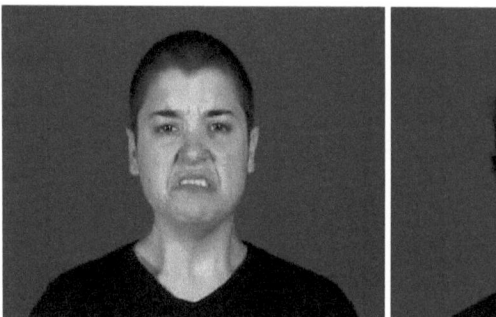 

Figure 7.2: Examples for facial expressions of actors in the DaFEx database [23]

existing approaches, for instances the acoustic feature sets in audio-visual recognition are often limited to pitch and energy features only, and the fusion scheme based on a Bayesian network has not been applied to audio-visual emotion recognition so far. The system is intended to be used for human-robot interaction in future work. The unimodal recognition modules as well as results and their interpretation will be presented in the following, preceded by a description of the database.

7.4.1 The DaFEx database

The *Da*tabase of *F*acial *Ex*pressions (DaFEx) [23] contains short videos of eight Italian actors (4 male, 4 female) that portray seven emotions (happiness, surprise, fear, sadness, anger, disgust, as well as neutral). Examples can be found in Figure 7.2. Each actor had six repetitions of each emotion in three intensities (high, medium, low), resulting in $8 \times 7 \times 6 \times 3 = 1008$ instances. In four of the repetitions, a phonetically rich and visemically balanced sentence ("In quella piccola stanza vuota c'era però soltanto una sveglia." — English: "In that little empty room there was only an alarm clock.") was uttered. In the other two repetitions, the actors remained silent.

Since the goal of the study described here was multimodal recognition, only the subset of DaFEx with speaking actors was used, consisting of 672 instances. Due to fan lights and air-conditioning in the recording room, there is a considerable background noise in the speech recordings which is even audible after noise filtering, thus degrading the quality of the speech. The video quality, in contrast, is very good.

The data was evaluated by 4-fold cross validation with each split containing one repetition. Since the sample size is very small, the evaluation was not speaker independent.

7.4.2 Recognition of emotions from facial expressions and speech

Now, the two unimodal systems to recognise emotions from speech and facial expressions as well as the fusion scheme will be described shortly. Though the analysis is offline, both unimodal systems are capable of online processing. For the speech module, EMOVOICE, this has already been shown in previous chapters of this book, but also for the facial expression module, real-time applicability has been demonstrated [187]. The classifier used for all evaluations was SVM.

Speech

For the recognition of emotions from speech, EMOVOICE as described in Section 6.1 was used. The original feature set of 1451 features was reduced by correlation-based feature subset selection to 71 pitch, energy, MFCC, spectral, voicing and voice quality features. One feature vector was obtained for each of the 672 utterances or video clips.

Facial expressions

The algorithm used for facial expression recognition has been described previously by Rabie et al. [187] and is illustrated by Figure 7.3. First, face pose and basic facial features, such as nose, mouth and eyes, were recognised by the face detection module [41]. Then, based on these detected features, facial shape and texture parameters were extracted with active appearance models (AAMs) [53] which were used as feature vector for the classification. Appearance models are calculated by multiple PCA, triangulation and image warping of a linear shape model that was obtained from a training set of faces with shape-defining landmarks. Active appearance models compute the parameters iteratively for new instances, starting from an initial estimation of its shape. One feature vector was calculated for each image frame and classified individually. In order to obtain a result for the whole video clip that can be fused with the acoustic recognition result majority voting over all image frames in one clip was applied.

Fusion scheme

Fusion was performed on the decision level using a Bayesian network. Input to the network were the unimodal recognition results with the prediction probabilities for each class. The probabilities of the network nodes were based on the confusion matrices of the individual classifiers. Using the class probabilities as input and basing the node probabilities on the confusion matrices led to a weighting of the modalities according to their ability to recognise certain classes, taking into account that different modalities predict particular classes with different accuracies. This is expected to give better results than a simple majority voting of the best result for each modality.

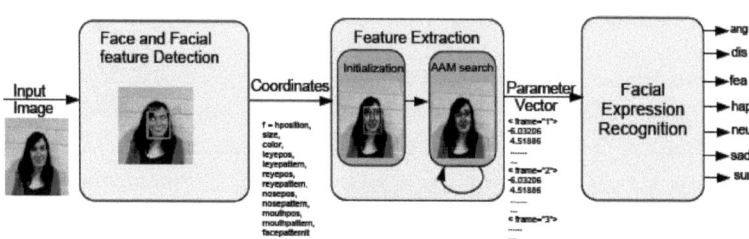

Figure 7.3: Overview of the architecture of the emotional facial expression recognition system [187].

Modality	Anger	Disgust	Fear	Happiness	Neutral	Sadness	Surprise	Total
Acoustic	68.1	51.4	48.6	50.0	87.5	69.4	58.3	61.9
Visual	94.4	73.6	58.3	80.6	79.2	72.2	62.9	74.5
Bimodal	81.9	87.5	52.8	86.1	86.1	75.0	77.8	78.2

Table 7.9: Unimodal and bimodal recognition results of speech and facial expressions in % on the DaFEx database.

7.4.3 Results and discussion

Table 7.9 shows the unimodal and bimodal recognition results, for each of the seven classes and in total. Obviously, results obtained from facial expressions are considerably higher than those from acoustic features. Only for neutral, the acoustic recognition exceeds the visual recognition. This may have several reasons, including the reduced quality of the speech recordings by background noises and that the visual modality had, because of frame-based evaluation, more training instances. Neutral speech may have been portrayed in a heterogeneous way by the actors, thus easily subsuming other classes as disgust, fear and surprise and reaching a high class accuracy.

It was further observed that the visual classifier makes only few confusions on the evaluation dimension, while the speech classifiers discriminates better along the activation dimension. Thus, it can be expected that the two modalities complement each other well.

The fact that class accuracies differ considerably between the modalities — for example anger, disgust and happiness are considerably better recognised by the visual modality while the opposite holds for neutral — argues in favour of the weighted fusion scheme. Indeed, a significant though not enormous improvement could be achieved by fusion, with an improvement of 4 % resp. 16 % over the visual resp. acoustic modality. Four classes, disgust, sadness, happiness, surprise were recognised more accurately in bimodal classification. Overall, bimodality leads to high accuracies of more than 75 % for all classes except fear where the accuracy lies between the unimodal rates, as both modalities seem to encode redundant information in this case.

7.4.4 Conclusion

In this section a study of decision level fusion of acoustic and visual affective cues for emotion recognition was presented. A fusion scheme weighting each class by the class accuracy of the individual modalities on a test set was applied as it was observed that acoustic and visual classifiers had different abilities to predict particular classes. This is in line with hypotheses of modality fusion in human perception [74]. In unimodal recognition, the visual modality was superior, which may be due to the database where the acoustic channel had worse quality. However, Caridakis et al. [38] and Zeng et al. [266] also achieved lower results for the acoustic modality (Busso et al. [36] not) though on different databases, and likewise Chetty and Wagner [46] who also used the DaFEx database but for the task of audio-visual speaker verification obtained worse results for speech than for visual or audio-visual analysis. This may hint at the visual modality giving better results when used alone than speech, but this cannot yet be taken as a general result as the databases on which evaluations have been conducted are very limited in size and number. As in the other studies, bimodal recognition could improve the accuracy significantly here. However, from the complementary performances of the unimodal systems an even higher improvement could have been expected and suggests further refinement of the fusion scheme.

7.5 Conclusion

This chapter presented four bimodal studies combining acoustic information on emotions with context, physiological signals, word information and facial expressions. Accuracy could indeed by increased by multimodal analysis in all four cases compared to unimodal performance. Several fusion schemes as well as hierarchical classification were explored, and feature level fusion could slightly outperform decision level fusion in the two cases where both schemes were applied. Overall, results suggest that multimodal analysis improves results and is more reliable, so a combination of more than two modalities seems promising. However, studies are limited by the sparsity of high quality multimodal corpora with arbitrary modality combinations. Furthermore, for application in practice, the problem of different time scales and signal sampling rates, and that some modalities are unavailable at certain points in time has to be solved.

Chapter 8

Final conclusion and outlook

This book investigated real-time automatic emotion recognition from acoustic features of speech under various aspects, including suitable methodology, integration into affective application and multimodal fusion. In particular, the research questions raised in Chapter 1 can be answered now:

1. **What is suitable methodology for emotion recognition when considering real-time constraints?**

   As a pattern recognition problem, speech emotion recognition can be decomposed into three main sub-problems, audio segmentation, feature extraction and classification that all need to consider real-time constraints.

   With regard to audio segmentation, a systematic comparison and discussion of optimal segment length was carried out that has not been conducted so far on this scale across databases. Furthermore, chunking an audio stream based on voice activity detection, which is a novel way of audio segmentation for speech emotion recognition, was found to give the best compromise in terms of accuracy, fast calculation (Section 5.2) and easy integration into an online system (Section 6.1). In contrast, most state-of-the-art systems use utterance-like units that are conveniently provided with the database annotation but are usually not suited for online recognition.

   Relevant acoustic features for emotion recognition proved to be very database and speech type dependent (Section 5.3). While for read, acted speech, pitch features were dominant, the less emotional the data was, the higher was the importance of MFCC and spectral features. Though recently, more spontaneous emotions databases exist and a considerable amount of studies on these have emerged, still many researchers base their investigations on acted speech, arguing that this is representative of natural emotions while at the same time easier to collect. The result that different features are relevant for acted and spontaneous emotions however is a strong recommendation towards the analysis of spontaneous emotions instead of acted emotions.

When evaluating classes individually in each database, MFCCs also proved to be the most generally successful feature type. In general, however, the proposed feature set consisting of pitch, energy, MFCC, duration, spectral, voicing and voice quality features proved to be powerful, especially if reduced by selecting features with low correlation (CFS) which proved to be the most robust selection method across databases.

A comparison of classification algorithms revealed that while with more prototypical data (Berlin), Support Vector Machines (SVM) and Multi-Layer Perceptrons (MLP) that are traditionally known as very accurate classifiers in speech emotion recognition performed slightly better, Naïve Bayes, a very simple classifier, yielded best results for more natural data, and is considerably faster at the same time (Section 5.4). However, there can be found more comprehensive classifier comparisons in the literature (e. g. [173, 207]), as classification algorithms were not the main focus of this book.

2. **To what extent is it possible to build application dependent recognisers? How can these recognisers be trained?**

In order to ease the creation of application specific classifiers compared to other speech emotion recognition toolboxes (e. g. OpenEar [73]), a workflow was designed for recording speech databases of emotions elicited from psychologically grounded stimuli (Section 6.2). The number of applications that have already been developed with EMOVOICE using this workflow shows that it is easily feasible for software developers to integrate EMO-VOICE in their application (Section 6.3) and the conducted user studies revealed that robustly working systems with good accuracy and user acceptance can be produced (Section 6.5).

3. **How much can further information such as words, gender, bio sensor data and facial gestures contribute to improve speech emotion recognition?**

Accuracy could indeed by increased by multimodal analysis in all four cases compared to unimodal performance which suggests that multimodality in general improves results and is more reliable (Chapter 7). However, more extensive studies are limited by the sparsity of high quality multimodal corpora. Furthermore, for application in practice, the problem of different time scales and signal sampling rates, and that some modalities are unavailable at certain points in time has to be solved.

Of course, in this book the field of emotion recognition could not be processed fully and the addressed problems not ultimately be solved. The major impediment for speech emotion recognition in practice remains accuracy which should reach values close to 100 % in the long term in order for emotion recognition to be distributed in a wide range of application scenarios. In artistic, playful applications that are made for entertainment, users are probably very sympathetic and may even later re-interpret their own input to suit the system response. With software that is purely functional and that is supposed to support work or learning, humans often implicitly assume machines to work perfect, though this is not realistic as even humans are not able to reach perfect recognition rates in this task. A further problem for emotion recognition in applications is that human-computer interaction is often not very emotional so that application fields are limited. This, however, could change as more and more affective applications emerge: currently, users may not interact emotionally because they do not expect an emotional response. Still, they would feel more comfortable to interact with an emotionally responsive machine.

Improving accuracy probably requires more work regarding features than regarding classifiers. For EMOVOICE this would also mean to integrate word information in the long run. Though this has been deliberately left out, it is needed to achieve human-comparable results for emotion recognition, as soon as more robust and more accurate speech recognition systems are available in the future.

Also temporal information, that has been included into the emotion model of E-Tree, would be useful to integrate already during classification, as the emotional state of a person is not likely to change very quickly or in an extreme direction. For instance, true anger usually lasts over more than just a few units of time (at least if they are reasonably short), and abrupt changes from strong anger to strong joy are not very likely to occur within a short time span. Therefore, it makes sense to use this knowledge to weight classification results or discard single occurrences of one emotion in a long sequence of another emotion.

Further concrete enhancements of EMOVOICE could include the improvement of the training stimuli, that is making them more natural and situation dependent, and integrating classification into continuous emotion dimensions, maybe not as regression from continuous training trace data, but as interpolation from base points in a dimensional model (corresponding to discrete classes). Classification models of the base points could be obtained from annotated training databases so that there is no need for continuously labelled databases. Moreover, the effects in online speech emotion recognition of situational factors such as different microphones or competing speakers have been identified as significant, here as well as in previous work, but have not yet been examined closely.

Finally, appropriate methodology for evaluating online systems, that differs from methodology for offline systems, will get more important, the more systems emerge. Thus, a formal framework for this methodology would be useful taking into account the interplay of application presentation and recognition module in user evaluation. In particular, it would be interesting which differences in accuracy are just noticeable by humans.

The most important factors in future speech emotion recognition will probably primarily concern further research on relevant acoustic features and the collection of more speech databases with natural emotions. Trends in classification are likely to concentrate on improvements on a meta-level (so for example intelligent class groupings in hierarchical classification) than on the algorithms themselves. The choice of investigated emotions should be oriented rather at what is relevant in specific applications and not at available databases. For example, it is arguable if an appropriate response to anger in a game can actually be found: may the game be so arrogant as to tell the user to calm down or should it rather refrain from reacting to anger? Moreover, the characteristics of some few emotions or emotion related states may be easier found empirically by observation. As an example, confusion is marked in many situations by a chopped speaking style interlaced with many small pauses and it would be straight-forward to model it directly with durational characteristics than with all kinds of possible acoustic features. Furthermore, multimodal approaches will certainly increase in the future.

Hopefully, the increasing interest in research on affect recognition from speech will remain and expand also to commercial products, so that with combined efforts soon powerful systems can be built letting many people benefit from software that considers their affect and therefore better meets human needs in interaction.

THE END

Bibliography

[1] W. H. Abdulla and N. Kasabov, "Improving speech recognition performance through gender separation," in *Proceedings of the International Conference on Artificial Neural Networks and Expert Systems (ANNES)*, Dunedin, New Zealand, 2001, pp. 218–222.

[2] D. W. Aha, D. Kibler, and M. K. Albert, "Instance-based learning algorithms," *Machine Learning*, vol. 6, no. 1, pp. 37–66, January 1991.

[3] H. Ai, D. J. Litman, K. Forbes-Riley, M. Rotaru, J. Tetreault, and A. Purandare, "Using system and user performance features to improve emotion detection in spoken tutoring dialogs," in *Proceedings of the 9th International Conference on Spoken Language Processing (INTERSPEECH)*, Pittsburgh, PA, USA, September 2006.

[4] K. Alter, E. Rank, S. A. Kotz, U. Toepel, M. Besson, A. Schirmer, and A. D. Friderici, "Affective encoding in the speech signal and in event-related brain potentials," *Speech Communication*, vol. 40, no. 1–2, pp. 61–70, April 2003.

[5] A. Álvarez, I. Cearreta, J. M. López, A. Arruti, E. Lazkano, B. Sierra, and N. Garay, "Feature subset selection based on evolutionary algorithms for automatic emotion recognition in spoken Spanish and standard Basque language," in *Proceedings of the 9th International Conference on Text, Speech and Dialogue (TSD)*, Brno, Czech Republic, September 2006, pp. 565–572.

[6] N. Amir, S. Ron, and N. Laor, "Analysis of an emotional speech corpus in Hebrew based on objective criteria," in *Proceedings of the ISCA Tutorial and Research Workshop on Speech and Emotion*, Newcastle, Northern Ireland, UK, September 2000, pp. 29–33.

[7] J. Ang, R. Dhillon, A. Krupski, E. Shriberg, and A. Stolcke, "Prosody-based automatic detection of annoyance and frustration in human-computer dialog," in *Proceedings of the 7th International Conference on Spoken Language Processing (INTERSPEECH)*, Denver, CO, USA, September 2002, pp. 2037–2040.

[8] F. Archetti, G. Arosio, E. Fersini, and E. Messina, "Audio-based emotion recognition for advanced automatic retrieval in judicial domain," in *Proceedings of the 1st International Conference on ICT Solutions for Justice (ICT4JUSTICE)*, Thessaloniki, Greece, October 2008.

[9] A. Austermann, N. Esau, L. Kleinjohann, and B. Kleinjohann, "Fuzzy emotion recognition in natural speech dialogue," in *Proceedings of the 14th IEEE International Workshop on Robot and Human Interactive Communication (RO-MAN)*, Nashville, TN, USA, August 2005, pp. 317–322.

[10] T. Bänziger and K. Scherer, "Using actor portrayals to systematically study multimodal emotion expression: The GEMEP corpus," in *Proceedings of the 2nd International Conference on Affective Computing and Intelligent Interaction (ACII)*, Lisbon, Portugal, September 2007, pp. 476–487.

[11] P. A. Barbosa, "Detecting changes in speech expressiveness in participants in a radio program," in *Proceedings of the 10th Annual Conference of the International Speech Communication Association (INTERSPEECH)*, Brighton, UK, September 2009, pp. 2155–2158.

[12] R. Barra-Chicote, F. Fernandez, S. Lufti, J. M. Lucas-Cuesta, J. Macias-Guarasa, J. M. Montero, R. San-Segundo, and J. M. Pardo, "Acoustic emotion recognition using dynamic Bayesian networks and multi-space distributions," in *Proceedings of the 10th Annual Conference of the International Speech Communication Association (INTERSPEECH)*, Brighton, UK, September 2009, pp. 336–339.

[13] C. Bartneck, "Integrating the OCC model of emotions in embodied characters," in *Proceedings of the Workshop on Virtual Conversational Characters: Applications, Methods, and Research Challenges*, Melbourne, Australia, November 2002.

[14] A. Batliner, J. Buckow, R. Huber, V. Warnke, E. Nöth, and H. Niemann, "Boiling down prosody for the classification of boundaries and accents in German and English," in *Proceedings of the 7th European Conference on Speech Communication and Technology (INTERSPEECH)*, Aalborg, Denmark, September 2001, pp. 2781–2784.

[15] A. Batliner, K. Fischer, R. Huber, J. Spilker, and E. Nöth, "How to find trouble in communication," *Speech Communication*, vol. 40, no. 1–2, pp. 117–143, April 2003.

[16] A. Batliner, V. Zeißler, C. Frank, J. Adelhardt, R. P. Shi, and E. Nöth, "We are not amused — But how do you know? User states in a multi-modal dialogue system." in *Proceedings of the 8th European Conference on Speech Communication and Technology (INTERSPEECH)*, Geneva, Switzerland, September 2003, pp. 733–736.

[17] A. Batliner, C. Hacker, S. Steidl, E. Nöth, S. D'Arcy, M. Russell, and M. Wong, " "You stupid tin box" — Children interacting with the AIBO robot: A cross-linguistic emotional speech corpus," in *Proceedings of the 4th International Conference on Language Resources and Evaluation (LREC)*, Lisbon, Portugal, April 2004, pp. 171–174.

[18] A. Batliner, C. Hacker, S. Steidl, E. Nöth, and J. Haas, "From emotion to interaction: Lessons from real human-machine-dialogues," in *Proceedings of the Tutorial and Research Workshop on Affective Dialogue Systems (ADS)*, Irsee, Germany, June 2004, pp. 1–12.

[19] A. Batliner, S. Steidl, C. Hacker, E. Nöth, and H. Niemann, "Tales of tuning — Prototyping for automatic classification of emotional user states," in *Proceedings of the 9th European Conference on Speech Communication and Technology (INTERSPEECH)*, Lisbon, Portugal, September 2005, pp. 489–492.

[20] A. Batliner, F. Burkhardt, M. van Ballegooy, and E. Nöth, "A taxonomy of applications that utilize emotional awareness," in *Proceedings of the 5th Slovenian and 1st International Language Technologies Conference (IS-LTC)*, Ljubljana, Slovenia, October 2006, pp. 246–250.

[21] A. Batliner, S. Steidl, B. Schuller, D. Seppi, K. Laskowski, T. Vogt, L. Devillers, L. Vidrascu, N. Amir, L. Kessous, and V. Aharonson, "Combining efforts for improving automatic classification of emotional user states," in *Proceedings of the 5th Slovenian and 1st International Language Technologies Conference (IS-LTC)*, Ljubljana, Slovenia, October 2006, pp. 240–245.

[22] A. Batliner, S. Steidl, C. Hacker, and E. Nöth, "Private emotions versus social interaction: A data-driven approach towards analysing emotion in speech," *User Modelling and User-Adapted Interaction — The Journal of Personalization Research (UMUAI)*, vol. 18, no. 1–2, pp. 175–206, February 2008.

[23] A. Battocchi, F. Pianesi, and D. Goren-Bar, "A first evaluation study of a database of kinetic facial expressions (DaFEx)," in *Proceedings of the 7th International Conference on Multimodal Interfaces (ICMI)*, Trento, Italy, October 2005, pp. 214–221.

[24] R. Bellman, *Adaptive control processes: A guided tour.* Princeton, USA: Princeton University Press, January 1961.

[25] S. Biersack and V. Kempe, "Exploring the influence of vocal emotion expression on communicative effectiveness," *Phonetica*, vol. 62, no. 2–4, pp. 106–119, 2005.

[26] C. M. Bishop, *Pattern Recognition and Machine Learning (Information Science and Statistics)*, 2nd ed. Secaucus, NJ, USA: Springer-Verlag New York, Inc., October 2007.

[27] D. Bitouk, A. Nenkova, and R. Verma, "Improving emotion recognition using class-level spectral features," in *Proceedings of the 10th Annual Conference of the International Speech Communication Association (INTERSPEECH)*, Brighton, UK, September 2009, pp. 2023–2026.

[28] P. Boersma, "Accurate short-term analysis of the fundamental frequency and the harmonics-to-noise ratio of a sampled sound," in *Proceedings of the Institute of Phonetic Sciences*, 1993, pp. 97–110.

[29] P. Boersma and D. Weenink, "Praat: Doing phonetics by computer (Version 5.1.25)," Software available at http://www.praat.org/, January 2010.

[30] L. Breiman, "Random forests," *Machine Learning*, vol. 45, no. 1, pp. 5–32, October 2001.

[31] F. Burkhardt, A. Paeschke, M. Rolfes, W. F. Sendlmeier, and B. Weiss, "A database of German emotional speech," in *Proceedings of the 9th European Conference on Speech Communication and Technology (INTERSPEECH)*, Lisbon, Portugal, September 2005, pp. 1517–1520.

[32] F. Burkhardt, M. van Ballegooy, R. Englert, and R. Huber, "An emotion-aware voice portal," in *Proceedings of the 16th Electronic Speech Signal Processing Conference*, Prague, Czech Republic, September 2005.

[33] C. Busso and S. Narayanan, "The expression and perception of emotions: Comparing assessments of self versus others," in *Proceedings of the 9th Annual Conference of the International Speech Communication Association (INTERSPEECH)*, Brisbane, Australia, September 2008, pp. 257–260.

[34] C. Busso and S. Narayanan, "Scripted dialogs versus improvisation: Lessons learned about emotional elicitation techniques from the IEMOCAP database," in *Proceedings of the 9th Annual Conference of the International Speech Communication Association (INTERSPEECH)*, Brisbane, Australia, September 2008, pp. 1670–1673.

[35] C. Busso and S. Narayanan, "Analysis of emotionally salient aspects of fundamental frequency for emotion detection," *IEEE Transactions on Audio, Speech and Language Processing*, vol. 17, no. 4, pp. 582–596, May 2009.

[36] C. Busso, Z. Deng, S. Yildirim, M. Bulut, C. M. Lee, A. Kazemzadeh, S. Lee, U. Neumann, and S. Narayanan, "Analysis of emotion recognition using facial

expressions, speech and multimodal information," in *Proceedings of the 6th International Conference on Multimodal Interfaces (ICMI)*, State College, PA, USA, October 2004, pp. 205–211.

[37] C. Busso, S. Lee, and S. Narayanan, "Using neutral speech models for emotional speech analysis," in *Proceedings of the 8th Annual Conference of the International Speech Communication Association (INTERSPEECH)*, Antwerp, Belgium, August 2007, pp. 2225–2228.

[38] G. Caridakis, L. Malatesta, L. Kessous, N. Amir, A. Raouzaiou, and K. Karpouzis, "Modeling naturalistic affective states via facial and vocal expressions recognition," in *Proceedings of the 8th International Conference on Multimodal Interfaces (ICMI)*, Banff, AL, Canada, November 2006, pp. 146–154.

[39] J. C. Carletta, "Assessing agreement on classification tasks: The Kappa statistic," *Computational Linguistics*, vol. 22, no. 2, pp. 249–254, June 1996.

[40] S. Casale, A. Russo, G. Scebba, and S. Serrano, "Speech emotion classification using machine learning algorithms," in *Proceedings of the IEEE International Conference on Semantic Computing*, Santa Clara, CA, USA, August 2008, pp. 158–165.

[41] M. Castrillón, O. Déniz, C. Guerra, and M. Hernández, "ENCARA2: Real-time detection of multiple faces at different resolutions in video streams," *Journal of Visual Communication and Image Representation*, vol. 18, no. 2, pp. 130–140, April 2007.

[42] M. Cavazza, D. Pizzi, F. Charles, T. Vogt, and E. André, "Emotional input for character-based interactive storytelling," in *Proceedings of the 8th International Conference on Autonomous Agents and Multiagent Systems (AAMAS)*, Budapest, Hungary, May 2009, pp. 313–320.

[43] C.-C. Chang and C.-J. Lin, *LIBSVM: A library for support vector machines (Version 2.9)*, November 2009, Software available at http://www.csie.ntu.edu.tw/~cjlin/libsvm.

[44] F. Charles, S. Lemercier, T. Vogt, N. Bee, M. Mancini, J. Urbain, M. Price, E. André, C. Pelachaud, and M. Cavazza, "Affective interactive narrative in the CALLAS project," in *Proceedings of the 4th International Conference on Virtual Storytelling (VS)*, Saint Malo, France, December 2007, Demo Paper, pp. 210–213.

[45] K. Chen, G. Yue, F. Yu, Y. Shen, and A. Zhu, "Research on speech emotion recognition system in E-Learning," in *Proceedings of the 7th International Conference on Computational Science (ICCS), Part III*, Beijing, China, May 2007, pp. 555–558.

[46] G. Chetty and M. Wagner, "Multimodal speaker verification using ancillary known speaker characteristics such as gender or age," in *Proceedings of the 10th Annual Conference of the International Speech Communication Association (INTERSPEECH)*, Brighton, UK, September 2009, pp. 1167–1170.

[47] J. Cho, S. Kato, and H. Itoh, "Bayesian-based inference of dialogist's emotion for sensitivity robots," in *Proceedings of the 16th IEEE International Conference on Robot & Human Interactive Communication*, Jeju Island, Korea, August 2007, pp. 792–797.

[48] J. Cichosz and K. Ślot, "Emotion recognition in speech signal using emotion-extracting binary decision trees," in *Proceedings of the 2nd International Conference on Affective Computing and Intelligent Interaction (ACII): Doctoral Consortium*, Lisbon, Portugal, September 2007, pp. 9–16.

[49] J. Clark, C. Yallop, and J. Fletcher, *An introduction to phonetics and phonology*, 3rd ed. Malden, MA, USA: Blackwell Publishers, January 2007.

[50] C. Clavel, L. Devillers, G. Richard, I. Vasilescu, and T. Ehrette, "Detection and analysis of abnormal situations through fear-type acoustic manifestations," in *Proceedings of the IEEE International Conference on Acoustics, Speech, and Signal Processing (ICASSP)*, Honolulu, Hawaii, April 2007, pp. IV – 21–24.

[51] W. W. Cohen, "Fast effective rule induction," in *Proceedings of the 12th International Conference on Machine Learning*, Tahoe City, CA, USA, July 1995, pp. 115–123.

[52] C. Conati and X. Zhou, "Modeling students' emotions from cognitive appraisal in educational games," in *Proceedings of the 6th International Conference on Intelligent Tutoring Systems (ITS)*, Biarritz, France, June 2002, pp. 944–954.

[53] T. F. Cootes, G. J. Edwards, and C. J. Taylor, "Active appearance models," *IEEE Transactions on Pattern Analysis and Machine Intelligence*, vol. 23, no. 6, pp. 681–685, June 2001.

[54] R. Cowie, E. Douglas-Cowie, B. Appoloni, J. Taylor, and W. Fellenz, "What a neural net needs to know about emotion words," in *Proceedings of the 3rd World Multiconference on Circuits, Systems, Communications and Computers*, Athens, Greece, July 1999, pp. 5311–5366.

[55] R. Cowie, E. Douglas-Cowie, S. Savvidou, E. McMahon, M. Sawey, and M. Schröder, "'Feeltrace': An instrument for recording perceived emotion in real time," in *Proceedings of the ISCA Tutorial and Research Workshop on Speech and Emotion*, Newcastle, Northern Ireland, UK, September 2000, pp. 19–24.

Bibliography

[56] R. Cowie, E. Douglas-Cowie, N. Tsapatsoulis, G. Votsis, S. Kollias, W. Fellenz, and J. Taylor, "Emotion recognition in human-computer interaction," *IEEE Signal Processing Magazine*, vol. 18, no. 1, pp. 32–80, January 2001.

[57] A. Damasio, *Looking for Spinoza*. Orlando, FL, USA: Harcourt, February 2003.

[58] C. Darwin, *The expression of emotions in man and animals*. London, UK: John Murray, November 1872.

[59] D. Datcu and L. J. M. Rothkrantz, "The recognition of emotions from speech using Gentle-Boost classifier. A comparison approach," in *Proceedings of the International Conference on Computer Systems and Technologies (CompSysTech)*, Veliko Tarnovo, Bulgaria, June 2006.

[60] I. Daubechies, *Ten lectures on wavelets*, ser. Regional Conference Series in Applied Mathematics, no. 61. Philadelphia, PA, USA: Society for Industrial and Applied Mathematics, June 1992.

[61] F. de Rosis, C. Pelachaud, I. Poggi, V. Carofiglio, and B. de Carolis, "From Greta's mind to her face: Modelling the dynamics of affective states in a conversational embodied agent," *International Journal of Human-Computer Studies*, vol. 59, no. 1–2, pp. 81–118, July 2003.

[62] F. Dellaert, T. Polzin, and A. Waibel, "Recognizing emotion in speech," in *Proceedings of the 4th International Conference on Spoken Language Processing (ICSLP)*, Philadelphia, PA, USA, October 1996, pp. 1970–1973.

[63] L. Devillers, L. Vidrascu, and L. Lamel, "Challenges in real-life emotion annotation and machine learning based detection," *Neural Networks*, vol. 18, no. 4, pp. 407–422, June 2005.

[64] E. Douglas-Cowie, N. Campbell, R. Cowie, and P. Roach, "Emotional speech: Towards a new generation of databases," *Speech Communication*, vol. 40, no. 1–2, pp. 33–60, April 2003.

[65] E. Douglas-Cowie, L. Devillers, J.-C. Martin, R. Cowie, S. Savvidou, S. Abrilian, and C. Cox, "Multimodal databases of everyday emotion: Facing up to complexity," in *Proceedings of the 9th European Conference on Speech Communication and Technology (INTERSPEECH)*, Lisbon, Portugal, September 2005, pp. 813–816.

[66] E. Douglas-Cowie, R. Cowie, I. Sneddon, C. Cox, O. Lowry, M. McRorie, J.-C. Martin, L. Devillers, S. Abrilian, A. Batliner, N. Amir, and K. Karpouzis, "The HUMAINE

database: Addressing the collection and annotation of naturalistic and induced emotional data," in *Proceedings of the 2nd International Conference on Affective Computing and Intelligent Interaction (ACII)*, Lisbon, Portugal, September 2007, pp. 488–500.

[67] E. Douglas-Cowie, R. Cowie, C. Cox, N. Amir, and D. Heylen, "The Sensitive Artificial Listener: An induction technique for generating emotionally coloured conversation," in *Proceedings of the LREC Workshop on Emotion: Corpora for Research on Emotion and Affect*, Marrakech, Marokko, May 2008, pp. 1–4.

[68] R. O. Duda, P. E. Hart, and D. G. Stork, *Pattern Classification*, 2nd ed. New York, NJ, USA: Wiley-Interscience Publication, October 2000.

[69] P. Dumouchel, N. Dehak, Y. Attabi, R. Dehak, and N. Boufaden, "Cepstral and long-term features for emotion recognition," in *Proceedings of the 10th Annual Conference of the International Speech Communication Association (INTERSPEECH)*, Brighton, UK, September 2009, pp. 344–347.

[70] P. Ekman, W. V. Friesen, and P. Ellsworth, "What emotion categories or dimensions can observers judge from facial behavior?" in *Emotion in the Human Face*, P. Ekman, Ed. New York, NJ, USA: Cambridge University Press, 1982, pp. 39–55.

[71] C. Elliott and J. Brzezinski, "Autonomous agents as synthetic characters," *AI Magazine*, vol. 19, no. 2, pp. 13–30, 1998.

[72] I. S. Engberg and A. V. Hansen, "Documentation of the Danish Emotional Speech Database (DES)," Aalborg University, Aalborg, Denmark, Technical Report, September 1996.

[73] F. Eyben, M. Wöllmer, and B. Schuller, "openEAR — Introducing the Munich open-source emotion and affect recognition toolkit," in *Proceedings of the 3rd International Conference on Affective Computing and Intelligent Interaction (ACII)*, Amsterdam, The Netherlands, September 2009, pp. 576–581.

[74] S. Fagel, "Emotional McGurk effect," in *Proceedings of the 3rd International Conference on Speech Prosody*, Dresden, Germany, May 2006.

[75] U. M. Fayyad and K. B. Irani, "Multi-interval discretization of continuous-valued attributes for classification learning," in *Proceedings of the 13th International Joint Conference on Artificial Intelligence (IJCAI)*, Chambéry, France, August–September 1993, pp. 1022–1027.

[76] R. Fernandez and R. W. Picard, "Modeling drivers' speech under stress," *Speech Communication*, vol. 40, no. 1–2, pp. 145–159, April 2003.

[77] R. Fernandez and R. W. Picard, "Classical and novel discriminant features for affect recognition from speech," in *Proceedings of the 9th European Conference on Speech Communication and Technology (INTERSPEECH)*, Lisbon, Portugal, September 2005, pp. 473–476.

[78] G. Fink, "Developing HMM-based recognizers with ESMERALDA," in *Proceedings of the 2nd International Workshop on Text, Speech and Dialogue (TSD)*, Plzen, Czech Republic, September 1999, pp. 229–234.

[79] K. Forbes-Riley and D. J. Litman, "Predicting emotion in spoken dialogue from multiple knowledge sources," in *Proceedings of Human Language Technologies: The Annual Conference of the North American Chapter of the Association for Computational Linguistics (HLT/NAACL)*, Boston, MA, USA, May 2004, pp. 201–208.

[80] N. Fries, "Sprachsystem und Emotionen," *Zeitschrift für Linguistik und Literaturwissenschaft (LiLi)*, vol. 101 (Sprache und Subjektivität I), pp. 37–69, 1996.

[81] N. H. Frijda, *The Emotions*. Cambridge and New York, USA: Cambridge University Press, 1986.

[82] R. Gajšek, V. Štruc, S. Dobrišek, and F. Mihelič, "Emotion recognition using linear transformations in combination with video," in *Proceedings of the 10th Annual Conference of the International Speech Communication Association (INTERSPEECH)*, Brighton, UK, September 2009, pp. 1967–1970.

[83] J. S. Garofolo, L. F. Lamel, W. M. Fisher, J. G. Fiscus, D. S. Pallett, N. L. Dahlgren, and V. Zue, "TIMIT acoustic-phonetic continuous speech corpus," Linguistic Data Consortium (LDC), Philadelphia, PA, USA, Technical Report, 1993.

[84] T. Giannakopoulos, A. Pikrakis, and S. Theodoridis, "A dimensional approach to emotion recognition of speech from movies," in *Proceedings of the IEEE International Conference on Acoustics, Speech, and Signal Processing (ICASSP)*, Taipei, Taiwan, April 2009, pp. 65–68.

[85] R. W. Gibbs, J. S. Leggitt, and E. A. Turner, "What's special about figurative language in emotional communication?" in *The Verbal Communication of Emotions: Interdisciplinary Perspectives*, S. R. Fussell, Ed. Mahwah, NJ, USA: Lawrence Erlbaum Associates, Inc., June 2002, pp. 125–149.

[86] S. W. Gilroy, M. Cavazza, R. Chaignon, S.-M. Mäkelä, M. Niranen, E. André, T. Vogt, J. Urbain, M. Billinghurst, H. Seichter, and M. Benayoun, "E-tree: emotionally driven augmented reality art," in *Proceedings of the 16th ACM International Conference on Multimedia*, Vancouver, BC, Canada, October 2008, pp. 945–948.

[87] S. Gilroy, M. Cavazza, R. Chaignon, S.-M. Mäkelä, M. Niiranen, E. André, T. Vogt, J. Urbain, H. Seichter, M. Billinghurst, and M. Benayoun, "An affective model of user experience for interactive art," in *Proceedings of the International Conference on Advances in Computer Entertainment Technology (ACE)*, Yokohama, Japan, December 2008, pp. 107–110.

[88] T. Goldbeck, F. Tolkmitt, and K. Scherer, "Experimental studies on vocal content communication," in *Facets of Emotion. Recent Research*, K. Scherer, Ed. Hillsdale, NJ, USA: Lawrence Erlbaum Associates, April 1988, ch. 6, pp. 121–137.

[89] M. Goudbeek, J. P. Goldman, and K. Scherer, "Emotion dimensions and formant position," in *Proceedings of the 10th Annual Conference of the International Speech Communication Association (INTERSPEECH)*, Brighton, UK, September 2009, pp. 1575–1578.

[90] J. Gratch, S. Marsella, N. Wang, and B. Stankovic, "Assessing the validity of appraisal-based models of emotion," in *Proceedings of the 3rd International Conference on Affective Computing and Intelligent Interaction (ACII)*, Amsterdam, The Netherlands, September 2009.

[91] M. Grimm, E. Mower, K. Kroschel, and S. Narayanan, "Combining categorical and primitives-based emotion recognition," in *Proceedings of the 14th European Signal Processing Conference (EUSIPCO)*, Florence, Italy, September 2006.

[92] M. Grimm, K. Kroschel, H. Harris, C. Nass, B. Schuller, G. Rigoll, and T. Moosmayr, "On the necessity and feasibility of detecting a driver's emotional state while driving," in *Proceedings of the 2nd International Conference on Affective Computing and Intelligent Interaction (ACII)*, Lisbon, Portugal, September 2007, pp. 126–138.

[93] M. Grimm, K. Kroschel, and S. Narayanan, "The Vera Am Mittag German Audio-Visual Emotional Speech Database," in *Proceedings of the IEEE International Conference on Multimedia & Expo (ICME)*, Hannover, Germany, June 2008, pp. 865–868.

[94] H. Gunes and M. Piccardi, "Affect recognition from face and body: Early fusion vs. late fusion," in *Proceedings of the IEEE International Conference on Systems, Man and Cybernetics (SMC)*, Waikoloa, HI, USA, October 2005, pp. 3437–3443.

[95] M. Hackel, S. Schwope, J. Fritsch, B. Wrede, and G. Sagerer, "A humanoid robot platform suitable for studying embodied interaction," in *Proceedings of the IEEE/RSJ International Conference on Intelligent Robots and Systems (IROS)*, Edmonton, AL, Canada, August 2005, pp. 56–61.

[96] T. Hacki and S. Heitmüller, "Development of the child's voice: Premutation, mutation," *International Journal of Pediatric Otorhinolaryngology*, vol. 49, Supplement 1, pp. 141–144, October 1999.

[97] M. Haindl, P. Somol, D. Ververidis, and C. Kotropoulos, "Feature selection based on mutual correlation," in *Proceedings of the 11th Iberoamerican Congress on Pattern Recognition*, Cancun, Mexico, November 2006, pp. 569–577.

[98] M. A. Hall, "Correlation-based feature subset selection for machine learning," Master's thesis, University of Waikato, Hamilton, New Zealand, April 1998.

[99] J. H. L. Hansen, S. E. Bou-Ghazale, R. Sarikaya, and B. Pellom, "Getting started with the SUSAS: Speech Under Simulated and Actual Stress Database," Robust Speech Processing Laboratory, Duke University, Durham, USA, Technical Report RSPL-98-10, April 1998.

[100] S. Harrison, P. Senger, and D. Tatar, "The three paradigms of HCI," in *Proceedings of the Conference on Human-Computer Interaction (CHI)*, San Jose, CA, USA, April–May 2007.

[101] A. Hassan and R. I. Damper, "Emotion recognition from speech using extended feature selection and a simple classifier," in *Proceedings of the 10th Annual Conference of the International Speech Communication Association (INTERSPEECH)*, Brighton, UK, September 2009, pp. 2043–2046.

[102] F. Hegel, T. Spexard, T. Vogt, G. Horstmann, and B. Wrede, "Playing a different imitation game: Interaction with an empathic android robot," in *Proceedings of the IEEE-RAS International Conference on Humanoid Robots (HUMANOIDS)*, Genoa, Italy, December 2006, pp. 56–61.

[103] D. Hillard, M. Ostendorf, and E. Shriberg, "Detection of agreement vs. disagreement in meetings: Training with unlabeled data," in *Proceedings of the Conference of the North American Chapter of the Association for Computational Linguistics on Human Language Technology (HLT/NAACL)*, Edmonton, AL, Canada, May–June 2003, pp. 34–36.

[104] F. Hönig, A. Batliner, and E. Nöth, "Real-time recognition of the affective user state with physiological signals," in *Proceedings of the 2nd International Conference on Affective*

Computing and Intelligent Interaction (ACII): Doctoral Consortium, Lisbon, Portugal, September 2007, pp. 1–8.

[105] H. Hu, M.-X. Xu, and W. Wu, "GMM supervector based SVM with spectral features for speech emotion recognition," in *Proceedings of the IEEE International Conference on Acoustics, Speech, and Signal Processing (ICASSP)*, Honolulu, HI, USA, April 2007, pp. IV – 413–416.

[106] R. Huang and C. Ma, "Toward a speaker-independent real-time affect detection system," in *Proceedings of the 18th International Conference on Pattern Recognition (ICPR)*, Hong Kong, China, August 2006, pp. 1204–1207.

[107] E. Hudlicka, "To feel or not to feel: The role of affect in human-computer interaction," *International Journal of Human-Computer Studies*, vol. 59, no. 1–2, pp. 1–32, July 2003.

[108] *Proceedings of the International Conference on Multimedia & Expo*, Amsterdam, The Netherlands, July 2005.

[109] Y. Ijima, M. Tachibana, T. Nose, and T. Kobayashi, "Emotional speech recognition based on style estimation and adaptation with multiple-regression HMM," in *Proceedings of the IEEE International Conference on Acoustics, Speech, and Signal Processing (ICASSP)*, Taipei, Taiwan, April 2009, pp. 4157–4160.

[110] *Proceedings of the 7th European Conference on Speech Communication and Technology (INTERSPEECH)*, Aalborg, Denmark, September 2001.

[111] *Proceedings of the 8th European Conference on Speech Communication and Technology (INTERSPEECH)*, Geneva, Switzerland, September 2003.

[112] *Proceedings of the 9th European Conference on Speech Communication and Technology (INTERSPEECH)*, Lisbon, Portugal, September 2005.

[113] *Proceedings of the 9th International Conference on Spoken Language Processing (INTERSPEECH)*, Pittsburgh, PA, USA, September 2006.

[114] *Proceedings of the 8th Annual Conference of the International Speech Communication Association (INTERSPEECH)*, Antwerp, Belgium, August 2007.

[115] *Proceedings of the 9th Annual Conference of the International Speech Communication Association (INTERSPEECH)*, Brisbane, Australia, September 2008.

[116] *Proceedings of 10th Annual Conference of the International Speech Communication Association (INTERSPEECH)*, Brighton, UK, September 2009.

[117] S. Ioannou, A. Raouzaiou, K. Karpouzis, and S. Kollias, "Adaptation of facial feature extraction and rule generation in emotion-analysis systems," in *Proceedings of the International Joint Conference on Neural Networks (IJCNN)*, Budapest, Hungary, July 2004, pp. 513–518.

[118] G. Jacucci, A. Spagnolli, A. Chalambalakis, A. Morrison, L. Liikkanen, S. Roveda, and M. Bertoncini, "Bodily explorations in space: Social experience of a multimodal art installation," in *Proceedings of the 12th IFIP Conference on Human-Computer Interaction (INTERACT)*, Uppsala, Sweden, August 2009, pp. 62–75.

[119] C. Jones and J. Sutherland, "Acoustic emotion recognition for affective computer gaming," in *Affect and Emotion in Human-Computer Interaction*, ser. Lecture Notes in Computer Science (LNCS), C. Peter and R. Beale, Eds. Berlin, Heidelberg, Germany: Springer, August 2008, vol. 4868, pp. 209–219.

[120] C. Jones and A. Deeming, "Affective human-robotic interaction," in *Affect and Emotion in Human-Computer Interaction*, ser. Lecture Notes in Computer Science (LNCS), C. Peter and R. Beale, Eds. Berlin, Heidelberg, Germany: Springer, August 2008, vol. 4868, pp. 175–185.

[121] C. Jones and I.-M. Jonsson, "Automatic recognition of affective cues in the speech of car drivers to allow appropriate responses," in *Proceedings of the Annual Conference of the Australian Computer-Human Interaction Special Interest Group (OZCHI)*, Canberra, Australia, November 2005, pp. 1–10.

[122] C. Jones and I.-M. Jonsson, "Using paralinguistic cues in speech to recognise emotions in older car drivers," in *Affect and Emotion in Human-Computer Interaction*, ser. Lecture Notes in Computer Science (LNCS), C. Peter and R. Beale, Eds. Berlin, Heidelberg, Germany: Springer, August 2008, vol. 4868, pp. 229–240.

[123] N. Kamaruddin and A. Wahab, "CMAC for speech emotion profiling," in *Proceedings of the 10th Annual Conference of the International Speech Communication Association (INTERSPEECH)*, Brighton, UK, September 2009, pp. 1991–1994.

[124] J. F. Kelley, "An iterative design methodology for user-friendly natural language office information applications," *ACM Transactions on Office Information Systems*, vol. 2, no. 1, pp. 26–41, March 1984.

[125] M. Kienast, A. Paeschke, and W. Sendlmeier, "Articulatory reduction in emotional speech," in *Proceedings of the 6th European Conference on Speech Communication and Technology (EUROSPEECH)*, Budapest, Hungary, September 1999, pp. 117–120.

[126] A. Kießling, "Extraktion und Klassifikation prosodischer Merkmale in der automatischen Sprachverarbeitung," Ph.D. dissertation, Technical Faculty, University Erlangen-Nuremberg, Germany, 1996.

[127] E. H. Kim, K. H. Hyun, S. H. Kim, and Y. K. Kwak, "Improved emotion recognition with a novel speaker-independent feature," *IEEE/ASME Transactions on Mechatronics*, vol. 14, no. 3, pp. 317–325, June 2009.

[128] J. Kim, S. Lee, and S. Narayanan, "A detailed study of word-position effects on emotion expression in speech," in *Proceedings of the 10th Annual Conference of the International Speech Communication Association (INTERSPEECH)*, Brighton, UK, September 2009, pp. 1987–1990.

[129] J. Kim and E. André, "Emotion recognition based on physiological changes in music listening," *IEEE Transactions on Pattern Analysis and Machine Intelligence*, vol. 30, no. 12, pp. 2067–2083, December 2008.

[130] J. Kim and F. Lingenfelser, "Ensemble approaches to parametric decision fusion for bimodal emotion recognition," in *Proceedings of the International Conference on Bio-inspired Systems and Signal Processing (BIOSIGNALS)*, Valencia, Spain, January 2010, pp. 460–463.

[131] J. Kim, E. André, M. Rehm, T. Vogt, and J. Wagner, "Integrating information from speech and physiological signals to achieve emotional sensitivity," in *Proceedings of the 9th European Conference on Speech Communication and Technology (INTERSPEECH)*, Lisbon, Portugal, September 2005, pp. 809–812.

[132] S. Kim, P. G. Georgiou., S. Lee, and S. Narayanan, "Real-time emotion detection system using speech: Multi-modal fusion of different timescale features," in *Proceedings of the 9th IEEE Workshop on Multimedia Signal Processing (MMSP)*, Chania, Greece, October 2007, pp. 48–51.

[133] M. Kotti and C. Kotropoulos, "Gender classification in two emotional speech databases," in *Proceedings of the 19th International Conference on Pattern Recognition (ICPR)*, Tampa, FL, USA, December 2008, pp. 1–4.

[134] O.-W. Kwon, K. Chan, J. Hao, and T.-W. Lee, "Emotion recognition by speech signals," in *Proceedings of the 8th European Conference on Speech Communication and Technology (INTERSPEECH)*, Geneva, Switzerland, September 2003, pp. 125–128.

[135] C.-C. Lee, C. Busso, S. Lee, and S. Narayanan, "Modeling mutual influence of interlocutor emotion states in dyadic spoken interactions," in *Proceedings of the 10th Annual*

Conference of the International Speech Communication Association (INTERSPEECH), Brighton, UK, September 2009, pp. 1983–1986.

[136] C.-C. Lee, E. Mower, C. Busso, S. Lee, and S. Narayanan, "Emotion recognition using a hierarchical binary decision tree approach," in *Proceedings of the 10th Annual Conference of the International Speech Communication Association (INTERSPEECH)*, Brighton, UK, September 2009, pp. 320–323.

[137] C. M. Lee and S. Narayanan, "Toward detecting emotions in spoken dialogs," *IEEE Transactions on Speech and Audio Processing*, vol. 13, no. 2, pp. 293–303, March 2005.

[138] C. M. Lee, S. Yildirim, M. Bulut, and A. Kazemzadeh, "Emotion recognition based on phoneme classes," in *Proceedings of the 8th International Conference on Spoken Language Processing (INTERSPEECH)*, Jeju Island, Korea, October 2004, pp. 889–892.

[139] W.-S. Lee, Y.-W. Roh, D.-J. Kim, J.-H. Kim, and K.-S. Hong, "Speech emotion recognition using spectral entropy," in *Proceedings of the 1st International Conference on Intelligent Robotics and Applications (ICIRA)*, Wuhan, China, October 2008, pp. 45–54.

[140] L. A. Liikkanen and L. Pearce, "MusicKiosk: When listeners become composers. An exploration into affective, interactive music," in *Proceedings of the 10th International Conference of Music Perception and Cognition (ICMPC)*, Sapporo, Japan, August 2008.

[141] L. A. Liikkanen, G. Jacucci, E. Huvio, T. Laitinen, and E. André, "Exploring emotions and multimodality in digitally augmented puppeteering," in *Proceedings of the Conference on Advanced Visual Interfaces (AVI)*, Naples, Italy, May 2008, pp. 339–342.

[142] L. A. Liikkanen, G. Jacucci, and M. Helin, "ElectroEmotion — A tool for producing emotional corpora collectively," in *Proceedings of the 3rd International Conference on Affective Computing and Intelligent Interaction (ACII)*, Amsterdam, The Netherlands, September 2009, pp. 332–338.

[143] D. Litman and K. Forbes-Riley, "Predicting student emotions in computer-human tutoring dialogues," in *Proceedings of the 42nd Annual Meeting of the Association for Computational Linguistics (ACL)*, Barcelona, Spain, July 2004, pp. 351–358.

[144] D. Litman, M. Rotaru, and G. Nicholas, "Classifying turn-level uncertainty using word-level prosody," in *Proceedings of the 10th Annual Conference of the International Speech Communication Association (INTERSPEECH)*, Brighton, UK, September 2009, pp. 2003–2006.

[145] J. Liu, C. Chen, J. Bu, M. You, and J. Tao, "Speech emotion recognition using an enhanced co-training algorithm," in *Proceedings of the IEEE International Conference on Multimedia & Expo (ICME)*, Beijing, China, July 2007, pp. 999–1002.

[146] I. Luengo, E. Navas, and I. Hernáez, "Combining spectral and prosodic information for emotion recognition in the INTERSPEECH 2009 Emotion Challenge," in *Proceedings of the 10th Annual Conference of the International Speech Communication Association (INTERSPEECH)*, Brighton, UK, September 2009, pp. 332–335.

[147] M. Lugger and B. Yang, "An incremental analysis of different feature groups in speaker independent emotion recognition," in *Proceedings of the International Congress of Phonetic Sciences (ICPhS)*, Saarbrücken, Germany, August 2007, pp. 2149–2152.

[148] M. Lugger and B. Yang, "Cascaded emotion classification via psychological emotion dimensions using a large set of voice quality parameters," in *Proceedings of the IEEE International Conference on Acoustics, Speech, and Signal Processing (ICASSP)*, Las Vegas, NV, USA, March–April 2008, pp. 4945–4948.

[149] M. Lugger and B. Yang, "On the relevance of high-level features for speaker independent emotion recognition of spontaneous speech," in *Proceedings of the 10th Annual Conference of the International Speech Communication Association (INTERSPEECH)*, Brighton, UK, September 2009, pp. 1995–1998.

[150] H.-R. Lv, Z.-L. Lin, W.-J. Yin, and J. Dong, "Emotion recognition based on pressure sensor keyboards," in *Proceedings of the IEEE International Conference on Multimedia & Expo (ICME)*, Hannover, Germany, June 2008, pp. 1089–1092.

[151] A. Madan, "Jerk-o-meter: Speech-feature analysis provides feedback on your phone interactions," http://www.media.mit.edu/press/jerk-o-meter/, 2005.

[152] B. Maeireizo, D. Litman, and R. Hwa, "Co-training for predicting emotions with spoken dialogue data," in *Proceedings of the 42nd Annual Meeting of the Association for Computational Linguistics (ACL): Interactive Posters/Demonstrations Session*, Barcelona, Spain, July 2004, pp. 202–205.

[153] A. Mehrabian, "Framework for a comprehensive description and measurement of emotional states," *Genetic, Social, and General Psychology Monographs*, vol. 121, no. 3, pp. 339–361, August 1995.

[154] P. Mermelstein, "Distance measures for speech recognition, psychological and instrumental," in *Proceedings of the Joint Workshop on Pattern Recognition and Artificial Intelligence*, Hyannis, MA, USA, June 1976, pp. 374–388.

[155] Merriam-Webster, "Online dictionary," http://www.merriam-webster.com, 2010.

[156] T. Mitchell, *Machine Learning*. New York: McGraw Hill, October 1997.

[157] N. Morgan and E. Fosler-Lussier, "Combining multiple estimators of speaking rate," in *Proceedings of the IEEE International Conference on Acoustics, Speech, and Signal Processing (ICASSP)*, Seattle, WA, USA, May 1998, pp. 729–732.

[158] E. Mower, M. J. Mataric, and S. Narayanan, "Evaluating evaluators: A case study in understanding the benefits and pitfalls of multi-evaluator modeling," in *Proceedings of the 10th Annual Conference of the International Speech Communication Association (INTERSPEECH)*, Brighton, UK, September 2009, pp. 1583–1586.

[159] I. R. Murray and J. L. Arnott, "Toward the simulation of emotion in synthetic speech: A review of the literature on human vocal emotion," *Journal of the Acoustical Society of America*, vol. 93, no. 2, pp. 1097–1108, February 1993.

[160] F. Nasoz, K. Alvarez, C. Lisetti, and N. Finkelstein, "Emotion recognition from physiological signals for presence technologies," *International Journal of Cognition, Technology and Work*, vol. 6, no. 1, pp. 4–14, February 2004.

[161] D. Neiberg and K. Elenius, "Automatic recognition of anger in spontaneous speech," in *Proceedings of the 9th Annual Conference of the International Speech Communication Association (INTERSPEECH)*, Brisbane, Australia, September 2008, pp. 2755–2758.

[162] D. Neiberg, K. Elenius, and K. Laskowski, "Emotion recognition in spontaneous speech using GMMs," in *Proceedings of the 9th International Conference on Spoken Language Processing (INTERSPEECH)*, Pittsburgh, PA, USA, September 2006, pp. 809–812.

[163] G. Nicholas, M. Rotaru, and D. Litman, "Exploiting word-level features for emotion prediction," in *Proceedings of the IEEE/ACL Workshop on Spoken Language Technology*, Palm Beach, Aruba, December 2006, pp. 110–113.

[164] A. Nogueiras, A. Moreno, A. Bonafonte, and J. Mariño, "Speech emotion recognition using Hidden Markov Models," in *Proceedings of the 7th European Conference on Speech Communication and Technology (INTERSPEECH)*, Aalborg, Denmark, September 2001, pp. 2679–2682.

[165] D. Norman, *The design of everyday things*. New York, NJ, USA: Doubleday, February 1990.

[166] D. A. Norman, "Emotion and design: Attractive things work better," *Interactions Magazine (IX)*, vol. 9, no. 4, pp. 36–42, July/August 2002.

[167] T. L. Nwe, S. W. Foo, and L. C. De Silva, "Speech emotion recognition using Hidden Markov Models," *Speech Communication*, vol. 41, no. 4, pp. 603–623, November 2003.

[168] K. Oatley and P. N. Johnson-Laird, "Towards a cognitive theory of emotions," *Cognition and Emotion*, vol. 1, no. 1, pp. 29–50, March 1987.

[169] A. Ortony and T. J. Turner, "What's basic about basic emotions?" *Psychological Review*, vol. 97, no. 3, pp. 315–331, July 1990.

[170] A. Ortony, G. L. Clore, and A. Collins, *The cognitive structure of emotions*. Cambridge, UK: Cambridge University Press, 1988.

[171] A. Osherenko and E. André, "Differentiated semantic analysis in lexical affect sensing," in *Proceedings of the 3rd International Conference on Affective Computing and Intelligent Interaction (ACII)*, Amsterdam, The Netherlands, September 2009, pp. 369–374.

[172] A. Osherenko, E. André, and T. Vogt, "Affect sensing in speech: Studying fusion of linguistic and acoustic features," in *Proceedings of the 3rd International Conference on Affective Computing and Intelligent Interaction (ACII)*, Amsterdam, The Netherlands, September 2009, pp. 320–325.

[173] P.-Y. Oudeyer, "The production and recognition of emotions in speech: Features and algorithms," *International Journal of Human-Computer Studies*, vol. 59, no. 1–2, pp. 157–183, July 2003.

[174] A. Paiva, M. Costa, R. Chaves, M. Piedade, D. Mourão, D. Sobral, K. Höök, G. Andersson, and A. Bullock, "SenToy: An affective sympathetic interface," *International Journal of Human-Computer Studies*, vol. 59, no. 1–2, pp. 227–235, July 2003.

[175] M. Paleari and C. Lisetti, "Toward multimodal fusion of affective cues," in *Proceedings of the 1st ACM International Workshop on Human-centered Multimedia (HCM)*, Santa Barbara, CA, USA, October 2006, pp. 99–108.

[176] V. A. Petrushin, "Creating emotion recognition agents for speech signal," in *Socially Intelligent Agents. Creating Relationships with Computers and Robots*, K. Dautenhahn, A. H. Bond, L. Cañamero, and B. Edmonds, Eds. Norwell, MA, USA: Kluwer Academic Publishers, May 2002, pp. 77–84.

[177] H. R. Pfitzinger and C. Kaernbach, "Amplitude and amplitude variation of emotional speech," in *Proceedings of the 9th Annual Conference of the International Speech Communication Association (INTERSPEECH)*, Brisbane, Australia, September 2008, pp. 1036–1039.

[178] R. W. Picard, *Affective Computing*. Cambridge, MA, USA: MIT Press, September 1997.

[179] R. W. Picard, E. Vyzas, and J. Healy, "Toward machine emotional intelligence: Analysis of affective physiological state," *IEEE Transactions on Pattern Analysis and Machine Intelligence*, vol. 23, no. 10, pp. 1175–1191, October 2001.

[180] S. Planet, I. Iriondo, J.-C. Socoró, C. Monzo, and J. Adell, "GTM-URL contribution to the INTERSPEECH 2009 Emotion Challenge," in *Proceedings of the 10th Annual Conference of the International Speech Communication Association (INTERSPEECH)*, Brighton, UK, September 2009, pp. 316–319.

[181] R. Plutchik, *The emotions: Facts, theories, and a new model*. New York, NJ, USA: Random House, 1962.

[182] T. S. Polzin and A. H. Waibel, "Emotion-sensitive human-computer interfaces," in *Proceedings of the ISCA Tutorial and Research Workshop on Speech and Emotion*, Newcastle, Northern Ireland, UK, September 2000, pp. 201–206.

[183] T. S. Polzin and A. H. Waibel, "Detecting emotions in speech," in *Proceedings of the 2nd International Conference on Cooperative Multimodal Communications (CMC)*, Tilburg, The Netherlands, January 1998.

[184] H. Pon-Barry and S. Shieber, "Identifying uncertain words within an utterance via prosodic features," in *Proceedings of the 10th Annual Conference of the International Speech Communication Association (INTERSPEECH)*, Brighton, UK, September 2009, pp. 1579–1582.

[185] P. Pudil, J. Novovičová, and J. Kittler, "Floating search methods in feature selection," *Pattern Recognition Letters*, vol. 15, no. 11, pp. 1119–1125, November 1994.

[186] A. Rabie, T. Vogt, M. Hanheide, and B. Wrede, "Evaluation and discussion of multi-modal emotion recognition," in *Proceedings of the 2nd International Conference on Computer and Electrical Engineering (ICCEE)*, Dubai, United Arab Emirates, December 2009, pp. 598–602.

[187] A. Rabie, C. Lang, M. Hanheide, M. Castrillon-Santana, and G. Sagerer, "Automatic initialization for facial analysis in interactive robotics," in *Proceedings of the 6th International Conference on Computer Vision Systems (ICVS)*, Santorini, Greece, May 2008, pp. 517–526.

[188] M. Rehm, T. Vogt, M. Wissner, and N. Bee, "Dancing the night away — Controlling a virtual karaoke dancer by multimodal expressive cues," in *Proceedings of the 7th International Conference on Autonomous Agents and Multiagent Systems (AAMAS)*, Estoril, Portugal, May 2008, pp. 1249–1252.

[189] E. Roesch, T. Bänziger, and K. Scherer, "Preliminary plans for exemplars: Theory," HUMAINE Network of Excellence, Deliverable D3c, May 2004.

[190] I. J. Roseman and C. A. Smith, "Appraisal theory: Overview, assumptions, varieties, controversies," in *Appraisal processes in emotion: Theory methods, research*, K. Scherer, A. Schorr, and T. Johnstone, Eds. New York, NJ, USA: Oxford University Press, April 2001, pp. 3–19.

[191] I. J. Roseman, A. A. Antoniou, and P. E. Jose, "Appraisal determinants of emotions: Constructing a more accurate and comprehensive theory," *Cognition and Emotion*, vol. 10, no. 3, pp. 241–277, May 1996.

[192] R. Sarikaya and J. N. Gowdy, "Subband based classification of speech under stress," in *Proceedings of the IEEE International Conference on Acoustics, Speech, and Signal Processing (ICASSP)*, Seattle, WA, USA, May 1998, pp. 569–572.

[193] N. Sato and Y. Obuchi, "Emotion recognition using Mel-frequency cepstral coefficients," *Information and Media Technologies*, vol. 2, no. 3, pp. 835–848, September 2007.

[194] N. Satoh, K. Yamauchi, S. Matsunaga, M. Yamashita, R. Nakagawa, and K. Shinohara, "Emotion clustering using the results of subjective opinion tests for emotion recognition in infants' cries," in *Proceedings of the 8th Annual Conference of the International Speech Communication Association (INTERSPEECH)*, Antwerp, Belgium, August 2007, pp. 2229–2232.

[195] K. Scherer, "Vocal communication of emotion: A review of research paradigms," *Speech Communication*, vol. 40, no. 1-2, pp. 227–256, April 2003.

[196] K. Scherer, "Criteria for emotion-antecedent appraisal: A review," in *Cognitive Perspectives on Emotion and Motivation*, V. Hamilton, G. H. Bower, and N. H. Frijda, Eds. Dordrecht, The Netherlands: Kluwer Academic Publishers, May 1988, pp. 89–126.

[197] K. Scherer, R. Banse, H. Walbott, and T. Goldbeck, "Vocal clues in emotion encoding and decoding," *Motivation and Emotion*, vol. 15, no. 2, pp. 123–148, June 1991.

[198] F. Schiel, S. Steininger, and U. Türk, "The SmartKom multimodal corpus at BAS," in *Proceedings of the 3rd International Conference on Language Resources and Evaluation (LREC)*, Las Palmas, Gran Canaria, Spain, May 2002, pp. 200–206.

[199] S. Schnall, "The pragmatics of emotion language," *Psychological Inquiry*, vol. 16, no. 1, pp. 28–31, January 2005.

[200] M. Schröder, H. Pirker, and M. Lamolle, "First suggestions for an emotion annotation and representation language," in *Proceedings of the LREC Workshop on Emotion: Corpora for Research on Emotion and Affect*, Genoa, Italy, May 2006, pp. 88–92.

[201] M. Schröder, R. Cowie, D. Heylen, M. Pantic, C. Pelachaud, and B. Schuller, "Towards responsive sensitive artificial listeners," in *Proceedings of the 4th International Workshop on Human-Computer Conversation*, Bellagio, Italy, October 2008.

[202] M. Schröder, P. Baggia, F. Burkhardt, C. Pelachaud, C. Peter, and E. Zovato, "Emotion Markup Language (EmotionML) 1.0," World Wide Web Consortium (W3C), Technical Report (Working draft), October 2009.

[203] B. Schuller, "Automatische Emotionserkennung," Ph.D. dissertation, Technical University Munich, Germany, April 2006.

[204] B. Schuller and G. Rigoll, "Timing levels in segment-based speech emotion recognition," in *Proceedings of the 9th International Conference on Spoken Language Processing (INTERSPEECH)*, Pittsburgh, PA, USA, September 2006, pp. 1818–1821.

[205] B. Schuller and G. Rigoll, "Recognising interest in conversational speech — Comparing bag of frames and supra-segmental features," in *Proceedings of the 10th Annual Conference of the International Speech Communication Association (INTERSPEECH)*, Brighton, UK, September 2009, pp. 1999–2003.

[206] B. Schuller, G. Rigoll, and M. Lang, "Hidden Markov Model-based speech emotion recognition," in *Proceedings of the IEEE International Conference on Acoustics, Speech, and Signal Processing (ICASSP)*, Hong Kong, China, April 2003, pp. II-1–4.

[207] B. Schuller, R. Müller, M. Lang, and G. Rigoll, "Speaker independent emotion recognition by early fusion of acoustic and linguistic features within ensembles," in *Proceedings of the 9th European Conference on Speech Communication and Technology (INTERSPEECH)*, Lisbon, Portugal, September 2005, pp. 805–808.

[208] B. Schuller, A. Batliner, D. Seppi, S. Steidl, T. Vogt, J. Wagner, L. Devillers, L. Vidrascu, N. Amir, L. Kessous, and V. Aharonson, "The relevance of feature type for the automatic classification of emotional user states: Low level descriptors and functionals," in *Proceedings of the 8th Annual Conference of the International Speech Communication Association (INTERSPEECH)*, Antwerp, Belgium, August 2007, pp. 2253–2256.

[209] B. Schuller, G. Rigoll, M. Grimm, K. Kroschel, T. Moosmayr, and G. Ruske, "Effects of in-car noise-conditions on the recognition of emotion within speech," in *Proceedings of the Deutsche Jahrestagung für Akustik (DAGA)*, Stuttgart, Germany, September 2007, pp. 305–306.

[210] B. Schuller, D. Seppi, A. Batliner, A. Maier, and S. Steidl, "Towards more reality in the recognition of emotional speech," in *Proceedings of the IEEE International Conference on Acoustics, Speech, and Signal Processing (ICASSP)*, Honolulu, HI, USA, April 2007, pp. IV-941–944.

[211] B. Schuller, B. Vlasenko, D. Arsic, G. Rigoll, and A. Wendemuth, "Combining speech recognition and acoustic word emotion models for robust text-independent emotion recognition," in *Proceedings of the IEEE International Conference on Multimedia & Expo (ICME)*, Hannover, Germany, June 2008, pp. 1333–1336.

[212] B. Schuller, A. Batliner, S. Steidl, and D. Seppi, "Emotion recognition from speech: Putting ASR in the loop," in *Proceedings of the IEEE International Conference on Acoustics, Speech, and Signal Processing (ICASSP)*, Taipei, Taiwan, April 2009, pp. 4585–4588.

[213] B. Schuller, S. Steidl, and A. Batliner, "The INTERSPEECH 2009 Emotion Challenge," in *Proceedings of the 10th Annual Conference of the International Speech Communication Association (INTERSPEECH)*, Brighton, UK, September 2009, pp. 312–315.

[214] N. Sebe, M. S. Lew, I. Cohen, A. Garg, and T. S. Huang, "Emotion recognition using a Cauchy Naïve Bayes classifier," in *Proceedings of the 16th International Conference on Pattern Recognition (ICPR)*, Québec City, QC, Canada, August 2002, pp. 17–20.

[215] T. Seppänen, E. Väyrynen, and J. Toivanen, "Prosody-based classification of emotions in spoken Finnish," in *Proceedings of the 8th European Conference on Speech Communication and Technology (INTERSPEECH)*, Geneva, Switzerland, September 2003, pp. 717–720.

[216] V. Sethu, E. Ambikairajah, and J. Epps, "Pitch contour parameterisation based on linear stylisation for emotion recognition," in *Proceedings of the 10th Annual Conference of the International Speech Communication Association (INTERSPEECH)*, Brighton, UK, September 2009, pp. 2011–2014.

[217] I. Shafran, M. Riley, and M. Mohri, "Voice signatures," in *Proceedings of the IEEE Automatic Speech Recognition and Understanding Workshop (ASRU)*, St. Thomas, Virgin Islands, USA, December 2003, pp. 31–36.

[218] S. Shahid, E. Krahmer, and M. Swerts, "Audiovisual emotional speech of game playing children: Effects of age and culture," in *Proceedings of the 8th Annual Conference of the International Speech Communication Association (INTERSPEECH)*, Antwerp, Belgium, August 2007, pp. 2681–2684.

[219] M. Shami and W. Verhelst, "Automatic classification of emotions in speech using multi-corpora approaches," in *Proceedings of the IEEE BENELUX/DSP Valley Signal Processing Symposium (SPS-DARTS)*, Antwerp, Belgium, March 2006, pp. 3–6.

[220] J. Sichert, *Visualisierung des emotionalen Ausdrucks in der Stimme*. Saarbrücken, Germany: Vdm Verlag Dr. Müller, September 2008.

[221] J. Sidorova, "Speech emotion recognition with TGI+.2 classifier," in *Proceedings of the 12th Conference of the European Chapter of the Association for Computational Linguistics (EACL): Student Research Workshop*, Athens, Greece, April 2009, pp. 54–60.

[222] M. Slaney and G. McRoberts, "Baby ears: A recognition system for affective vocalizations," in *Proceedings of the IEEE International Conference on Acoustics, Speech, and Signal Processing (ICASSP)*, Seattle, WA, USA, May 1998, pp. 985–988.

[223] C. A. Smith and P. C. Ellsworth, "Patterns of cognitive appraisal in emotion," *Journal of Personality and Social Psychology*, vol. 48, no. 4, pp. 813–838, April 1985.

[224] P. Somol, P. Pudil, J. Novovičová, and P. Paclík, "Adaptive floating search methods in feature selection," *Pattern Recognition Letters*, vol. 20, no. 11–13, pp. 1157–1163, November 1999.

[225] S. Steidl, *Automatic Classification of Emotion-Related User States in Spontaneous Children's Speech*. Berlin, Germany: Logos Verlag, February 2009.

[226] S. Steidl, M. Levit, A. Batliner, E. Nöth, and H. Niemann, ""Of all things the measure is man" — Automatic classification of emotions and inter-labeler consistency," in *Proceedings of the IEEE International Conference on Acoustics, Speech, and Signal Processing (ICASSP)*, Philadelphia, PA, USA, March 2005, pp. 317–320.

[227] S. Steidl, B. Schuller, A. Batliner, and D. Seppi, "The hinterland of emotions: Facing the open-microphone challenge," in *Proceedings of the 3rd International Conference on Affective Computing and Intelligent Interaction (ACII)*, Amsterdam, The Netherlands, 2009, pp. 690–697.

[228] S. Steininger, S. Rabold, O. Dioubina, and F. Schiel, "Development of user-state conventions for the multimodal corpus in SmartKom," in *Proceedings of the LREC Workshop on*

Multimodal Resources and Multimodal Systems Evaluation, Las Palmas, Gran Canaria, Spain, June 2002, pp. 733–37.

[229] R. Sun, E. Moore, II, and J. F. Torres, "Investigating glottal parameters for differentiating emotional categories with similar prosodics," in *Proceedings of the IEEE International Conference on Acoustics, Speech, and Signal Processing (ICASSP)*, Taipei, Taiwan, April 2009, pp. 4509–4512.

[230] R. Tato, R. Santos, R. Kompe, and J. M. Pardo, "Emotional space improves emotion recognition," in *Proceedings of the 7th International Conference on Spoken Language Processing (INTERSPEECH)*, Denver, CO, USA, September 2002, pp. 2029–2032.

[231] M. A. Tischler, C. Peter, M. Wimmer, and J. Voskamp, "Application of emotion recognition methods in automotive research," in *Proceedings of the 2nd Workshop on Emotion and Computing — Current Research and Future Impact*, Oldenburg, Germany, September 2007, pp. 50–55.

[232] K. P. Truong and S. Raaijmakers, "Automatic recognition of spontaneous emotions in speech using acoustic and lexical features," in *Proceedings of the 5th International Workshop on Machine Learning for Multimodal Interaction (MLMI)*, Utrecht, The Netherlands, September 2008, pp. 161–172.

[233] K. P. Truong and D. A. van Leeuwen, "An 'open-set' detection evaluation methodology for automatic emotion recognition in speech," in *Proceedings of the 8th Annual Conference of the International Speech Communication Association (INTERSPEECH)*, Antwerp, Belgium, August 2007, pp. 338–341.

[234] K. P. Truong, M. A. Neerincx, and D. A. van Leeuwen, "Assessing agreement of observer- and self-annotations in spontaneous multimodal emotion data," in *Proceedings of the 9th Annual Conference of the International Speech Communication Association (INTERSPEECH)*, Brisbane, Australia, September 2008, pp. 318–321.

[235] K. P. Truong, D. A. van Leeuwen, M. A. Neerincx, and F. M. G. de Jong, "Arousal and valence prediction in spontaneous emotional speech: Felt versus perceived emotion," in *Proceedings of the 10th Annual Conference of the International Speech Communication Association (INTERSPEECH)*, Brighton, UK, September 2009, pp. 2027–2030.

[236] R. J. J. H. van Son and L. C. W. Pols, "An acoustic description of consonant reduction," *Speech Communication*, vol. 28, no. 2, pp. 125–140, June 1999.

[237] E. Velten, Jr., "A laboratory task for induction of mood states," *Behavior Research and Therapy*, vol. 6, no. 4, pp. 473–482, November 1968.

[238] D. Ververidis and C. Kotropoulos, "A review of emotional speech databases," in *Proceedings of the 9th Panhellenic Conference on Informatics (PCI)*, Thessaloniki, Greece, November 2003, pp. 560–574.

[239] D. Ververidis and C. Kotropoulos, "Automatic speech classification to five emotional states based on gender information," in *Proceedings of the 12th European Signal Processing Conference (EUSIPCO)*, Vienna, Austria, September 2004, pp. 341–344.

[240] D. Ververidis and C. Kotropoulos, "Fast sequential floating forward selection applied to emotional speech features estimated on DES and SUSAS data collections," in *Proceedings of the 14th European Signal Processing Conference (EUSIPCO)*, Florence, Italy, September 2006.

[241] O. Villon and C. Lisetti, "Toward recognizing individual's subjective emotion from physiological signals in practical application," in *Proceedings of the 20th IEEE International Symposium on Computer-Based Medical Systems (CBMS)*, Maribor, Slovenia, June 2007, pp. 357–362.

[242] B. Vlasenko, B. Schuller, A. Wendemuth, and G. Rigoll, "Combining frame and turn-level information for robust recognition of emotions within speech," in *Proceedings of the 8th Annual Conference of the International Speech Communication Association (INTERSPEECH)*, Antwerp, Belgium, August 2007, pp. 2249–2252.

[243] B. Vlasenko, B. Schuller, K. T. Mengistu, G. Rigoll, and A. Wendemuth, "Balancing spoken content adaptation and unit length in the recognition of emotion and interest," in *Proceedings of the 9th Annual Conference of the International Speech Communication Association (INTERSPEECH)*, Brisbane, Australia, September 2008, pp. 805–808.

[244] T. Vogt and E. André, "Comparing feature sets for acted and spontaneous speech in view of automatic emotion recognition," in *Proceedings of the IEEE International Conference on Multimedia & Expo (ICME)*, Amsterdam, The Netherlands, July 2005, pp. 474–477.

[245] T. Vogt and E. André, "Improving automatic emotion recognition from speech via gender differentiation," in *Proceedings of the 5th International Conference on Language Resources and Evaluation (LREC)*, Genoa, Italy, May 2006, pp. 1123–1126.

[246] T. Vogt and E. André, "Exploring the benefits of discretization of acoustic features for speech emotion recognition," in *Proceedings of the 10th Annual Conference of the International Speech Communication Association (INTERSPEECH)*, Brighton, UK, September 2009, pp. 328–331.

[247] T. Vogt, E. André, and J. Wagner, "Automatic recognition of emotions from speech: A review of the literature and recommendations for practical realisation," in *Affect and Emotion in Human-Computer Interaction*, ser. Lecture Notes in Computer Science (LNCS), C. Peter and R. Beale, Eds. Berlin, Heidelberg, Germany: Springer, August 2008, vol. 4868, pp. 75–91.

[248] T. Waaramaa, P. Alku, and A.-M. Laukkanen, "The role of F3 in the vocal expression of emotions," *Logopedics Phoniatrics Vocology*, vol. 31, no. 4, pp. 153–156, December 2006.

[249] J. Wagner, J. Kim, and E. André, "From physiological signals to emotions: Implementing and comparing selected methods for feature extraction and classification," in *Proceedings of the IEEE International Conference on Multimedia & Expo (ICME)*, Amsterdam, The Netherlands, July 2005, pp. 940–943.

[250] J. Wagner, T. Vogt, and E. André, "A systematic comparison of different HMM designs for emotion recognition from acted and spontaneous speech," in *Proceedings of the 2nd International Conference on Affective Computing and Intelligent Interaction (ACII)*, Lisbon, Portugal, September 2007, pp. 114–125.

[251] J. Wagner, E. André, and F. Jung, "Smart Sensor Integration: A framework for multimodal emotion recognition in real-time," in *Proceedings of the 3rd International Conference on Affective Computing and Intelligent Interaction (ACII)*, Amsterdam, The Netherlands, September 2009, pp. 209–216.

[252] H. L. Wang and L.-F. Cheong, "Affective understanding in multimedia," *IEEE Transactions on Circuits and Systems for Video Technology*, vol. 16, no. 6, pp. 689–704, June 2006.

[253] B. Weiner and S. Graham, "An attributional approach to emotional development," in *Emotions, Cognition, and Behavior*, C. E. Izard, J. Kagan, and R. B. Zajonc, Eds. New York, NJ, USA: Cambridge University Press, July 1984, pp. 167–191.

[254] J. Wilting, E. Krahmer, and M. Swerts, "Real vs. acted emotional speech," in *Proceedings of the 9th International Conference on Spoken Language Processing (INTERSPEECH)*, Pittsburgh, PA, USA, September 2006, pp. 805–808.

[255] I. H. Witten and E. Frank, *Data Mining: Practical machine learning tools and techniques*, 2nd ed. San Francisco, CA, USA: Morgan Kaufmann, June 2005.

[256] M. Wöllmer, F. Eyben, S. Reiter, B. Schuller, C. Cox, E. Douglas-Cowie, and R. Cowie, "Abandoning emotion classes — Towards continuous emotion recognition with modelling

of long-range dependencies," in *Proceedings of the 9th Annual Conference of the International Speech Communication Association (INTERSPEECH)*, Brisbane, Australia, September 2008, pp. 597–600.

[257] B. Wrede and E. Shriberg, "Spotting "Hot Spots" in meetings: Human judgement and prosodic cues," in *Proceedings of the 8th European Conference on Speech Communication and Technology (INTERSPEECH)*, Geneva, Switzerland, September 2003, pp. 2805–2808.

[258] S. Wrede, J. Fritsch, C. Bauckhage, and G. Sagerer, "An XML based framework for cognitive vision architectures," in *Proceedings of the International Conference on Pattern Recognition (ICPR)*, Cambridge, UK, August 2004, pp. 757–760.

[259] S. Wu, T. H. Falk, and W.-Y. Chan, "Long-term spectro-temporal information for improved automatic speech emotion classification," in *Proceedings of the 9th Annual Conference of the International Speech Communication Association (INTERSPEECH)*, Brisbane, Australia, September 2008, pp. 638–641.

[260] W. Wu, T. F. Zheng, M.-X. Xu, and H.-J. Bao, "Study on speaker verification on emotional speech," in *Proceedings of the 9th International Conference on Spoken Language Processing (INTERSPEECH)*, Pittsburgh, PA, USA, September 2006, pp. 2102–2105.

[261] Z. Xiao, E. Dellandrea, W. Dou, and L. Chen, "Hierarchical classification of emotional speech," Laboratoire d'Informatique en Image et Systèmes d'Information (LIRIS), Université de Lyon, France, Technical Report RR-LIRIS-2007-006, March 2007.

[262] S. Yildirim, C. M. Lee, S. Lee, A. Potamianos, and S. Narayanan, "Detecting politeness and frustration state of a child in a conversational computer game," in *Proceedings of the 9th European Conference on Speech Communication and Technology (INTERSPEECH)*, Lisbon, Portugal, September 2005, pp. 2209–2212.

[263] M. You, C. Chen, J. Bu, J. Liu, and J. Tao, "Manifolds based emotion recognition in speech," *Computational Linguistics and Chinese Language Processing*, vol. 12, no. 1, pp. 49–64, March 2007.

[264] S. Yun and C. D. Yoo, "Speech emotion recognition via a max-margin framework incorporating a loss function based on the Watson and Tellegen's emotion model," in *Proceedings of the IEEE International Conference on Acoustics, Speech, and Signal Processing (ICASSP)*, Taipei, Taiwan, April 2009, pp. 4169–4172.

[265] Z. Zeng, Y. Fu, G. I. Roisman, Z. Wen, Y. Hu, and T. S. Huang, "Spontaneous emotional facial expression detection," *Journal of Multimedia*, vol. 1, no. 5, pp. 1–8, August 2006.

[266] Z. Zeng, Y. Hu, Y. Fu, T. S. Huang, G. I. Roisman, and Z. Wen, "Audio-visual emotion recognition in adult attachment interview," in *Proceedings of the 8th International Conference on Multimodal interfaces (ICMI)*, Banff, AL, Canada, November 2006, pp. 139–145.

[267] T. Zhang, M. Hasegawa-Johnson, and S. E. Levinson, "Mental state detection of dialogue system users via spoken language," in *Proceedings of the ISCA/IEEE Workshop on Spontaneous Speech Processing and Recognition (SSPR)*, Tokyo, Japan, April 2003.

[268] T. Zhang, M. Hasegawa-Johnson, and S. E. Levinson, "Cognitive state classification in a spoken tutorial dialogue system," *Speech Communication*, vol. 48, no. 6, pp. 616–632, June 2006.

[269] G. Zhou, J. H. L. Hansen, and J. F. Kaiser, "Nonlinear feature based classification of speech under stress," *IEEE Transactions on Speech and Audio Processing*, vol. 9, no. 3, pp. 201–216, March 2001.

[270] J. Zhou, G. Wang, Y. Yang, and P. Chen, "Speech emotion recognition based on rough set and SVM," in *Proceedings of the 5th IEEE International Conference on Cognitive Informatics (ICCI)*, Beijing, China, July 2006, pp. 53–61.

I want morebooks!

Buy your books fast and straightforward online - at one of world's fastest growing online book stores! Environmentally sound due to Print-on-Demand technologies.

Buy your books online at
www.morebooks.shop

Kaufen Sie Ihre Bücher schnell und unkompliziert online – auf einer der am schnellsten wachsenden Buchhandelsplattformen weltweit! Dank Print-On-Demand umwelt- und ressourcenschonend produziert.

Bücher schneller online kaufen
www.morebooks.shop

KS OmniScriptum Publishing
Brivibas gatve 197
LV-1039 Riga, Latvia
Telefax +371 686 204 55

info@omniscriptum.com
www.omniscriptum.com

Printed by Books on Demand GmbH, Norderstedt / Germany